Also by
STEPHANIE &
JEREMY PUGLISI

◇ ◇ ◇

Where Should We Camp Next?

Where Should We Camp Next?: Camping 101

Where Should We Camp Next?: National Parks

RV Vacations

WHERE SHOULD WE CAMP NEXT?

BUDGET CAMPING

A 50-State Guide to
Budget-Friendly Campgrounds
and Free and Low-Cost Outdoor Activities

STEPHANIE AND JEREMY PUGLISI

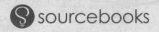 sourcebooks

This publication is designed to provide accurate and authoritative information in regard to the subject
matter covered. It is sold with the understanding that the publisher is not engaged in rendering legal,
accounting, or other professional service. If legal advice or other expert assistance is required, the
services of a competent professional person should be sought. —*From a Declaration of Principles Jointly
Adopted by a Committee of the American Bar Association and a Committee of Publishers and Associations*

Published by Sourcebooks
P.O. Box 4410, Naperville, Illinois 60567-4410
(630) 961-3900
sourcebooks.com

Cataloging-in-Publication data is on file with the Library of Congress.

Printed and bound in the United States of America.
KP 10 9 8 7 6 5 4 3 2 1

To Maggie the Camping Dog.

You are the guardian and protector of our family and our constant travel companion. you were born to live your best life at the campground and out on the trail—and you were born to be ours. We love you very much.

CONTENTS

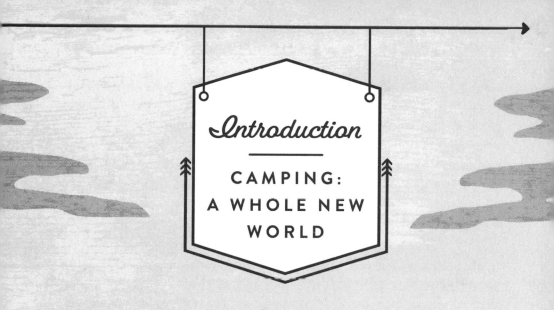

Introduction

CAMPING: A WHOLE NEW WORLD

For decades, camping has been characterized as an affordable way to vacation. Many of us grew up in working-class homes where airfare tickets and hotel stays were far out of reach, but a weeklong camping trip with friends and family was a fun and attainable way to use those vacation days.

The campground industry has changed dramatically over the last decade, and today camping trips are not necessarily always budget-friendly experiences. Many campgrounds have invested heavily in pricey amenities like water parks, lazy rivers, and fitness centers. A night at a resort campground can cost more than a night at a budget hotel, and longtime campers are feeling the hit to their wallet.

We know that right now, some folks are pricing out camping trips and wondering if the numbers work for their personal budgets. When we started camping as a family, we were two teachers who had a lot of time to spend with our kids in the summer, but we did not have a lot of money to spend on vacations. Camping was the perfect way for us to stretch those dollars and make lifelong memories without breaking the bank. In a world of $200+/night campground fees, is it still possible to plan amazing camping trips on a budget?

The answer is yes—absolutely—and this book will help you do it.

We will walk you through the landscape of state park, national forest, U.S. Army Corps of Engineers, and mom-and-pop campgrounds that offer amazing camping experiences at affordable prices. These campgrounds may not have water slides or zip lines, but instead you'll find swimming, fishing, hiking trails, wildlife viewing, and campfires to make lifelong memories.

PRICING

In this book, we've created three tiers of budget campgrounds, all under $100 per night, and most well below that threshold.

- →→ $ 0–40 dollars per night
- →→ $$ 40–70 dollars per night
- →→ $$$ 70–100 dollars per night

While a $100/night campground may not seem like a budget option for many campers, we know that for a family with multiple children, this price is far below what they would pay for hotel or rental home accommodations, and it can be viewed as a great value, especially combined with on-site amenities that keep those kids busy for free.

We also created a simple badge system to highlight campgrounds that stand out in one of two ways.

 Most Bang for the Buck: This badge is awarded to campgrounds that are incredibly affordable but still manage to offer campers a lot of value at the low end of our pricing scale. For the most part, we awarded this badge to state parks or U.S. Army Corps of Engineers campgrounds that include hookups of some kind—but they do so without jacking up the price. The U.S. Army Corps of Engineers does dominate when it comes to winning this badge, because their campgrounds are, quite simply, the best value in American camping right now.

Worth the Splurge: This badge is awarded to campgrounds that are in the upper range of our pricing system but offer an excellent array of amenities and/or activities that actually make them seem like a bargain in the grand scheme of things. Most of the campgrounds that win the Worth the Splurge badge are private campgrounds that offer quite a lot, but they have still managed to keep their prices down.

The campgrounds that we have selected in each state are also divided into Best in State and Also Great subcategories. In some cases, we feel that the campgrounds earning Best in State are objectively better in every way. In other cases, the differences are slight, and we are merely giving a nod to the campgrounds that we would choose if we were returning to that region. All the campgrounds selected in this book are wonderful in some way or another. We did not struggle to find enough great campgrounds for this book. In fact, the opposite was true. There were too many great campgrounds, and we simply couldn't include all of them.

CAMPING ON ANY BUDGET: THE FIVE MOST IMPORTANT WAYS TO CONTROL YOUR COSTS

Camping trips provide several ways to control your vacation costs. Campground costs are the primary focus of this book, but don't forget there are many other ways to save money when planning a camping trip, including picking a budget-friendly destination, preparing your own food, and looking for free or low-cost activities.

1 Campgrounds: Campground reservation fees are the number one way you can control your costs when planning a camping trip. If you are staying at multiple campgrounds over the length of a trip, think about the average nightly cost to stay on budget. On many of our trips, we will combine state or national park campgrounds with some private campgrounds, averaging out at about $60 to $70 per night, well below what it would cost our family of five to stay in more traditional accommodations.

2 Traveling Distance: The farther you travel, the more your camping trip is going to cost. Gas, tolls, and wear and tear on your vehicle can all add up, so picking a location close to home can significantly reduce the total cost of your camping vacation.

3 Equipment: Some folks are attracted to the low cost of a camping vacation and then go and blow their budget on a bunch of bells and whistles that they really don't need. These splurges can range from expensive tents to pricey RVs. We encourage everyone to keep these costs as low as possible until you know you will get enough value out of those purchases.

4 Food: We save hundreds of dollars on every camping trip by eating at the campground instead of out at restaurants. With a bit of planning, we can keep our food costs the same as they are at home if the budget is particularly tight. When we do eat out, we go during lunch service, which can cut the bill in half.

5 Activities: Maximize your enjoyment of the free to low-cost activities that camping provides. Every campground will have unique amenities, but many will offer fishing, hiking, and biking opportunities. Geocaching is a popular campground activity. We also pack our kayaks, paddleboards, or tubes if there are lakes or rivers nearby. We look for swimming holes and local festivals. Many campgrounds will offer a recreation schedule with free activities throughout the day for people of all ages. Some state parks will have frisbee golf courses or archery targets. It is absolutely possible to have an adventurous, jam-packed camping trip without spending a ton of money on activity fees.

CAMPGROUNDS IN THIS BOOK

There are certain types of campgrounds that offer a great budget camping experience, so you'll find many state park, national forest, and U.S. Army Corps of Engineers locations in this book. Here's a bit more information about these types of campgrounds.

State Park Campgrounds

Each state funds and runs its own state park system, so the campground experience will vary widely from state to state. Some states, such as South Carolina, Delaware, and Oregon, have invested heavily in their campgrounds and offer modern online reservation systems, water and electric hookups, and robust recreation schedules. Others—like our home state of New Jersey— have outdated bathhouses and limited options for RVers.

Nevertheless, state parks offer the most prevalent and accessible option for budget campgrounds in this country, and you will find hundreds of amazing state park campgrounds in this book. Some will be rustic, others will have some hookups, and a few rare gems offer full hook-up campsites with paved pads, picnic tables, and fire rings. In general, state park campgrounds have bathhouses with showers, laundry facilities, and supplies like ice and firewood. Most have playgrounds, educational programming, and other recreational offerings. Some offer access to water parks, climbing walls, and spray grounds.

Make sure to research regulations in advance of making reservations at state parks. Some—we're looking at you New Hampshire—have extensive pet restrictions. Others are entirely pet friendly, asking that you simply leash and clean up after your pup. Some have alcohol prohibitions and strict quiet hours. Ensure that the state park policies are aligned with your camping style before you book.

National Forest Campgrounds

The U.S. Forest Service manages millions of acres of public lands across the country, and there are thousands of campgrounds on these lands with RV and tenting sites that can be reserved in advance for a nightly fee between $10 and $35. There are also many more thousands of dispersed camping sites— unreservable and undesignated camping areas—that are free. In this book, we've focused on designated campgrounds in the national forests that offer, and often require, reservations in advance. Because first-come, first-served campgrounds are risky for out-of-state campers, we have tried to limit the number of them that we recommend in this book—but there are a few.

National forest campgrounds are rustic and will offer only the most basic facilities, such as a vault toilet—if there is any toilet at all. Some sites will have fire rings and picnic tables. Never expect reliable cell service or Wi-Fi. For the most part, you'll want to be prepared for self-contained camping at these campgrounds. Many national forests will have their fair share of dirt or gravel roads, so while the beauty is exceptional and the price is right, you'll want to do research and leg work in advance of a stay to make sure you can navigate the campground safely with your equipment.

U.S. Army Corps of Engineers Campgrounds

Over 4,300 recreation areas and over 450 lakes in 43 states are managed by the U.S. Army Corps of Engineers (COE), and there are more than 450 COE campgrounds scattered across the country. Since they are mostly located on rivers and lakes, they are the perfect base camp for water-centric activities, such as boating, skiing, canoeing, kayaking, swimming, and fishing. Even if you don't plan on getting in the water, the views alone are sure to keep you coming back again and again.

COE campgrounds share many similarities with state parks. Most will offer roomy, scenic campsites, with somewhat simple amenities. Some have full hookups, but many offer electric or water/electric campsites only. You'll usually find a dump station on-site, as well as basic—but clean—restrooms/shower facilities.

Simple playgrounds, swim beaches, boat launches, hiking trails, and more are often found in COE campgrounds, but there is usually not much else in the way of amenities. Despite this, the views and prime locations make them worth it, especially considering the inexpensive prices. Rates vary depending on location, amenities offered, and the season, with some offering basic tent camping for only $10 per night. Most COE campsites will be in the range of $30 to $50. The most expensive caps out at around $70. COEs also have cabins that are offered at various prices, depending on the site and size of cabin. Visitors age sixty-two and older receive a 50 percent discount on camping.

Private Campgrounds

The landscape for budget-friendly private camping options has changed dramatically over the last decade. Real estate developers and private equity funds have turned many of what used to be affordable family-owned campgrounds into pricey resort chains and franchises. You can still find some simple, clean, affordable, privately owned campgrounds, mostly in the East and the Midwest, and we've included many of those options in this book. In the West, where there are more public lands and many more affordable public camping options, private campgrounds are often not the best budget option, and you won't find as many of them featured here.

In general, great budget-friendly private campgrounds have nicely sized, landscaped campsites, full hookups, picnic tables, and fire rings. We look for classic campground features like playgrounds, basketball courts, fishing ponds, hand-dipped ice cream, and simple recreational activities such as kickball tournaments or craft times. These types of immersive, affordable camping experiences have become less prevalent in recent years, but they are still available and are a wonderful, budget-friendly family experience.

National Park Campgrounds

There is no doubt national park campgrounds are amazing budget camping options. However, since we wrote an entire book about our favorite national park campgrounds—*Where Should We Camp Next?: National Parks*—we've only included the most obvious choices in this book. Check out our previously published book to read about hundreds of fantastic national park campgrounds that also happen to be budget friendly.

County Park Campgrounds

It is not common to find extraordinary county park campgrounds, but they do exist, and we feature the best ones in this book. Most county park campgrounds have similar qualities as state parks, offering simple amenities in picturesque, natural settings. Some county park campgrounds will offer a tremendous variety of recreational and educational programs, from fishing derbies to birding walks to nature programs. Many will have picnic pavilions and boating rentals, so they can be the perfect place to camp with family and friends.

Harvest Hosts Locations

We have featured a smattering of worthy Harvest Hosts locations throughout this book, mostly to illustrate that this membership program offers a unique and special way to camp on a budget. The membership includes thousands of overnight camping options, so check out more details about the affordable annual membership later in this chapter.

CAMPGROUND AND CAMPING MEMBERSHIPS

There are many camping and campground memberships that will save you money...but only if you use them. Do your research and make sure the value matches the way you camp.

Good Sam Club

The Good Sam Club membership is popular with RVers since it provides discounts at over 2,400 RV parks and campgrounds, as well as a discount on fuel at Pilot Flying Js. You'll also get members-only pricing at Camping World retail stores. Additional membership add-ons include travel insurance, tire discounts, and extended service warranties.

Passport America

Members of Passport America receive 50 percent off camping fees at their network of almost 2,000 campgrounds. There are no blackout dates for members, and their online search tool allows for easy campground discovery.

Thousand Trails

The Thousand Trails membership is unique in that it offers members the opportunity to camp fee free at any of their network campgrounds once they have purchased a membership. There are only about eighty campgrounds in the system, so buyers need to make sure they would want to stay at these locations before slapping down the hefty fees required for the lifetime membership.

KOA Rewards

This loyalty program offers a 10 percent discount on all KOA campgrounds as well as exclusive savings on partner products and services. Membership also allows campers to build up reward points that can be cashed in for discounts off future stays. In general, campers who stay at KOAs more than a few nights per year will benefit from purchasing a rewards card, since it only costs $36 per year.

Escapees RV Club

Escapees caters to the full-time RV crowd, offering campground discounts but also mail-forwarding services and specialized RV insurance quotes. They host events and rallies, so if you are looking for community and support for the full-time RV lifestyle, this membership may be valuable for you.

Harvest Hosts

Harvest Hosts is an annual membership program that allows those with self-contained RVs to stay overnight—for twenty-four hours maximum—at more than 4,000 wineries, breweries, farms, museums, aquariums, and other unique attractions. For your RV to be considered "self-contained" it must have an interior toilet, water tank, and inside cooking facilities. You may use a porta-potty if it stays inside your trailer at all times. Harvest Hosts does not allow the use of tents of any kind, including rooftop tents, and host locations do not provide hookups, bathrooms, or shower facilities.

At under $100 per year, we believe a Harvest Hosts membership is a terrific option for budget campers, as long as they are using it for two to three stays per year. It's a unique program, so here are some tips for making the most of a Harvest Hosts membership if you do decide to join.

TIP #1: USE HARVEST HOSTS TO BREAK UP LONGER DRIVES

Because an official Harvest Hosts stay is limited to one night, most RV owners use them as stops on their way to and from destinations. Staying at a Harvest Hosts location is a great way to rest up after a long drive, or to extend a great vacation just a little bit longer. Some locations may invite you to stay longer than one night, but that will vary from location to location.

TIP #2: USE HARVEST HOSTS FOR QUICK GETAWAYS CLOSE TO HOME

A Harvest Hosts stay is also great for a quick overnight trip close to home. You may not want to travel very far for a one-night stay—but there is a pretty good chance they have some awesome locations within striking distance of your home. Why not escape for a quick night away and check out a winery or a brewery within a few hours of your house? Because your overnight stay can last for twenty-four hours, you can linger in the morning and enjoy the location before heading home.

TIP #3: ALWAYS CHECK IN WITH YOUR HOST

When camping at a Harvest Hosts location you are required to check in with your host, and for good reason. The farm or winery you are visiting is not a campground with defined sites. You need to get specific information about where you can—and cannot—park for the night.

TIP #4: CONSIDER STAYING HITCHED UP FOR THE NIGHT

If you don't plan on exploring the area in your tow vehicle after setting up camp, then you may want to stay hitched up for the night. It will save you some time and effort upon arrival and departure if your rig stays hitched up and ready to go. Just make sure you unplug your RV's seven-pin connection from your tow vehicle—and plug it back in when it is time to drive home.

TIP #5: LEARN SOMETHING NEW IF YOUR HOST ALLOWS IT

One of the best parts about visiting a Harvest Hosts location is that many hosts will invite you to take a behind-the-scenes look at the inner workings of their operation. At a recent Harvest Hosts stay, we were invited to watch our hosts make a special, limited-edition cranberry wine. Watching them crush the cranberries and learning about the wine-making process was a highlight of the trip.

TIP #6: MAKE A PURCHASE BEFORE YOU LEAVE

Harvest Hosts recommends that you purchase at least $20 worth of wine, produce, or gifts from your host's gift shop before you leave. Of course, you are welcome to spend more to show your appreciation for an awesome and unique overnight camping experience.

TIP #7: DON'T ASSUME YOU CAN COOK OUTSIDE

Most Harvest Hosts locations do not allow you to cook outside of your RV. This is why your RV must have an interior kitchen of some kind. Some locations will allow you to cook outside, but you must receive direct permission from your host to do so.

TIP #8: DOGS ARE OFTEN ALLOWED, BUT CHECK GUIDELINES BEFORE YOU GO

Dogs are allowed at the vast majority of Harvest Hosts locations. However, it is incredibly important that you ask your host about their specific guidelines. There may be areas, like a section of a vineyard, where your dog is not permitted. Know before you go and always keep your dog on leash when it is outside of your RV. That rule never changes.

TIP #9: DON'T OVERSTAY YOUR WELCOME

An official Harvest Hosts stay should be for one night, and for no more than twenty-four hours. To stay longer without the direct invitation of your host would be to overstay your welcome. Please don't wait for your hosts to ask you to leave.

BOONDOCKERS WELCOME

A Boondockers Welcome membership can be added to your Harvest Hosts membership for an additional annual fee. They offer almost 3,000 locations for members to camp on private property, many of which allow you to get off-road, at least a little bit. About 30 percent of these locations do not offer hookups of any kind. Some hosts charge campers a nominal fee if guests use water or electric hookups.

BUDGET CAMPING OPTIONS NOT FOUND IN THIS BOOK

There are ways to camp on a budget that we have not included in this book, which you can explore further online if you are dedicated to maximizing travel while minimizing expenses. We've largely focused on traditional campgrounds with designated campsites. However, there are more creative—and cheap—ways to camp, especially if you are traveling by RV.

Boondocking

People often confuse boondocking with dry camping. Dry camping is simply staying in a designated campsite without any water, electric, or sewer hook-ups. Boondocking is staying outside of a designated campground or campsite in a national forest, Borough of Land Management area, or any other dispersed camping property. Boondocking is largely free, and you'll need to be entirely self-contained with your own water and power source...plus you need a plan to dispose of your waste. Boondocking is most definitely a budget-camping option, but because of the challenges involved in locating and navigating to boondocking locations, we stuck to recommending only designated campgrounds and campsites in this book.

Wallydocking

"Wallydocking" is a term used to describe overnight camping in a Walmart parking lot or other similar retail parking lots, such as a Home Depot, Cracker Barrel, or truck stops. The term "Wally" refers to Walmart, as it is one of the most popular retail chains that has traditionally allowed overnight parking in many of their stores' parking lots.

Wallydocking is typically done by RVers who need a safe and free place to park and sleep for a night while on the road en route to another destination. It can be a great way to control costs and avoid paying campground fees for short, overnight stays. Some Walmart locations allow overnight parking in their parking lots, but policies can vary by store and by local regulations. It's important to check with the store manager or call ahead to confirm that overnight parking is allowed.

While Wallydocking can be a convenient and free option for overnight parking, it's important to keep in mind that these parking lots are not camp-sites and do not offer any amenities or facilities, such as water, electricity, or waste disposal. It can also be a noisy experience, with trucks and RVs pulling in and out at all hours of the night. Do your research in advance to ensure you won't get a knock on the door from local law enforcement asking you to move along to another location.

Moochdocking

Moochdocking is RV camping on a friend or family's property for free. This might mean parking in their driveway, on the street, or somewhere on their land. It's a great way to save some money, but it does come with some risks— like ticking off grouchy neighbors or getting a citation for parking illegally. However, with a little bit of planning, it has some big rewards: free camping all over the country and getting to visit loved ones at the same time.

Check HOA and local municipal code before parking your rig in front of a friend's house. More importantly, double and triple check the conditions before pulling down someone's driveway or driving into a wide-open field. People who do not own RVs may think their property is perfectly suited for an overnight stay, but they may not understand the logistics involved in making a U-turn or the risks involved of getting stuck in muddy ground. Do your own research and be prepared for some surprises.

BUDGET HACK: BORROW OR RENT CAMPING EQUIPMENT

It's not uncommon for folks to run out and buy a ton of camping equipment before they have even taken their first camping trip. This can be a big budget buster, as you may not even know your equipment preferences or how much you will end up using it. If you are new to camping, try borrowing the basics from a friend or family member. Ask if anyone has a tent and sleeping bags gathering dust in the garage. They may also have a camp stove and cooler for you to try out. We personally love loaning out our camping equipment since it helps us introduce friends to the camping lifestyle without emptying their pockets.

If you don't have a friend like ours, renting equipment has become easier than ever. Here are a few of our favorite outdoor retailers that rent tents, sleeping bags, backpacks, and other gear. Many offer shipping throughout the United States and also offer the option to purchase gear that you wish to keep.

- REI
- Outdoors Geek
- LowerGear
- Camp Crate
- Ruffwear
- Eastern Mountain Sports
- The Clymb
- Arrive Outdoors
- GearCommons

BUDGET HACK: RENT AN RV

If you are thinking about purchasing an RV and haven't done a ton of camping, we encourage you to take advantage of RV rental options and try before you buy. The upfront cost of an RV rental may seem a bit high for a budget-conscious traveler, but believe us, it's cheaper than buying an RV. An RV purchase will come along with a variety of hidden costs, including insurance, maintenance, and storage fees. We own an RV and love it, but we encourage you to crunch the numbers before writing a check.

There is a wide range of RV models available for rent, especially if you are looking at peer-to-peer rental platforms like Outdoorsy, RVezy, or RVshare. It may be tempting to choose based on price, but you should dig a little deeper to make sure your rental will be a good fit for your family. Make sure there's a designated bed for every traveler—changing the dinette or couch into a bed every night will get old fast. You'll also want to find a kitchen that is stocked with essentials and well-equipped for any meal preparation that you might be planning. If you don't want to use the campground bathhouse, look for an RV rental with a full bath on board. If you're looking to travel with any four-legged family members, search for a rental that is pet friendly. Lastly, you'll want to think about the gear you're bringing on your RV adventure. Make sure your rental can accommodate any bikes, kayaks, or canoes you plan to bring along.

Many rental companies will deliver an RV to the campground of your choice. This might be an attractive option if you are looking for a change of scenery without the hassle of driving, towing, or parking an RV. There are a lot of good reasons to camp close to home, and some rental companies will even recommend their favorite campgrounds and help navigate the reservation process.

There is a range of rental options available, and you'll want to choose one that offers the level of comfort and support you are looking for. Here are some of the most reputable RV rental companies out there right now.

Cruise America

You've probably seen Cruise America's Class C rentals in national parks around the country. They've been in business since the 1970s and know how to offer a ton of support for the first-time renter. Their RVs are built to be virtually unbreakable, and many units are pet friendly. You will pay a premium price with Cruise America, but you're likely to have a seamless user experience.

Road Bear RV

Road Bear RV is another rental company that has been around for decades and has its customer service fine-tuned. There are only seven locations in the country, but they are all located around major metropolitan areas like Los Angeles, Denver, and New York City. Again, you'll find higher prices than the peer-to-peer marketplace, but Road Bear RV will offer a ton of planning support and RV education.

Outdoorsy

This peer-to-peer rental platform connects RV owners with RV renters in the United States and Canada. There are a wide variety of rigs and price points, and you'll find everything from a $50-per-night pop-up camper to a $350-per-night motorhome. Outdoorsy offers liability insurance policies up to $1 million, providing peace of mind to both parties.

RVShare

RVshare is another peer-to-peer rental platform with thousands of privately owned RVs available to rent around the United States. They offer renters' insurance and roadside assistance, plus a website full of resources for first-time RVers.

RVezy

This peer-to-peer RV rental platform has private RV rentals available for those traveling in North America. The platform provides insurance coverage, 24-7 roadside assistance, an app, and customer support to renters and owners. Their handy matchmaking tool, a quick survey, helps renters find the RV that's right for their trip.

BUDGET HACK: RENT YOUR PERSONAL RV

Some folks help defray the costs of an RV by renting out their personal rig on peer-to-peer rental networks like RVShare and Outdoorsy. We personally know people who rent out their RV just enough to pay their RV expenses and fund their travel budget for the year. Be aware this is not in any way a form of passive income—it takes a lot of work to manage an RV rental listing, clean and stock the RV, and answer the seemingly endless questions of a first-time RV renter. But if you have the time and patience, this is a great way to defray the cost of camping trips.

BUDGET HACK: LOW-COST, HIGH-VALUE GEAR

We have found that buying the cheapest camping gear is not very budget friendly, since we end up having to replace it every year. Instead of looking for the cheapest items, we focus on finding items that give us the most bang for our buck. Here are some pieces of gear that have paid for themselves multiple times over by lasting for one camping season after another. There are many more recommendations for budget-camping gear spread throughout the book in easy-to-find sidebars. They are all items that we love and have used for years.

Nebo Slyde King Flashlight

The Nebo Slyde King rechargeable USB flashlight is affordable and rugged at a surprisingly budget price point. The main 500 lumen LED flashlight is excellent, but it also offers a retractable work light that hides inside the flashlight body when not in use. This work light, when coupled with the magnetic base and red hazard flasher, turns this casual flashlight into a powerful tool for roadside emergencies on your way to and from the campground. We keep one in our RV and one in our car.

Lodge Cast Iron

How many things can you buy for $15 that will last you a lifetime? Maybe just one—the 10.25-inch Lodge cast-iron skillet. This iconic piece of cookware is a workhorse at the campground. The pre-seasoning process means even a cast-iron amateur can use and maintain it. We have a few other Lodge cast-iron pieces in our camp kitchen, including a Dutch oven, but this one wins the award for best value.

Blackstone Griddle

The Blackstone 22-inch tabletop griddle may end up being an iconic piece of gear for this generation of campers. Our parents loved their suitcase-style Coleman stoves that were powered by white gas, but current camping enthusiasts have fallen head over heels in love with their Blackstone griddles, and we think the 22-inch is the most perfectly designed in the bunch. It heats up easily and evenly, and it is fairly simple to use and maintain. The two burners allow you to create two cooking zones and use direct and indirect heat. The hood makes melting cheese and keeping your food warm easy, but it can also be removed if you want a more compact and easily stored product.

Estwing Fireside Friend Splitting Tool

The Estwing Fireside Friend is not just a camp ax, it is an indestructible splitting tool made of solid steel that will help make your campfires burn brighter and warmer. Smaller pieces of firewood burn faster, and the four-pound head allows you to split large pieces of firewood with ease. The 14-inch Fireside Friend has a hand-sharpened edge and is made in America.

Leatherman Signal

The Leatherman Signal is designed more for those who love the great outdoors than for the handyman who loves projects around the house. The Signal packs a fire starter, hammer, one-handed blade, emergency whistle, bottle opener, and so much more. If you take your camp kitchen seriously, then you'll want to pack a Signal in your kit. It will make your life easier in nineteen different ways and last for many camping seasons.

RTIC 45 Cooler

We know that RTIC coolers are not the cheapest, and many people will balk at one being included in a roundup of budget gear. But these coolers are built to last, cost a lot less than a Yeti, and if you pack the ice correctly, you will save a huge amount of money on both ice and food waste while camping. We like this size in particular because it is big enough to fit a hefty amount of food, but not too big to carry or move without throwing out your back.

The North Face Recon Backpack

Our North Face backpacks have held up to heavy use for more than a decade. This one is perfectly designed for day hikes because of its mesh front compartment, superior interior organization, and spacious water bottle holders that easily secure two Camelback Chutes. The Recon gets this, and everything else, perfectly right.

IKEA Kitchen Items

If you are stocking a camp kitchen or RV from scratch, don't buy products at specialty camping stores. Go right to an IKEA if you have one nearby. From pots and pans to can openers and colanders, we've never found a more affordable place to load up on the basics. Since IKEA design is centered around small spaces, you'll gather lots of space-saving ideas while you shop.

NEW ENGLAND

RECOMMENDED CAMPGROUNDS

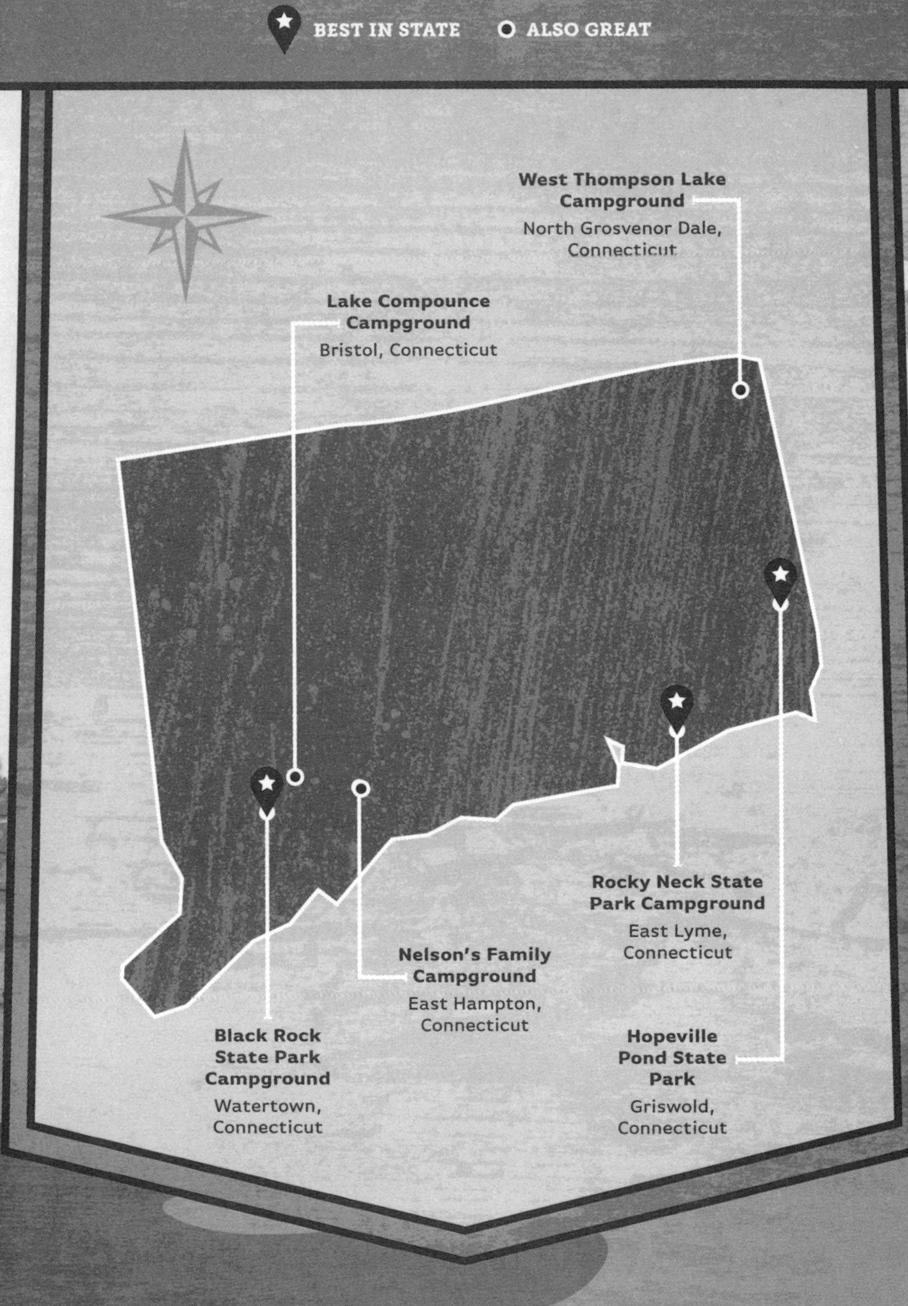

★ BEST IN STATE ○ ALSO GREAT

West Thompson Lake Campground

North Grosvenor Dale, Connecticut

Lake Compounce Campground

Bristol, Connecticut

Rocky Neck State Park Campground

East Lyme, Connecticut

Black Rock State Park Campground

Watertown, Connecticut

Nelson's Family Campground

East Hampton, Connecticut

Hopeville Pond State Park

Griswold, Connecticut

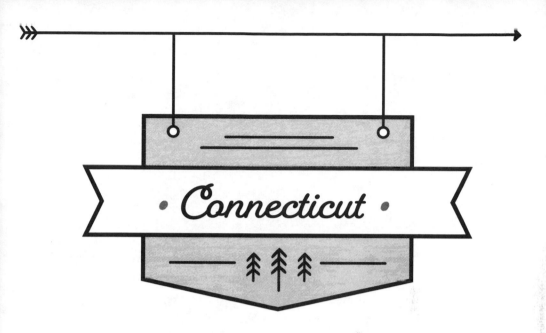

Connecticut

Connecticut is too often thought of as just a suburb of New York City. But in reality, only a small part of the Constitution State feels connected to New York. The state has lovely rolling hills in the countryside, dozens of quaint towns with great food and quirky local shopping, and an underrated coastal area that draws visitors back summer after summer. Connecticut is one of the most expensive states to live in, but surprisingly, it is a terrific state for budget camping. This is not just because of its excellent and underrated state park system of campgrounds—which, unfortunately, for the most part, does not allow pets. There are also a solid handful of family-friendly private campgrounds that have kept their prices down, and even a U.S. Army Corps of Engineers campground, which is a rarity in the Northeast. Connecticut is often overlooked because of the grandeur and beauty of its New England neighbors, but it shouldn't be. This state is beautiful—and so are many of its excellent and affordable campgrounds.

Please note that pets are not allowed in most of Connecticut's state park campgrounds.

BEST IN STATE

Black Rock State Park

▷ Watertown, Connecticut

▷ portal.ct.gov

▷ RV and Tent Sites, Cabins

▷ $

Black Rock State Park is situated in one of the prettiest and most "New England–like" sections of the state. The rolling hills of the Western Highlands are quiet and lovely, and this state park is an absolute gem. There are many lovely rambles to take around this park—and you can take off right from your campsite. The walks around the pond are particularly lovely, and there are several small waterfalls in the park as well. There are a wide variety of campsites in the campground, but almost all of them are spacious. Some are tucked into the woods and others are located in open grassy areas—a few even have water views. Some sites, like the ones in Gypsy Circle, can easily accommodate larger RVs. If you are tent camping or camping in an RV without a bathroom you can breathe easy. The bathrooms are very clean. Every inch of this campground seems loved and cared for by park staff and by the campers who return here year after year.

--------------------- **Budget-Camping Hack:** ---------------------
Boondocking with Cabela's in East Hartford

If you are looking for a free place to park your RV for one night on your way to points farther north, then boondock at the Cabela's location in East Hartford, Connecticut. Just make sure you park in the back of the building at this particular location. It is a good idea to call first and ask a manager for permission before showing up unannounced. It's also customary to make a purchase before you leave.

Rocky Neck State Park

▷ East Lyme, Connecticut

▷ portal.ct.gov

▷ RV and Tent Sites, Cabins

▷ $

The half-mile stretch of beach along the Long Island Sound in Rocky Neck State Park is an absolute delight, especially if you have small kids. The sand is soft, the waves are gentle, and the water is warm and shallow in the summer. The campground is not located directly on the beach, but it is just a short drive away. There is a walking path from the campground to the beach, but it will take you fifteen to twenty minutes to get there by foot. Not super fun if you are carrying lots of beach stuff with you. This coastal park is filled with great spots for crabbing and fishing that are quite close to the campground proper. Many of the sites here are on a grassy, parklike field with minimal privacy, and variable shade—but the community vibe here is part of the fun. Neighbors pull up chairs around each other's campfires here, and the sounds of conversation and children playing fill the air on summer nights.

Hopeville Pond State Park

▷ Griswold, Connecticut

▷ portal.ct.gov

▷ RV and Tent Sites, Cabin

▷ $

Hopeville Pond State Park has a heavenly little campground—especially for RV owners. Many of the sites are large and level, and the roads are easy to navigate. Tent campers love it here too, but most of the sites lack privacy. The campground is surrounded by water on three sides, and the best sites have water views. If you can get a water-view site in the A or C sections, then you should do so. There is even a swimming beach just for campers right next to the C section, so grab a site there if you want a short walk back to your tent or

RV after taking a dip. Hopeville Pond is also terrific for fishing and is chockful of chain pickerel, channel catfish, largemouth bass, northern pike, and yellow perch, so make sure to wet a line while you are camping here. If you get hungry and don't feel like cooking, head over to Charlene's Diner in Jewett City. It's 4 miles away and serves up classic diner grub at an affordable price.

------ **Budget-Camping Gear: GCI Outdoors Camp Chairs** ------

Connecticut-based GCI Outdoors makes the best budget-friendly camp chair we have ever tested. Its Comfort Pro chairs are just a few bucks more than the el cheapos you can find at big-box stores across the country every spring, but they are way sturdier and way more comfortable. They also come in a variety of colors, so you can match them up with the rest of your camping kit.

ALSO GREAT

West Thompson Lake Campground

▷ North Grosvenor Dale, Connecticut

▷ recreation.gov

▷ RV and Tent Sites, Lean-to Shelters

▷ $

The U.S. Army Corps of Engineers has very few campgrounds in the Northeast, and most of them are delightful little gems. This tiny and rustic campground, which is nestled into the northeast corner of Connecticut, is no exception. There are only twenty-two sites here and two lean-to shelters. Half of the sites have water and electric, and half of them have no hookups. Each campsite is large, wooded, and private—and the lake is gorgeous. If you are looking for simplicity and tranquility in nature, then this is your place.

Lake Compounce Campground

▷ Bristol, Connecticut

▷ lakecompounce.com/lake-compounce-campground

▷ RV and Tent Sites, Cabins, Huts, Tipis

▷ $$$

Lake Compounce Amusement Park opened in 1846, making it the longest continually running amusement park in the country. This charming park has thrilling roller coasters like the Phobia Fear Coaster and Boulder Dash—and plenty of great rides for the littles too. It also has its own campground. You can take a complimentary tram from the campground and arrive at the gates of the amusement park in just a few minutes. The sites here lack privacy, but the campground is clean, comfortable, and well maintained. Amusement park tickets are budget friendly and so are the RV sites. The cabins, huts, and tipis at the campground are definitely on the pricier side.

------------------ **Raising Young Naturalists:** ------------------
Free and Low-Cost Nature Centers

✧ **Melgs Point Nature Center** in Hammonasset Beach State Park is twenty-five minutes away from Rocky Neck State Park and has a wonderful campground of its own. It has excellent programs and exhibits that appeal to all ages, and admission is free.

✧ **Bent of the River Audubon Center** in Southbury is twenty-five minutes away from Black Rock State Park and thirty-five minutes away from Lake Compounce. It has a lovely nature sanctuary and education center. A small donation is encouraged for each visitor.

✧ **The Roaring Brook Nature Center** in Canton is thirty minutes away from Lake Compounce and Black Rock State Park. Admission for nonmembers is inexpensive, and it has educational exhibits on local wildlife and Native American history.

Nelson's Family Campground

▷ **East Hampton, Connecticut**

▷ **nelsonscampground.com**

▷ **RV Sites**

▷ **$$$**

Nelson's Family Campground has solid amenities, such as a nice pool and playground and fun themed weekends (like Bingo is my Thingo and Jingle & Mingle) from June to early October. There are many seasonal sites here, but the vibe is welcoming to those just popping in for the weekend. We also love that Gustine's RV Service is right next door. Tent camping is no longer allowed at Nelson's. It only offers RV sites with hookups.

------------------ Angler's Delight! ------------------

If you love fly fishing and you love camping, then Austin Hawes Campground in Barkhamstead, Connecticut, might be perfect for you. Most of the campers are here to fish early and fish often. Clean and comfortable cabins are also available.

RECOMMENDED CAMPGROUNDS

★ BEST IN STATE   ○ ALSO GREAT

South Branch Pond
Baxter State Park

Cobscook Bay State Park
Edmunds Township, Maine

Hadley's Point Campground
Bar Harbor, Maine

Blackwoods Campground
Mount Desert, Maine

Searsport Shores Ocean Campground
Searsport, Maine

Papoose Pond Family Campground and Cabins
Waterford, Maine

Sebago Lake State Park Campground
Casco, Maine

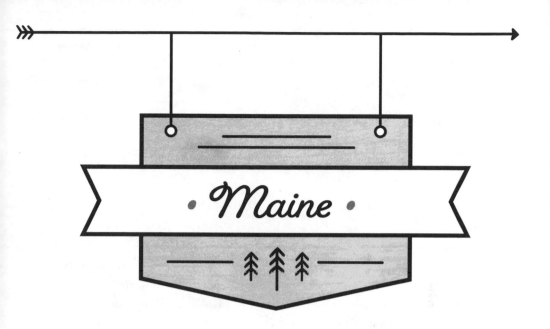

· Maine ·

Maine is filled with great options for budget camping. Its state park campgrounds are excellent and immensely affordable. A few of the most popular state park campgrounds, such as Camden Hills State Park and Sebago Lake State Park, are difficult to book, but if you look at other great state park options you can always find a site. Affordable camping can also be found at the campgrounds inside and outside of Acadia National Park, though booking sites on busy summer weekends can require quite a bit of patience and planning. Some of the campgrounds right outside of Acadia have jacked up their prices in recent years—but many of them, like Hadley's Point (featured in this chapter), still offer an excellent value. The rugged and resourceful campers who live in the great state of Maine seem to have little interest in fancy resort camping, and this has probably helped keep prices down for all of us. Taking a road trip to Vacationland in the summer or early fall can be downright heavenly, and you don't have to spend a fortune to feel like you are camping in a coastal Northwoods paradise.

BEST IN STATE

Cobscook Bay State Park
▷ Edmunds Township, Maine
▷ apps.web.maine.gov
▷ RV and Tent Sites
▷ $

Most campers who visit Maine don't go farther north than Acadia National Park, which is a shame, because that means they will miss Cobscook Bay State Park, which is just two hours northeast on Route 1. There are some truly spectacular campsites here for both tent campers and RV owners. Many of the sites here are long, private, pull-throughs that are easy to navigate—and some of them have water views. This makes Cobscook a real favorite among those who own longer RVs but still like to camp in state parks. There are no hookups at the individual sites, but there is a dump station, potable water, and a dated bathhouse with warm showers. Just make sure to bring change because the showers are not free. Spending time at Cobscook is all about unwinding and enjoying the water. There are few state parks for paddling and fishing—and clamming is even allowed here without a license. This is a quiet and uncrowded section of Vacationland, so plan on making your own fun and enjoying a few sweet summer days filled with nothing but simplicity, simplicity, simplicity.

Blackwoods Campground/Acadia National Park
▷ Mount Desert, Maine
▷ nps.gov
▷ RV and Tent Sites
▷ $

When it comes to camping in Acadia National Park, it is hard to beat the location (and the rustic beauty) of Blackwoods Campground. You cannot drive directly onto the ever-popular Park Loop Road from Blackwoods in a vehicle, but you can use the relatively new Village Connector Trail and walk to it. This makes Blackwoods Campground an absolute godsend for those who want to hike to many of the most popular trails in the park without having to drive to them and fight for parking spots at the crowded trail-heads. After a long day of hiking, you can head back to your campsite on foot and enjoy a quiet evening around the campfire. There are 221 tent sites here and sixty sites that can accommodate RVs. However, none of them have hookups—and there are no showers at the campground. You will have to head to a nearby concessionaire for a hot shower. It's a small price to pay for camping deep in the heart of Acadia National Park—the most breathtakingly beautiful national park in the East.

Searsport Shores Ocean Campground

▷ Searsport, Maine

▷ maineoceancamping.com

▷ RV and Tent Sites, Cabins, RV Rentals

▷ $$$

Searsport Shores Ocean Campground has an absolutely delightful location directly on Penobscot Bay. The waterfront sites are pricey here, but the rest of the sites are moderately priced considering the overall quality of the campground. There are also a wide variety of cabin and RV rentals that won't break the bank. All campers have access to the beach (with kayak launch and lobster pit) at Searsport Shores, so you won't feel deprived if you grab a site a few rows in from the water to save a few bucks. Searsport Shores has a quirky, artsy vibe that is all its own. It has lovely gardens, often offers live music, and even has an artist-in-residence program every summer. Make sure you partake in an old-fashioned lobster bake while you camp here. Every bite will be delicious and enhanced by the ocean views and the friendly company of your fellow campers.

------ **Other Campgrounds Inside Acadia National Park** ------

✧ **Seawall:** This popular campground is located on the west side of Mount Desert Island in a terrific location just steps away from the water. If you can't book Blackwoods, this is almost as good. There are no hookups at Seawall, so be prepared to dry camp.

✧ **Schoodic Woods:** The Schoodic Woods Campground is an absolute gem in the NPS system, but it is an hour away from Mount Desert Island on the Schoodic Peninsula. If you want a quiet retreat far from the madness of the Park Loop Road, then this is where you should camp next. Water and electric are available on many of the sites.

✧ **Duck Harbor:** This remote campground is located on Isle au Haut and can only be reached by mailboat. There are five tenting sites with lean-to shelters near the water that can each accommodate six people—and reservations are strictly required. If you can handle the logistics of getting here, the payoff (in solitude and scenery) is huge.

ALSO GREAT

South Branch Pond/Baxter State Park

▷ Baxter State Park, Maine

▷ baxterstatepark.org

▷ Tent sites, Lean-to Sites, Bunkhouse Cabin

▷ $

Adventurous souls should head to Baxter State Park for a rugged tent or cabin camping experience they will never forget. Just make sure you come prepared because this area is remote. South Branch Pond campground is Baxter's largest and most popular option for tent campers—and its waterfront location is peaceful and beautiful. There are twenty-one tent sites here, twelve lean-to sites, and one bunkhouse cabin. Before COVID-19, this was a shared cabin that could accommodate several different groups, so you could be bunked up with strangers. Since the pandemic, it is only reservable for one group. Check before you go to see if that has changed since the time of this writing.

Hadley's Point Campground

▷ Bar Harbor, Maine

▷ hadleyspoint.com

▷ RV and Tent Sites, Cabins

▷ **$$**

Several of the private campgrounds around Bar Harbor that offer full hook-up sites have become very expensive in recent years—but Hadley's Point has a done a great job of staying budget friendly. The campground is clean and attractive, but the amenities like the pool and playground are quite basic. But why should that matter? The main entrance to Acadia National Park is only ten minutes away, and most campers will be spending the entire day there anyway.

------- **Acadia National Park Hiking for Thrill Seekers** -------

Acadia has plenty of family-friendly hikes that are relatively easy but have big payoffs in terms of ocean views and spectacular scenery. But those seeking out more adventurous hikes with breathtaking views should strap on their boots and head to the Beehive or Precipice Trails, which are not for the faint of heart.

The Beehive is a 1.4-mile round-trip trail that zig zags back and forth on a 450-foot cliff. Several of the sections utilize Acadia's famous rungs and ladders, and the views of the Atlantic Ocean become more spectacular as you work your way up.

The initial 0.9-mile ascent on the Precipice Loop Trail requires even more physical fitness and mental toughness than the Beehive. Hikers should not descend on the Precipice Trail—there is another path back down which extends the hike to 3.2 miles. We recommend that you try the Beehive first before attempting Precipice.

Papoose Pond Family Campground and Cabins

▷ Waterford, Maine

▷ papoosepondcamping.com

▷ RV and Tents Sites, Cabins, Tree House, RV Rentals

▷ $$$

Papoose Pond offers classic family "summer camp"–style camping at its best. If you want full hook-up RV sites, or a clean and cozy cabin rental, then this is your place. It also has a few really cool tent sites that come with a covered picnic table and kitchenette (with electric stove, sink, and prep space) and a private bathroom. The activities here are excellent for kids of all ages, and the pool, playground, and other amenities are very good considering this campground's budget-friendly pricing.

Sebago Lake State Park

▷ Casco, Maine

▷ apps.web.maine.gov

▷ RV and Tent Sites

▷ $

Sebago Lake is one of the oldest state parks in Maine, and its centerpiece is the second largest lake in the state. Families return to this campground year after year to swim in its cool, clear waters. Many of the sites here lack privacy, and those that have been spoiled by the massive sites at places like Cobscook State Park may feel disappointed by the hustle and bustle of this place—but many campers with kids absolutely love it and couldn't imagine spending a summer without camping here. Many of the sites here also have water and electric hookups at a budget-friendly price.

-------------------- **Budget-Camping Gear:** --------------------

Gear Up 24/7/365 at L.L Bean in Freeport

L.L Bean's flagship store in Freeport, Maine, has been open twenty-four hours a day all year long since 1951. If you need to grab some budget-friendly camping gear on your way to Baxter or Acadia, then this is your place. The L.L. Bean Stowaway Pack is great for those needing a simple and lightweight day hiking bag. Need a pair of hiking shoes that don't cost a small fortune? Try L.L. Bean's Trail Model hikers for men, women, or your lively little campers.

RECOMMENDED CAMPGROUNDS

 BEST IN STATE ○ **ALSO GREAT**

**Spacious Skies
Minuteman Campground**
Littleton, Massachusetts

Clarksburg State Park
Clarksburg, Massachusetts

**Shady Knoll
Campground**
Brewster,
Massachusetts

**Hardwick Vineyard
and Winery
(Harvest Hosts)**
Hardwick,
Massachusetts

**Myles Standish
State Forest**
Carver,
Massachusetts

**Sperry Road
Campground at
Mount Greylock
State Reservation**
Williamstown,
Massachusetts

**Horseneck Beach
State Reservation**
Westport,
Massachusetts

Massachusetts

Much like the rest of New England, Massachusetts has an excellent infrastructure for budget camping. Its state park system is well run and has many campgrounds, such as Nickerson State Park, that are famous across the country, while simultaneously having some incredible hidden gems, like Clarksburg State Park, that are quite a bit less crowded. Massachusetts has one of the country's first true RV resorts in the legendary Normandy Farms, but those who want to spend less money and still have full hookups will find many other clean and comfortable family-owned campgrounds across the state. Even Cape Cod, which is expensive in almost every way imaginable, has several good budget-friendly campgrounds with full hookups. New Englanders like their camping plain and simple. When your surroundings are astonishingly beautiful and filled with lakes, rivers, mountains, and seascapes that have been celebrated in countless books and songs—who needs a fancy camping experience anyway?

BEST IN STATE

Myles Standish State Forest

▷ Carver, Massachusetts

▷ mass.gov

▷ RV and Tent Sites, Yurts

▷ $

Some of the campsites at Myles Standish that are directly situated on kettle ponds are absolutely breathtaking. Get one if you can and plan on spending some time sitting in your camp chair and soaking in the beauty and tranquility of the sparkling water. Kettle ponds form in holes left by retreating glaciers, and they are a particularly lovely feature of this excellent state forest. There are fifty-eight kettle ponds in Myles Standish, and four of them (Barretts Pond, Charge Pond, Curlew Pond, and Fearing Pond) have camping areas built around them. Charge Pond has one loop that is exclusively set aside for horse camping. These four camping areas are in different locations in this massive park and combined they offer 400 sites, none of which have hookups. The yurt rentals (which have two sets of bunk beds and are great for families) do have electric hookups, but there are only a small handful of them, and they book up fast on summer weekends. Myles Standish is designated as a state forest, but residents of Massachusetts consider it a state treasure—and it clearly is.

------------------ **Budget-Camping Hack** ------------------

Spacious Skies Campgrounds is a relatively new collection of campgrounds in the eastern half of the country that has larger aspirations. Their campgrounds (like the one reviewed in this chapter) offer up clean facilities and fun amenities for a reasonable price. Consider joining their loyalty program for a discount on your reservations and other fun perks. You could easily earn back the price of the membership if you camp with them a few times during the year.

Horseneck Beach State Reservation

▷ Westport, Massachusetts

▷ mass.gov

▷ RV and Tent Sites

▷ $

Sunsets at Horseneck Beach are beautiful, and so is just about everything else. During your stay make sure to take a walk up to the beach when the time is right. Or, if you have a site right over the dunes from the water, you can watch from the cozy comfort of your tent or RV. Your site will not have shade or privacy (which is common for East Coast beach camping). But many of the sites will have electric hookups, and all of them are spacious. The 2-mile stretch of sand in front of the campground is located along Buzzard's Bay and has excellent swimming and surfcasting, and it is also a lovely spot for a morning or evening hike. While you are camping here, make sure to drive over to nearby Gooseberry Island. It's one of the prettiest spots in the entire state.

Clarksburg State Park

▷ Clarksburg, Massachusetts

▷ mass.gov

▷ RV and Tent Sites

▷ $

The campground at Clarksburg State Park is something of a hidden gem in the Massachusetts State Park System. Its location in the northwest corner of the state just 3 miles from the Vermont border is pretty far off the radar for most campers in the Northeast. So, if you are seeking peace and quiet on your way to Vermont, this could be an excellent stop for a couple of nights. But please note that the campsites have no hookups, and the campground does not have a dump station. Camping here in an RV might work best if you have another stop with full hookups planned next. Tent campers will not share this concern and will love the sites and the setting surrounded by the Berkshire

Hills and the Green Mountains. The campground itself is relatively small, with only forty-five sites in a deeply forested setting. It is situated just steps away from Mauserts Pond, which has a lovely sand beach with a designated swimming area. This is also an excellent spot for fishing and kayaking.

ALSO GREAT

Spacious Skies Minuteman Campground

- ▷ Littleton, Massachusetts
- ▷ spaciousskiescampgrounds.com/minute-man/
- ▷ RV and Tent Sites, Cabins
- ▷ $$$

Are you planning an epic RV trip through New England and looking for a campground with full hookups near Boston? Then definitely check out Spacious Skies Minuteman Campground, which was formerly known as Boston Minuteman. The campground can be a little tricky to navigate for those in the largest rigs, but otherwise there is much to like here. The sites are large and private, and the facilities are clean and well kept. Boston is about an hour away.

Shady Knoll Campground

▷ Brewster, Massachusetts

▷ shadyknoll.com

▷ RV and Tent Sites

▷ $$$

Shady Knoll offers up comfortable camping in a rustic setting on beautiful Cape Cod. Pretty much everything is expensive on the Cape, but Shady Knoll keeps things simple and affordable. There are not many amenities here, but the sites are spacious and private with (surprise, surprise) ample shade, which is quite nice when you are camping near the beach. The campground's mid-Cape location puts you close to everything and makes this a great base camp for exploring one of the most magical places in New England. Atlantic Oaks in Eastham is owned by the same family and is also an excellent budget camping option for exploring all that Cape Cod has to offer.

Hardwick Vineyard and Winery (Harvest Hosts)

▷ Hardwick, Massachusetts

▷ harvesthosts.com

▷ Self-contained RVs Only

▷ $

If you find yourself traveling anywhere near central Massachusetts (perhaps on your way to or from Vermont or New Hampshire), then make sure you stop and spend the night at the Hardwick Vineyard and Winery. The vibe here is warm, welcoming, and lots of fun—and there is often live music at night. After a long day of travel, does it get much better than pulling up a chair, ordering a few glasses of New England wine, and relaxing to the sounds of jazz or acoustic guitar? The best part is you can walk right back home to your RV when the evening is over.

Sperry Road Campground/Mount Greylock State Reservation

▷ Williamstown, Massachusetts

▷ mass.gov

▷ Tent Sites

▷ $

More adventurous tent campers will definitely want to check out the Sperry Road Campground on Mount Greylock. This is hike-in camping, so you will need to pack light and be ready to haul your gear just over a mile from the nearest parking lot. The campground is tucked away in the woods and is a little slice of heaven surrounded by fragrant trees and lovely hiking trails. Nights can get chilly here, especially in the spring, so pack layers and bring a sleeping bag that is rated for cold temperatures.

Get the Most out of Your Cape Cod Vacation

Read Before You Go: Henry David Thoreau's *Cape Cod*

Thoreau's *Cape Cod* is often overshadowed by *Walden*, but it is a classic in its own right. This book was originally published as a series of articles in *Putnam's Monthly* starting in 1855, six years after *Walden* was published. The chapters can be read sequentially, or you can just pick any one that strikes your fancy. Every page brings an older and wilder Cape Cod to life with vivid descriptions of its people and its quiet ponds and windswept shores.

Visit Cape Cod's Wonderland

Nickerson State Park is a natural wonderland in the middle of Cape Cod. Here you will find eight freshwater ponds and hiking and biking trails galore. The fishing is great here and so is the camping. Several of the ponds are stocked with trout, and the campground has over 400 sites for tent campers and RV owners. If you love to fish and you love to camp, this might be your next favorite place.

Attend a Free Cape Cod Baseball League Game

Catching a game in the wood bat–only Cape Cod Baseball League may be one of the best free activities in all of New England. This collegiate summer league hosts some of the most talented prospects in the country, and the quality of play is excellent. Depending on the field, you may want to bring your own lawn chairs, and make sure you bring a few bucks for a hot dog or a cup of chowder. Let's play ball!

RECOMMENDED CAMPGROUNDS

★ BEST IN STATE ○ ALSO GREAT

Twin Mountain/Mt. Washington KOA Holiday

Twin Mountain, New Hampshire

Dolly Copp Campground

Gorham, New Hampshire

Lafayette Place Campground

Franconia Notch State Park

Dry River Campground

Crawford Notch State Park

Hancock Campground

Lincoln, New Hampshire

Ellacoya State Park RV Park

Gilford, New Hampshire

Wakeda Campground

Hampton Falls, New Hampshire

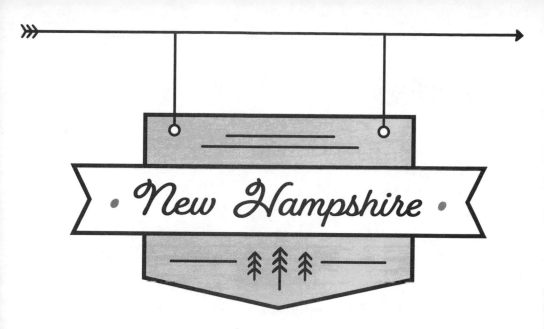

There are twenty-two campgrounds in White Mountain National Forest and twenty-one campgrounds in New Hampshire's state parks. Almost all of these campgrounds are beautiful—and every single one of them is affordable. For such a small state, New Hampshire is an absolute powerhouse when it comes to budget camping. When most people think of camping in the Granite State, they think of camping in the Whites—and for good reason. This national forest is every bit as epic as our most iconic national parks, but the rest of the state is great too. There is beach camping on and around the coast, and there are beautiful campgrounds in the often-overlooked Lakes Region. You could spend your entire life camping in New Hampshire—and some people do, returning summer after summer. Many of them return to knock another peak from the Presidential Range off their bucket lists, while others return to take their kids to budget-friendly theme parks like Storyland and Santa's Village. When it comes to camping and outdoor adventure, New Hampshire truly has something for everyone.

BEST IN STATE

Hancock Campground/White Mountain National Forest

▷ Lincoln, New Hampshire

▷ fs.usda.gov

▷ RV and Tent Sites

▷ $

There are six White Mountain National Forest campgrounds that can be found alongside the Kancamagus Highway, and Hancock is probably the prettiest and most popular, even if in need of updating and sometimes major repairs. Hancock also wins points because it is one of the few on the Kanc to be open year-round. But please take note: no services (such as bathrooms and running water) are open during the winter months, although the roads are plowed. In the summer and fall you will find a sylvan paradise nestled along the East Branch Pemigewasset River. There are swimming holes and tubing runs if you feel like getting wet, and there are lovely and private campsites for tents and RVs. The best sites here are the tent-only walk-in sites directly on the river. Just be prepared to carry all your gear about 100 yards from the group parking area down to your site. The walk is well worth it. These are some of the best campsites in all of New England. Reservations are not accepted here.

------------------- **Budget-Camping Gear:** -------------------
Trekking Poles That Won't Break the Bank

Hiking in the White Mountains is not for the faint of heart. While there are easy, family-friendly hikes everywhere, the region is more well-known for challenging hikes for experienced hikers. We recommend bringing along a pair of trekking poles like the aluminum ones made by Cascade Mountain Tech. These sturdy and attractive poles come with a carry bag and are incredibly affordable and well made. They also have over 15,000 five-star reviews on Amazon. Nuff said, right?

Lafayette Place Campground/Franconia Notch State Park

▷ Franconia, New Hampshire

▷ nhstateparks.org

▷ RV and Tent Sites

▷ $

Franconia Notch State Park is filled with natural wonders (like the Flume Gorge, The Basin, and Echo Lake) and some of the best hiking in the entire Northeast. Lafayette Place Campground is right smack in the middle of the action, and it is a bustling and popular campground. Though it does get crowded, most of the sites are large and private, so you can still have a peaceful camping experience. There is a well-stocked camp store here with souvenirs and essentials, and there is a cabin near the entrance where you can grab maps and safety information before heading out on a hike. Many of the guests here are using the campground as a base camp for some serious hiking, so you will often see them departing in the mornings and heading back in the late afternoon hours. The hustle and bustle of hikers gives this campground a distinctively outdoorsy vibe that we love very much.

Dry River Campground/Crawford Notch State Park

▷ Bartlett, New Hampshire

▷ nhstateparks.org

▷ RV and Tent Sites

▷ $

Dry River Campground is located directly off Route 302, and you can hear some road noise from the campground, though it quiets down at night. If you can, get a site as far away from the road as possible. Besides that single complaint, this small campground is an absolute gem that is surrounded by the many natural wonders of Crawford Notch. If you like hiking to waterfalls, then you will find the area around the campground to be absolutely magical. There are only thirty-six sites here, but more than half of them can accommodate RVs—especially smaller units like pop-up campers. Most of the sites here are huge and private, so if you don't like camping near your neighbors, you will love it. While you are camping here make sure to head over to the AMC Highland Center for great food and local brews that won't break the bank.

ALSO GREAT

Dolly Copp Campground/White Mountain National Forest

▷ Gorham, New Hampshire

▷ recreation.gov

▷ RV and Tent Sites

▷ $

Dolly Copp Campground is one of the most beloved campgrounds in the White Mountains, and in all of New Hampshire. The campground received a facelift in 2016 and even added sites with water and some with water and electric—a rarity in national forest campgrounds. Dolly Copp Campground is situated in a lovely spot along the Peabody River with the Presidential Range in the background. This campground is over one hundred years old and is filled with the magic of innumerable summer camping memories.

Twin Mountain/Mt. Washington KOA Holiday

▷ Twin Mountain, New Hampshire

▷ koa.com

▷ RV and Tent Sites, Cabins, Caboose, Glamping Tent

▷ $$$

If you are looking for a full-service campground to utilize as your White Mountains base camp, then you should certainly consider this charming and well-managed KOA. There is definitely a price jump here compared to the national forest campgrounds in the Whites, but we think it is worth the splurge, especially if you want full hookups, a pool, a laundry room, a dog park, and the other standard amenities that KOA is known for providing.

------------------- **Don't Bring Fido?** -------------------

The New Hampshire State Park system does not allow pets on many of its trails, campgrounds, and public spaces. Campers who bring a pet to Lafayette Campground, among others, will immediately have their reservations canceled. However, pets are allowed at Dry River Campground in Crawford Notch State Park. Because there is no consistent pet policy across this state park system, you should always check before you go.

Six Campgrounds along "The Kanc"

The Kancamagus Highway, which cuts across the White Mountains from Lincoln to Conway, is one of the prettiest drives in all of New England. It also happens to have six campgrounds to choose from for those who want to pull over and spend a few nights getting off the road and exploring this magical sliver of the magnificent Whites. Hancock is featured in this chapter, but campers from the Granite State may argue that one of the others is better. Check them all out before you book a site—they all make great base camps for a White Mountains camping adventure.

1. **Hancock Campground:** 56 Sites, Open Year-Round
2. **Big Rock Campground:** 28 Sites, Open Mid-May to Mid-October
3. **Passaconaway Campground:** 33 Sites, Open Mid-May to Mid-October
4. **Jigger Johnson Campground:** 75 Sites, Open Mid-May to Mid-October
5. **Blackberry Crossing Campground:** 26 Sites, Open Year-Round
6. **Covered Bridge Campground:** 49 Sites, Open Mid-May to Mid-October

Wakeda Campground

▷ Hampton Falls, New Hampshire

▷ wakedacampground.com

▷ RV and Tent Sites, Cabins

▷ $$

The Wakeda Campground is a classic family-style (and family-owned) private campground that has been making its guests smile since 1965. This rustic and charming woodsy campground is located just 8 miles from Hampton Beach, so the location is also excellent for day tripping. Wakeda is hustling and bustling in a good way. The sound of children laughing and the smell of campfires fill the air here on warm summer nights. When you pull in, you instantly feel like you are home.

Ellacoya State Park RV Park

▷ Gilford, New Hampshire

▷ nhstateparks.org

▷ RV Sites Only

▷ $$

The RV park at Ellacoya State Park is located directly on the shores of Lake Winnipesaukee, which is a lovely spot for swimming or paddling. There are only about forty RV sites here, and tent camping is not allowed. The sites lack privacy and have a parking lot–like feeling to them, but this is still an excellent place to camp because you get a full hook-up site at a bargain-basement price inside a lovely state park.

RECOMMENDED CAMPGROUNDS

 BEST IN STATE   ○ **ALSO GREAT**

George Washington State Campground
Chepachet, Rhode Island

Oakleaf Family Campground
Chepachet, Rhode Island

Fishermen's Memorial State Park Campground
Naragansett, Rhode Island

Wawaloam Campground
Richmond, Rhode Island

Burlingame State Park Campground
Charlestown, Rhode Island

Charlestown Breachway Campground
Charlestown, Rhode Island

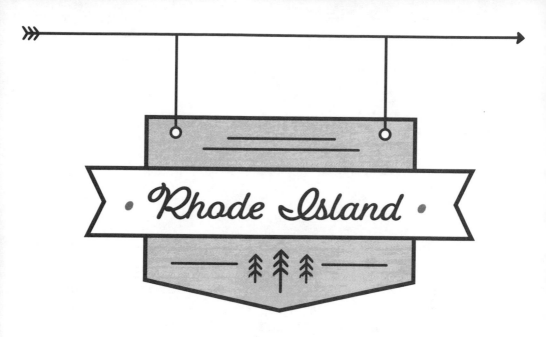

· Rhode Island ·

R hode Island is the smallest state in the country, and real estate is very expensive in many parts of the state—especially anywhere near the water—so there are not many private family-owned campgrounds. But there are a few good ones listed in this chapter that are reasonably priced and well worth a visit. Thankfully, the state park campground system is very good here. Burlingame State Park has over 700 sites, which really makes up for a lack of campsites elsewhere. Excellent coastal camping is also available at Charleston Breachway and East Beach State Campground.

You can't camp right inside of Providence and Newport, but both are within striking distance of several of the campgrounds listed below. Overall, finding a great campsite in Rhode Island can feel challenging—especially during the summer months—but this coastal state is beautiful, and campers of all kinds should consider stopping here during a tour of New England.

BEST IN STATE

Fishermen's Memorial State Park

▷ Naragansett, Rhode Island

▷ riparks.ri.gov/campgrounds

▷ RV and Tent Sites

▷ $

Fishermen's Memorial has long, spacious, paved sites that are often grassy and partially shaded. Many of them even have water and electric or full hook-ups. These qualities make the campground very popular with RV owners, especially in a state that is somewhat starved when it comes to private campgrounds with utilities and amenities. Fisherman's Memorial also has a playground and basketball, tennis, and horseshoe courts—so make sure you come prepared. The location here is also very good. Salty Brine State Beach, Scarborough State Beach, and Roger Wheeler State Beach are all within striking distance. The campground is also just a minute or two away from the Block Island Ferry and thirty minutes away from Newport. This campground books up fast. If you want to reserve a summer weekend, you had best get on it early.

--------- **Four-Wheel-Drive Camping at East Beach** ---------

East Beach State Campground offers twenty sites directly on the sand for those with self-contained RVs and four-wheel-drive capabilities. For the most part, this means truck campers and class B vans with permanently affixed bathrooms and holding tanks. If you have the right rig, this place is nothing short of spectacular.

Burlingame State Park

▷ Charlestown, Rhode Island

▷ riparks.ri.gov/campgrounds

▷ RV and Tent Sites, Cabins

▷ $

With over 700 campsites and twenty cabins, this campground is one of the largest in New England. With that many campsites you might think that each one of them is small, but you would be wrong. The sites here are almost universally large and level, and many of them are quite shady. The park is nestled alongside the Watchuag Pond, and it is packed with options for outdoor activities. There are six different camping areas here that all have a slightly different vibe to them, but we like the "main camp area" and the "fish camp area" best because they are closest to the water. While you are here, make sure to hike over to the Kimball Wildlife Refuge located on the south shore of the pond. If you don't camp with your own canoe or kayak, don't fret. You can rent them inside the park for a budget-friendly price.

ALSO GREAT

Charlestown Breachway

▷ Charlestown, Rhode Island

▷ riparks.ri.gov/campgrounds

▷ RV Sites

▷ $

This spare and simple campground is a water lover's paradise, at least for those who own self-contained, hard-walled RVs, because tents and RVs with any kind of canvas are not allowed here—and neither are pets. The campground runs along the Breachway, where excellent fishing abounds and RVers can cast a line just steps from their sites. A lovely sandy beach right on the Block Island Sound is also just steps away, so bring your beach chairs, your bathing suits, and lots of suntan lotion—at least if you are visiting in the summer when the water is warm enough for swimming.

George Washington State Campground

▷ Chepachet, Rhode Island

▷ riparks.ri.gov/campgrounds

▷ RV and Tent Sites, Cabins

▷ $

This rustic and charming campground has large, shaded sites that can fit larger rigs, but the roads can be tight and difficult to navigate, so tent campers and small RV owners will probably do best here. The campground is nestled alongside Bowdish Reservoir, which is great for swimming and paddling— and Providence is less than 25 miles away and offers excellent dining and shopping.

------------------- **Budget-Camping Gear:** -------------------

Petzl Headlamps for Dark Nights at the Campground

Having a good headlamp handy when you are camping is very smart. It can be used to read in your tent at night or help you change a diaper in the middle of the night if you are camping with little ones. We think that Petzl makes the best headlamps in the outdoor industry, because they are comfortable, afford-able, and very bright. If you are tent camping, these are terrific for midnight potty runs. They are also great for curling up and reading a good book at night without disturbing the other campers in your tent or RV. To save some money, we recommend getting one of the Petzl models that comes with a rechargeable battery, because alkaline batteries are very expensive.

Wawaloam Campground

▷ Richmond, Rhode Island

▷ wawaloam.com

▷ RV Sites

▷ $$$

The sites at Wawaloam Campground are more spacious than the sites at comparable family campgrounds across New England—and we think they are worth the splurge. The pool here is also large and clean, and there are two large water slides nearby. Other amenities include a modern playground, a miniature golf course, and a snack stand and coffee bar that serves up a quality cup of joe from local roasters. Excellent beaches are less than thirty minutes away.

Oakleaf Family Campground

▷ Chepachet, Rhode Island

▷ oakleafcampground.com

▷ RV and Tent Sites, RV Rentals

▷ $$

Oakleaf Family Campground offers full hook-up sites and clean family-friendly amenities (such as a pool, playground, and basketball and bocce ball courts) at a very reasonable price. It also offers a robust list of activities for kids and adults. Your littles will enjoy themed weekends like the Super Soaker Water Weekend, and Mom and Dad will enjoy events like the bourbon tastings and bingo bonanza. There are many seasonal campers here, but they make weekend visitors feel welcome, and so do the owners.

RECOMMENDED CAMPGROUNDS

📍 BEST IN STATE ⬭ ALSO GREAT

Smugglers' Notch State Park
Stowe, Vermont

Mountain View Campground
Morrisville, Vermont

Grand Isle State Park
Grand Isle, Vermont

North Beach Campground
Burlington, Vermont

Quechee State Park
Hartford, Vermont

Emerald Lake State Park
East Dorset, Vermont

Jamaica State Park
Jamaica, Vermont

Brattleboro North KOA Journey
East Dummerston, Vermont

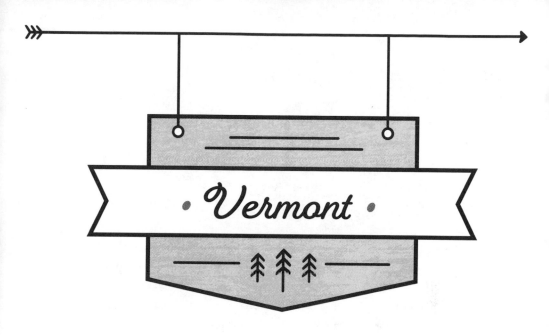

· Vermont ·

Vermont is one of the least populated states in the country, yet it boasts a robust network of affordable state park campgrounds. Many of the mom-and-pop campgrounds here are also affordable. Most New Englanders like to keep their camping simple, and this may be why the resort camping trend has not exploded here like it has elsewhere in the country. People camp in Vermont because they want to strap on their hiking boots and get out and explore, not because they want to spend their days enjoying amenities at a campground. This Zen-like camping mentality certainly seems to favor tent campers over RV owners. There are a fair number of places that can accommodate owners of large RVs in Vermont, but this is truly a tent camper's paradise. At least for a few precious months every summer.

BEST IN STATE

Grand Isle State Park

▷ Grand Isle, Vermont

▷ vtstateparks.com

▷ RV and Tent Sites, Lean-to Sites, Cabins

▷ $

Grand Isle State Park is the most-visited state park in Vermont, and its excellent campground is the second largest in the state (Lake Carmi State Park has the largest). The quality of campsites at Grand Isle varies from site to site. Some have privacy and shade, while others lack privacy and get plenty of sunlight. Most of the sites are spacious and easy to access, making this one of the most RV-friendly state park campgrounds in Vermont, though smaller RVs will still have more options here. There are no hookups at the sites, but a dump station is available. The campground is nestled along a gorgeous stretch of the Lake Champlain shoreline with views of the Adirondack Mountains, and there is a small swimming beach and a small beach for dogs to enjoy. In addition to the RV and tent sites, there are over thirty excellent lean-to sites and four adorable cabins with electric and covered front porches. Just remember to bring your own linens, as they are not included.

Smugglers' Notch State Park

▷ Stowe, Vermont

▷ vtstateparks.com

▷ Tent Sites and Lean-to Sites

▷ $

It is hard to imagine a better place for tent camping in all of New England. The campground at Smugglers' Notch State Park only has twenty tent sites and fourteen lean-to sites, and most of them are walk-in. These terrific sites have a parking area near the road, and then steps or a short path that lead to private campsites with handmade brick and stone firepits. Very small RVs can technically fit into a few of the non-walk-in sites, but the state park discourages you from even trying. It would require very specific firsthand knowledge to determine whether your RV could make it into one of these sites, so don't try it your first time here. Outdoor adventure can be found around every corner in this astonishingly beautiful state park, so strap on your hiking boots and head into the woods for some of the best hiking in Vermont. Bingham Falls is nearby, and so are the caves where smugglers camped out during Thomas Jefferson's Embargo Act of 1807.

Quechee State Park

▷ Hartford, Vermont

▷ vtstateparks.com

▷ RV and Tent Sites, Lean-to Sites, Cabins

▷ $

The campground at Quechee State Park is lovely, just like many other Vermont state park campgrounds are lovely. But this campground wins extra points for three reasons: it is big rig friendly, it has several excellent buddy sites for those camping with friends, and it boasts an excellent location in an area that is jam packed with affordable activities and outdoor recreation. The Quechee Gorge is within walking distance and will keep young kids occupied for hours. We also love the nearby Vermont Institute of Natural Science where you can take a forest canopy walk or watch an excellent live bird program. Admission is reasonably priced, and children three and under enter for free.

--------------- Affordable Roadside Grub ---------------

✧ **Honeypie** in Jamaica

✧ **Bob's Diner** in Manchester

✧ **White Cottage Snack Bar** in Woodstock

✧ **Curtis BBQ** in Putney

✧ **The Skinny Pancake** in Stowe

ALSO GREAT

North Beach Campground

▷ Burlington, Vermont

▷ enjoyburlington.com/place/north-beach-campground

▷ RV and Tent Sites

▷ $$

Many of the sites at North Beach Campground are small, packed in close to neighbors, and lacking in shade and privacy. But the location on Lake Champlain near downtown Burlington is excellent, so griping about the quality of the sites is beside the point. Urban camping also requires compromise, no matter where you go. Make sure you bring your bikes to this campground and hop on the bike path right inside the campground. Downtown Burlington is about a mile and a half away and filled with great food, shopping, and affordable cultural activities like the Echo Leahy Center and the Ethan Allan Homestead.

- - - - - - - - -   **Great Swimming Holes (and Cliff Jumping!)**   - - - - - - - - -

✧ **Lake Shaftsbury State Park** has a wide sandy beach and dirt-cheap kayak rentals.

✧ The area below the **West Dummerston Bridge** is great for swimming— just mind the current.

✧ The **Dorset Marble Quarry** has beginner to advanced cliff jumping for a small parking fee.

✧ **Bingham Falls** in Smugglers' Notch State Park is a great place for a cool summer dip.

Emerald Lake State Park

▷ East Dorset, Vermont

▷ vtstateparks.com

▷ RV and Tent Sites, Lean-to Sites

▷ $

A gem among gems, Emerald Lake State Park is one of the prettiest places to swim, kayak, and fish in all of Vermont. The campsites here are spacious, shaded, and surrounded by lush green trees—and many of them can accommodate small- to medium-sized RVs. Adventurous campers will swim to the island across the lake and seek out the rope swing. Just take caution— accidents do happen here.

Mountain View Campground

▷ Morrisville, Vermont

▷ mountainviewcamping.com

▷ RV and Tent Sites, Cabins

▷ $$

This is a great family-owned campground for those who want to camp in a pretty location but still have hookups and amenities for the kids without breaking the bank. There are two pools and a small, adults-only hot tub, along with clean and comfortable shower and laundry facilities. Reasonably priced kayak and tube rentals are also available, and the campground has direct access to the Lamoille River, which is reason enough to camp here. The store is also well-stocked, and the staff are friendly and quick to offer great recommendations for exploring nearby Stowe, Waterbury, and Montpelier.

Jamaica State Park

- ▷ Jamaica, Vermont
- ▷ vtstateparks.com
- ▷ RV and Tent Sites, Lean-to Sites
- ▷ $

Jamaica State Park is in a cell signal dead zone—just one of many reasons why it is a great place to reconnect with nature. The campground's main loop is located just steps away from the West River, which is a great spot for swimming and fishing. There is also a row of highly desirable lean-tos right on the river, which are great for tent campers. Owners of small RVs (like teardrops and pop-up campers) also try to snag them and use the lean-to for extra living space.

------------------- **Budget-Camping Gear:** -------------------
Are Your Hiking Socks Darn Tough?

Recommending $20 to $30 hiking socks in a budget-camping book may seem counterintuitive, but we think it makes perfect sense. Darn Tough socks are made in Northfield, Vermont, and they have a lifetime guarantee. So, if you get holes in them, just send them back for a new pair. Sounds budget friendly to us—plus, these socks are darn comfortable.

Brattleboro North KOA Journey

▷ East Dummerston, Vermont

▷ koa.com

▷ RV and Tent Sites, Cabins, Vintage RV Rental

▷ $$$

This charming KOA offers full hook-up RV sites, tent sites, and cabins at very reasonable prices. The surrounding area is also packed with great hikes and classic New England scenery. You can walk right next-door to Walker Farm and stock up on organic fruits and veggies, or you can take the short drive to downtown Brattleboro for a wide variety of quirky shopping and dining experiences. Just don't forget to head back to this KOA's delightful camp store for a maple creamy after dinner. Trust us, you won't regret it.

THE MID-ATLANTIC

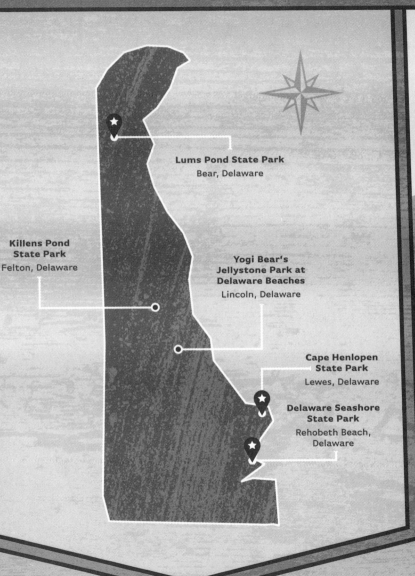

RECOMMENDED CAMPGROUNDS

★ BEST IN STATE   ○ ALSO GREAT

Lums Pond State Park
Bear, Delaware

Killens Pond State Park
Felton, Delaware

Yogi Bear's Jellystone Park at Delaware Beaches
Lincoln, Delaware

Cape Henlopen State Park
Lewes, Delaware

Delaware Seashore State Park
Rehobeth Beach, Delaware

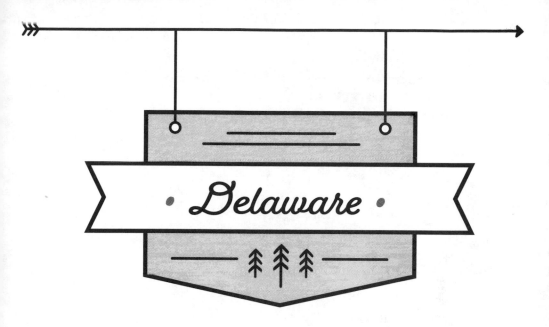

Delaware

When it comes to camping, "The First State" is small but mighty and punches way above its weight class. This is almost entirely because of its state park campgrounds and their excellent cabins, cottages, RV sites, and tent-camping sites. Delaware has seventeen state parks, and five of them have beautiful and well-maintained campgrounds. Two of them are close to the ocean (just steps away), and the other three are situated along the edge of wooded ponds. Delaware's state park campgrounds outshine those in many other states because they offer campsites with hookups and delightful alternative camping accommodations like cabins, cottages, and yurts.

Another reason why we love camping in the Delaware state park system is because of its excellent online reservation system. It's easy to navigate and you can also (in most cases) see a picture of the exact site you're considering. The "Camping This Weekend" feature allows you to see availability at each campground in a single glance. This feature even gives you a snapshot of what types of sites are available in terms of cabin sites, tent sites, RV sites, etc.

All of Delaware's state park campgrounds are pet friendly and open year-round.

If you want a camping experience with even more amenities and activities, then check out Jellystone Park Delaware Beaches. Just make sure you keep a close eye on your pic-a-nic baskets!

BEST IN STATE

Delaware Seashore State Park

▷   Rehobeth Beach, Delaware

▷   destateparks.com/Beaches/DelawareSeashore

▷   RV and Tent Sites, Cottages

▷ $

The campsites here are on the smaller side, they have little to no shade, and you can't have a campfire at your site. But once you get past those three things, everything at this campground is an absolute delight. This is, quite simply, one of the very best places for beach camping on the entire Eastern Seaboard. Families return here season after season for their weeklong summer vacations—and for some of them, this is the only place they camp all year. There are actually two campgrounds here that fly under one banner. The campground on the north side of the Indian River Inlet is newer and has full hookups at each site. It also has a delightful row of lovely waterfront cottages that can be reserved through the adjacent Indian River Marina. The campsites and cottages are just steps away from Delaware's best surfing beach. The campground on the south side of the inlet is a bit more family friendly. Some have full hookups, and some don't. The beach there has a lifeguard in the summer, and there is a modern playground and a well-stocked camp store. Make sure you head up to the Big Chill Beach Club for dinner and drinks. You can walk back to your campsite when you are done. The bridge also has a wide, gated-off pedestrian lane, so getting back and forth from either campground is easy peasy.

Cape Henlopen State Park

▷ Lewes, Delaware

▷ destateparks.com/Beaches/CapeHenlopen

▷ RV and Tent Sites, Cabins

▷ $

Cape Henlopen State Park boasts a scenic location that straddles the Atlantic Ocean and the Delaware Bay. The campground is just a five-minute walk from the beach, and the trails are also great for biking. Didn't bring your bike? You can borrow one for free, thanks to the Friends of Cape Henlopen nonprofit organization. There are a wide variety of great sites here including walk-in tent sites and RV sites with water and electric hookups. Some of the sites here can even accommodate big rigs, which is something of a rarity in East Coast state park campgrounds. The cabins here are rustic but clean and comfortable. Many of the sites are nicely shaded by scrubby, pine covered dunes, and they offer much-needed shade on hot summer days when the sun along the beach can feel relentless. Cute shopping and lots of great food can be found nearby—but many campers never leave once they settle into this coastal camping oasis.

-------------------- **Budget-Camping Gear** --------------------

Delaware is a terrific state for bird-watching, so make sure you bring a quality pair of binoculars when you camp here. If you are dropping into Delaware from the north, we recommend stopping at the Cabela's store in Christiana and picking up a pair of Cabela's Intensity HD Binoculars. They are incredibly well made and won't break the bank. They make a perfect first pair of serious binoculars for the young naturalist or adult hobbyist in your family.

Lums Pond State Park

▷ Bear, Delaware

▷ destateparks.com/PondsRivers/LumsPond

▷ RV and Tent Sites, Yurt

▷ $

Lums Pond is Delaware's largest freshwater pond, and it is the centerpiece of this large and fairly quiet state park. The campground here has the look and feel of a lovely RV park situated upon a grassy field. There are shady trees throughout, but there is little privacy between most of the sites. That is why RV owners probably love this place a bit more than tent campers. However, there is a very nice cluster of tent sites that would be great for group camping. Bring your fishing poles and your hiking shoes when you come to Lums— the fishing pier is a great spot to wet a line, and the Swamp Forest Trail that runs along the pond makes for a nice ramble. If you want to rent a kayak or a canoe, there is a concessionaire that does so inside of the park, but you will have to drive over to the other side of the pond to get equipped and launch. More adventurous souls will want to check out the zip-lining courses offered by Going Ape, an excellent concessionaire located within the park.

ALSO GREAT

Yogi Bear's Jellystone Park at Delaware Beaches

▷ Lincoln, Delaware

▷ delawarejellystone.com

▷ RV and Tent Sites, Cabins, Safari Tents

▷ $$$

This Jellystone Park will cost you at least twice as much as nearby state park options, but Yogi has more amenities and activities for the kids, so we think it is worth the splurge. The park recently added a splash pad and waterslides, and hayrides, family movie nights, and organized laser tag are offered on select nights. Older kids will enjoy the basketball and volleyball courts, and there is even a netted batting cage for soft toss. The pull-through RV sites are spacious and easy to access for those with big rigs. If you rent a cabin or safari tent, please remember to bring your own linens.

Killens Pond State Park

▷ Felton, Delaware

▷ destateparks.com/PondsRivers/KillensPond

▷ RV and Tent Sites, Cabins, Cottage

▷ $

Killens Pond flies under the radar when compared to Cape Henlopen and Delaware Seashore, but it does get busy in the summer when its excellent water park is open. The six loops here all have water and electric, and they have reasonably priced cabins and a rental cottage. You can immerse yourself in nature here by hiking the pondside trail or paddling to a stand of bald cypress trees, or you can enjoy modern amenities like the speed slides and pool at the water park located across the pond from the campground.

RECOMMENDED CAMPGROUNDS

 BEST IN STATE ○ **ALSO GREAT**

Deep Creek Lake State Park
Swanton, Maryland

Ramblin' Pines Campground
Woodbine, Maryland

Susquehanna State Park
Havre De Grace, Maryland

Rocky Gap State Park
Flintstone, Maryland

HopScratch Farm (Harvest Hosts)
Harwood, Maryland

Assateague Island National Seashore
Berlin, Maryland

Assateague State Park
Berlin, Maryland

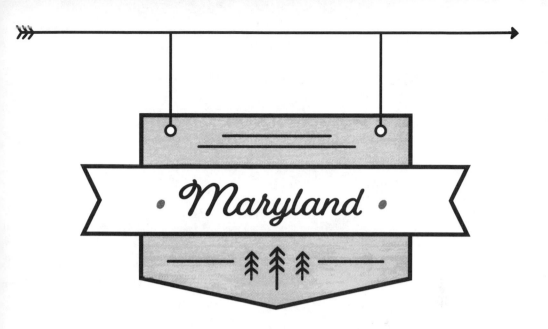

Maryland

Maryland's system of state park campgrounds has a little bit of everything. There are great campgrounds located near rivers, mountains, lakes, and beaches—and many of them fly way under the radar. Except for one. Assateague Island State Park is one of the most famous state parks in the country, and it is easy to see why. For many campers, this is the very definition of exquisite beach camping. The park has wide sandy beaches, rolling dunes, magical sunrises and sunsets, and wild horses that are legendary among campers. Assateague may be the crown jewel of the system—but it is far from the only great state-managed campground in Maryland. The other campgrounds in the system are most often enjoyed by locals and not by those traveling through the state, which is a total shame because there are some truly excellent options for camping in the Old Line State. The state park system is the first place to look for good camping, but there are many other public and private options spread throughout the state. Here are our favorite choices for budget camping.

BEST IN STATE

Assateague State Park

▷ Berlin, Maryland
▷ dnr.maryland.gov
▷ RV and Tent Sites
▷ $

In the spring, when Assateague State Park first opens for the season, it can be blustery and cold but lovely nonetheless. Summer has its magical moments if you have the gumption and the smarts to dodge the mosquitoes. The stickers and magnets that say "I Gave Blood at Assateague" are #jokingnotjoking. But when fall rolls around, the real magic begins. The bugs are gone and so are the crowds, and the water is still warm and inviting. Campsites at this perennially popular, and almost legendary, state park are also easier to nab in the fall, especially during the week. The sites on the electric loop are always hard to grab—and they aren't the prettiest anyway. We like the sites right up against the dunes, even though they don't have an ocean view, because we can fall asleep to the sound of the waves at night. This state park is equally popular among tent campers and RV owners, and for good reason: it's heavenly for both. If you are tent camping, research the sites carefully and try to find one that has some dunes around it to get privacy and protection from the wind. We recommend the state park over the national seashore for family campers, because the bathhouses have hot water and comfortable stalls for getting dressed. Bathrooms and showers at the national seashore are much sparser and more difficult to navigate. Those in self-contained rigs who can conserve water and electric use will probably prefer the even wilder beauty of the NPS campground right next door.

Assateague Island National Seashore

▷ Berlin, Maryland
▷ nps.gov

- ▷   RV and Tent Sites
- ▷ $

Some of the oceanfront campsites at the Oceanside Campground at Assateague Island National Seashore are just steps away from the Atlantic Ocean, and you can walk directly from your site down to the beach. These campsites are among the finest oceanfront campsites in the entire country—and perhaps the entire world. They are, of course, difficult to reserve, but far from impossible, especially if you are willing to camp here during the shoulder seasons. The Bayside Campground is much easier to book, and many of the sites are absolutely lovely—but you will need to walk a bit or ride your bike up to the beach. It's a small price to pay to be able to camp in paradise, and some folks like the bayside even better. After all, you can fish or launch a kayak on the bayside as well. The vibe at the national seashore is quieter and more peaceful than at the state park where families tend to congregate. But that's a fairly nuanced difference—both the state and national facilities are wonderful and welcoming whether you have kids or not. We could camp at Assateague again and again and again—and so could our kids. And that's exactly what we plan on doing.

Deep Creek Lake State Park

- ▷   Swanton, Maryland
- ▷   dnr.maryland.gov
- ▷   RV and Tent Sites, Cabins, Yurt, Bear Den
- ▷ $

The lake life is the good life, especially at Deep Creek Lake State Park in the northwest corner of Maryland. This state park has a sandy beach where campers and day-trippers can cool off in the summer. The entire campground is excellent, but many campers prefer the Meshach Browning loop because of its proximity to the aforementioned lake and swimming area. There are plenty of options for hiking here as well, so make sure you bring your hiking boots with you. Many campers are surprised to find mountains in western Maryland—but this entire section of the state is filled with delightful surprises. It's very possible you could even be surprised with a black bear sighting in this part of the state, so make sure you take the necessary precautions with your food and on the trails around the campground. Twenty-three of the eighty-two sites have electric hookups, and they are, of course, a bit harder to reserve. Deep Creek Lake also offers two mini cabins and a yurt, all with electricity and heat (but no running water), and what the park calls a "Bear's Den," which is an Adirondack-style shelter. The Delphia Brant loop is pet-free, so choose another loop if you are camping with a furry friend. Deep Creek Lake is truly an underappreciated gem in an underappreciated corner of this beautiful and diverse state.

ALSO GREAT

Susquehanna State Park

▷   Havre de Grace, Maryland
▷   dnr.maryland.gov
▷   RV and Tent Sites, Cabins
▷ $

Susquehanna State Park is situated on the lower banks of the Susquehanna River near the charming waterfront town of Havre de Grace. The camp-ground here is small and cozy, though the roads are wide and easy to navi-gate, and the individual campsites are large. There is a modern playground for the kids and an amphitheater that has educational programming in season. There is really good paddling here, but the fishing in the immediate area can be a bit temperamental. Make sure to head into Havre de Grace for breakfast or lunch at the Vintage Cafe and dinner at the Promenade Grill—both are budget friendly.

Ramblin' Pines Campground

▷ Woodbine, Maryland

▷ ramblinpinescampground.com

▷ RV and Tent Sites, Cabins

▷ $$

If you are looking for fun and affordable family camping just thirty minutes away from Baltimore and one hour away from Washington, DC, then look no further than Ramblin' Pines. This clean and well-managed campground has lots for the kids to do, including catch-and-release fishing in its charming pond, horseshoes, basketball, volleyball, and a jumping pillow and game room for rainy days. For the most part, the streets are wide and easy to navigate, and the campsites are spacious, private, and shady. The activities here are excellent, and the campground runs tournaments and contests of all kinds on the regular. Check its website for a complete calendar of events.

Rocky Gap State Park

▷ Flintstone, Maryland

▷ dnr.maryland.gov

▷ RV and Tent Sites, Cabins, Yurts

▷ $

Rocky Gap Campground has almost 300 sites, and the vast majority of them are large and level. The campsites are surrounded by trees and provide much-needed shade in the heat of summer. The campground's nine loops are not directly on the water, but they are situated along Lake Habeeb's long and skinny shoreline. Walking to the water is quick and easy, and there is a nice, guarded beach for swimming. Thirty of the sites here have electric, and the cabins and yurts are cute and affordable.

HopScratch Farm (Harvest Hosts)

▷ Harwood, Maryland

- ▷ harvesthosts.com
- ▷ **Self-contained RVs Only**
- ▷ **$**

HopScratch Farm is a lovely 12-acre property just outside charming down-town Annapolis, which is also the home of the United States Naval Academy. Baltimore and Washington, DC, are also close to HopScratch—so its location is hard to beat, and so are its steaks. Call ahead to have world-class filets or porterhouses waiting for you. The property is easy to navigate, and big rigs can easily be accommodated. Make sure you say hello to the friendly owners (and their horses, sheep, and cows) before you leave.

Budget-Friendly Games for Beach Camping

Planning on spending a week beach camping at Assateague? Then check out these four affordable games that are perfect for playing in the sand.

▷ *Pro Kadima Beach Paddles* can be found at just about any beach-themed shop in the country, and they are fun and super affordable. Grab some extra balls on Amazon—the one that comes with the set always seems to go missing halfway through the summer.

▷ *Wiffle ball* is a classic summer game that can be played with little risk of damaging anything or anyone, making it perfect for the campground and the beach. When playing on the beach, use the bat to draw a field and bases in the sand.

▷ *GSI's Freestyle Outdoors Bocce Set* comes with soft Bocce balls that are perfect for the campsite or the beach. An official court is sixty feet long by twelve feet wide, but you can make the playing field any size you want in the sand. Build a small court for the littles to play—or go the full size if you are feeling ambitious.

▷ *Wham-O's Frisbee* is a classic summer game for the beach, though we advise not using it at the campground around cars or RVs. We recommend the Frisbee Heavyweight for its sturdy design and unrivaled sailing power.

RECOMMENDED CAMPGROUNDS

★ BEST IN STATE   ○ ALSO GREAT

Mahlon Dickerson Reservation

Jefferson Township, New Jersey

Camp Gateway

Gateway National Recreation Area

The Family Campground at Turkey Swamp Park

Freehold, New Jersey

The Campground at Allaire State Park

Farmingdale, New Jersey

The Depot Travel Park

West Cape May, New Jersey

New Jersey

Budget camping in New Jersey is a somewhat tricky proposition. Real estate and property taxes are very expensive, especially in the northern and central parts of the state, so very few private campgrounds exist. That leaves only a handful of public campgrounds in those regions—and many of those are not friendly for those with large RVs. So ironically, this densely populated state is much more friendly for tent camping than it is for RVing. The southern Jersey Shore is the exception to the rule. RV parks abound in the areas surrounding Cape May and Atlantic City—but the prices for camping in those locations are much higher—and many tent campers will not enjoy camping next to large motorhomes and fifth wheels. Despite all these complexities, there are still a bunch of great places to camp in New Jersey that won't break the bank, and several of them are within striking distance of beautiful beaches. It costs money to get onto most beaches in New Jersey from Memorial Day to Labor Day, but spending a summer day enjoying the surf and sand is still a budget-friendly option when you find yourself in the Garden State.

BEST IN STATE

Mahlon Dickerson Reservation

▷   Jefferson Township, New Jersey

▷   morrisparks.net

▷   RV and Tent Sites, Adirondack Shelters

▷ $

Located an hour from New York City in far northern New Jersey, and named after the seventh governor of New Jersey, Mahlon Dickerson Reservation offers up a peaceful camping retreat in one of the most densely populated regions of the country. There are actually two separate camping areas here. One is for RVs, and one is for tent campers and those staying in Adirondack shelters. No matter how you camp, classic recreational activities such as hiking, biking, fishing, and horseback riding abound. The RV sites here are spacious and shaded and they come with water and electric hookups—something of a rarity for a public campground in the Northeast.

---------------- Free and Low-Cost Activities ----------------

✧   When camping at Gateway National Recreation Area in Sandy Hook, make sure to visit **Twin Lights** in nearby Highlands—self-guided tours are free, and it only costs a few bucks to climb the North and South Towers.

✧   **Monmouth Battlefield State Park** is less than fifteen minutes away from the Family Campground at Turkey Swamp Park in nearby Manalapan. The battle that took place here was one of the longest of the American Revolutionary War. Admission is free.

✧   Admission to the **Cape May County Park and Zoo** is also free. The zoo is charming and always popular with younger campers.

Camp Gateway/Gateway National Recreation Area

▷ Sandy Hook, New Jersey

▷ recreation.gov

▷ Tent Sites Only

▷ $

Nestled in the far northern corner of the Jersey Shore in the much beloved Sandy Hook unit of Gateway National Recreation Area, Camp Gateway is an under-the-radar gem (with less than twenty sites) that is for walk-in tent campers only. Thankfully the walk is not far. The parking lot is a quarter mile away from the nearest sites. Sandy Hook Bay is nearby, but walking to the ocean side would take a while. Hop on a bike or drive, and you will be relaxing on the warm sand in just a few minutes. The campground has restrooms but no showers, so plan accordingly. The beaches here are among the most beautiful beaches in the Garden State.

Family Campground at Turkey Swamp Park

▷ Freehold, New Jersey

▷ monmouthcountyparks.com

▷ RV and Tent Sites, Cabins

▷ $

This thickly wooded campground offers large, private sites that come with water and electric. On-site facilities include bathrooms with showers and a nice playground for the kids. If you have little ones, you should book a site with a playground view so you can watch them while you relax in your favorite camp chair. There is an archery range within walking distance of the campground and a small lake for boating and fishing is also nearby, but no swimming is allowed within the park. Bruce Springsteen grew up right here in Freehold, so the entire area is rich with his history and lore. The legendary Stone Pony is only thirty minutes away and offers live music all year long.

ALSO GREAT

Allaire State Park

- ▷ Farmingdale, New Jersey
- ▷ nj.gov
- ▷ RV and Tent Sites, Cabins
- ▷ $

The campground at Allaire State Park is rustic and peaceful, and the sites are mostly large and shaded. Thoreau would be happy here, surrounded by simplicity, simplicity, simplicity—but with hot showers in a brand-new bathhouse. The campground itself is somewhat unremarkable, but it is located in one of New Jersey's best state parks. Mountain bikers come from far and wide to ride the park's excellent network of trails. There are some tight turns inside the campground, so we do not recommend coming here with a large RV. Smaller trailers will do just fine, and so will tent campers and cabin campers. Excellent beaches can be found nearby in Manasquan and Point Pleasant.

------------------ **Budget-Camping Gear:** ------------------

Don't Forget to BYOT (Bring Your Own Toilet)!

Many of New Jersey's state park cabin rentals do not have bathrooms. Consider adding a portable toilet to your camping kit to add comfort and convenience to any cabin or tent-camping trip. When campground cabins do have bathrooms, they often cost a lot more than those without them—so why not save some money and BYOT? Camco Manufacturing makes super nifty portable travel toilets that are compact, easy to pack, and budget friendly. Their detachable holding tanks seal in bad odors, and they are easy to empty when you get back home.

The Depot Travel Park

▷ West Cape May, New Jersey

▷ thedepottravelpark.com

▷ RV and Tent Sites

▷ $$$

The Depot Travel Park has been providing a clean and comfortable place to camp near Cape May's gorgeous beaches since 1972. It is just a mile away from the ocean and all that downtown Cape May has to offer, so make sure you bring your bikes to make getting around easy. While so much of the camping industry has gravitated toward expensive glamping-type accommodations, this park has managed to keep things simple in a way that is delightfully old-fashioned. The facilities here are simple, but we think Depot Travel Park is still worth the splurge because the location is excellent. Cape May may just be the most beautiful town in New Jersey, and this is a great way to see it without busting the bank.

------ **Legendary Burgers and Dogs at the Jersey Shore** ------

Looking for cheap, casual eats on your next New Jersey camping adventure? Try the original Windmill location in Long Branch for the best hot dogs at the Jersey Shore. It's just down the road from Camp Gateway at Sandy Hook. It's shaped like a miniature windmill, so it's hard to miss!

Camping at Turkey Swamp Park in Freehold? Take a short drive to Stewart's Root Beer of Howell and order a burger, fries, and a couple of frosty bottles. Grab a table inside or just beep your horn for fast and friendly carhop service.

RECOMMENDED CAMPGROUNDS

★ **BEST IN STATE**   ○ **ALSO GREAT**

Cranberry Lake Campground

Cranberry Lake, New York

Selkirk Falls State Park

Pulaski, New York

Fish Creek Pond Campground and Rollins Pond Campground

Saranac Lake, New York

Four Mile Creek State Park

Youngstown, New York

North-South Lake Campground

Haines Falls, New York

Keuka Lake State Park

Bluff Point, New York

Yogi Bear's Jellystone Park Camp-Resort Binghamton

Endicott, New York

Glimmerglass State Park Campground

Cooperstown, New York

New York

N ew York is one of the best states for budget camping in the country. This is largely because of its robust list of more than seventy state park campgrounds and the additional fifty-two campgrounds that are managed by the DEC in the Catskill and Adirondack Mountain regions. Compared to many other states in the Northeast, when it comes to camping, New York has an embarrassment of riches. Reservations at the most popular of these campgrounds, like Fish Creek Pond Campground and North-South Lake, can be challenging on busy summer weekends—but nabbing a great spot is totally doable if you plan in advance.

The sheer geographical variety of camping in New York state is astonishing. From world-class coastal camping in Montauk on the far edge of Long Island, to the splendor of the Catskill and Adirondack Mountain Ranges (both within striking distance of New York City), to the vastly underappreciated Finger Lakes region, to the jaw-dropping power of Niagara Falls—New York really does have it all. In fact, the birth of modern camping is often credited to have taken place in the Adirondacks. Many campers love to escape the densely crowded regions around New York City and head to the mountains for a weekend, but you could also spend an entire summer (or an entire life-time) camping in New York and never get bored.

BEST IN STATE

Fish Creek Pond Campground and Rollins Pond Campground

▷   Saranac Lake, New York

▷   dec.ny.gov/outdoor

▷   RV and Tent Sites

▷ $

Experienced Adirondack campers often debate which campground is better—Fish Creek Pond or Rollins Pond. You have to drive through Fish Creek to get to Rollins, so they are inextricably joined in many people's minds. We don't think that one is better than the other, but they are quite different. The sites at Fish Creek offer less privacy than the sites at Rollins. So, if you want seclusion, choose Rollins. Fish Creek is more busy and more bustling—but for good reason. Most of the sites are directly on the water and most of them have absolutely stunning views. For the most part, the sites at Fish Creek are also easy to navigate for those in small- and moderately sized RVs. Fish Creek is filled with all types of campers, while Rollins Pond tends to have mostly tent campers. If you said that Fish Creek is for extroverts and Rollins is for introverts, you wouldn't be wrong. RVs are allowed in Rollins, but the roads are tighter and more difficult to navigate. At the end of the day, both of these campgrounds offer up stunning natural beauty with pristine waters surrounded by fragrant trees. Collectively, these two campgrounds serve as the crown jewel of Adirondack Park camping—especially for those who love kayaking or canoeing.

North-South Lake Campground

▷   Haines Falls, New York

▷ dec.ny.gov/outdoor

▷ RV and Tent Sites

▷ $

Most campers who visit North-South Lake for the first time fall in love with its fragrant wildflowers and pristine waters. The campground wraps around the top of North Lake, and the waterfront sites are cherished by New Yorkers who camp here season after season. This is one of the most popular campgrounds in the Catskills, so don't be too picky about what site you get. Take whatever you can get—even if it's not directly on the water. Creek-side sites make a great second choice if lakefront is not available. Almost all the sites are spacious, private, and wooded. Don't forget to bring your hiking boots when you camp here. The trailhead to Kaaterskill Falls can be accessed on the far side of South Lake. Get up early and go if you want peace and quiet—this iconic hike gets crowded, especially on summer weekends.

------- **Take Me Out to the (Minor League) Ball Game!** -------
Make sure you catch a Binghamton Rumble Ponies baseball game while you are camping at the nearby Jellystone Park. Tickets are affordable, and so are the snacks and hot dogs. You may just catch a rising star on their way up to the big leagues, where tickets can easily cost ten times more.

Cranberry Lake Campground

▷ Cranberry Lake, New York

▷ dec.ny.gov/outdoor

▷ RV and Tent Sites

▷ $

When it comes to swimming or paddling on a summer day, Cranberry Lake offers up a delightful slice of near-wild heaven. The rock-bottomed lake is quiet and peaceful and ringed by shady trees and delightful campsites. There is an unguarded swimming beach in the campground, but those with water-front sites will probably wade into the water just steps from their tents or RVs. Located in a remote section of the Adirondack State Park, this is yet another example of nearly perfect New York State camping. If you have kayaks, canoes, or paddleboards, then strap them on the roof and get going. The season is short this far north—and summer never lasts forever.

ALSO GREAT

Selkirk Falls State Park

▷   Pulaski, New York
▷   parks.ny.gov/parks/selkirkshores
▷   RV and Tent Sites, Cabins and Lodging
▷ $

If you are looking for a remote and relaxing getaway in an uncrowded part of the state, head to Selkirk Falls State Park on the Lake Ontario Bluffs for great fishing, hiking, and bird-watching. The sites here are large, but many lack privacy, so some sections of the park are much better for RVs than tents. The cabins here are rustic and tucked away in the woods, so if you want privacy, consider renting one of them instead of bringing your tent.

------------ **How to Become a Junior Naturalist** ------------
Kids ages five to twelve can ask for a Junior Naturalist Journal at participating campgrounds run by the New York DEC, such as the campgrounds at North-South Lake, Cranberry Lake, and Rollins Pond. If your child completes the activities in the booklet and turns it back in, they will receive a Junior Naturalist Patch. What a great (free!) keepsake from their New York State camping trip!

----- **Budget-Camping Gear: Stay Hydrated with Nalgene** -----

When you are hiking in the Catskills or Adirondacks, staying hydrated is a must. Nalgene water bottles are affordable and come in a wide variety of colors and sizes—and they are made in Rochester, New York. But be forewarned, you might be tempted to spend another $10 or $20 bucks covering yours with stickers from your travels.

Glimmerglass State Park

▷ Cooperstown, New York

▷ parks.ny.gov/parks/glimmerglass

▷ RV and Tent Sites, Cabins and Lodging

▷ $

James Fenimore Cooper called Otsego Lake "the Glimmerglass" in his 1841 novel *The Deerslayer*. Apparently, the name stuck. This lovely and underrated state park campground offers a terrific budget camping option for those who want to visit the (also affordable) Baseball Hall of Fame in Cooperstown, which is only ten minutes away. The sites here are spacious, but many are much less private than at a typical New York state park. If you need full hook-up sites on your visit to Cooperstown, check out Hartwick Highlands or the Cooperstown KOA Journey. They are both very good and won't break the bank.

--- **Stock Up and Chow Down at the Circle W General Store** ---

Forget something for your camping adventure at North-South Lake? Don't despair. The Circle W General Store has been serving customers in a pinch since 1908. Also consider grabbing sandwiches here and shoving them in your rucksack for a picnic lunch after a classic Catskills hike. There are a bunch of them nearby.

Other New York State Park Camping Gems

The entire New York state park camping system is amazing. Make sure you also check out these gems that have been reviewed in our other books:

▷ Hither Hills State Park (Montauk, New York)
▷ Letchworth State Park (Castile, New York)
▷ Robert H. Treman State Park (Ithaca, New York)
▷ Watkins Glen State Park (Watkins Glen, New York)

Keuka Lake State Park

▷ Bluff Point, New York

▷ parks.ny.gov/parks/keukalake

▷ RV and Tent Sites

▷ $

This is probably the most beloved campground in the entire Finger Lakes region. While the sites are not directly on the lake, they are just a short bike ride away from a lovely day-use area with exceptional swimming. The campground has three loops (Twin Fawns, Deer Run, and Esperanza View) that all have spacious and shaded sites. Some of them are private and some of them are not. About half of the sites in the Twin Fawns and Esperanza View loops have electric hookups at a ridiculously low price. There are no electric hookups in Deer Run.

Yogi Bear's Jellystone Park Camp-Resort Binghamton

▷ Endicott, New York

▷ binghamtonbearcamp.com

▷ RV and Tent Sites, Conestoga Wagons, Glamping Tents

▷ $$$

There are other excellent Jellystone Park campgrounds in New York that are worth visiting, but they cost much more. This Jellystone does a great job of offering up tons of family fun for a reasonable price. There isn't a pool or water park here, but there is a rustic lake with a swimming beach, floating obstacle course, and great fishing. Nonstop daily activities make this Yogi feel like a summer sleepover camp from the golden days of yesteryear.

Four Mile Creek State Park

▷ Youngstown, New York

▷ parks.ny.gov/parks/fourmile

▷ RV and Tent Sites, Yurts

▷ $

This underrated and RV-friendly state park is only fifteen minutes away from Niagara Falls, its more popular sister park. Four Mile Creek has a large campground with 275 spacious sites, so getting a spot there is relatively easy. The best part is that about half of those sites have 30-amp hookups for RV owners. The park even has a handful of 50-amp sites for larger rigs. Even if you are camping here to visit Niagara, plan on spending time enjoying the flora and fauna of this lovely park located directly on the shores of Lake Ontario.

RECOMMENDED CAMPGROUNDS

★ BEST IN STATE   ○ ALSO GREAT

Clear Creek State Park
Sigel, Pennsylvania

Willow Bay Campground
Bradford, Pennsylvania

The Campgrounds at Promised Land State Park
Greentown, Pennsylvania

Seven Points Recreation Area at Raystown Lake
Hesston, Pennsylvania

Old Mill Stream Campground (at Dutch Wonderland)
Lancaster, Pennsylvania

French Creek State Park
Elverson, Pennsylvania

Country Acres Campground
Gordonville, Pennsylvania

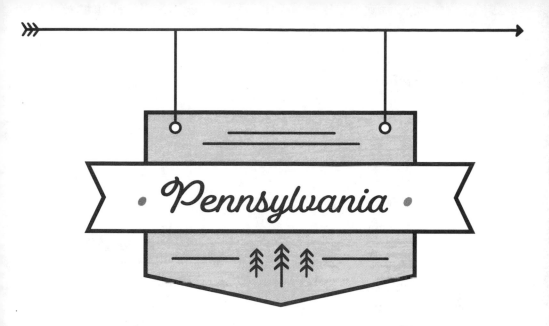

Pennsylvania

When it comes to budget camping and state park campgrounds, Pennsylvania is an absolute powerhouse in the East. Its state park campgrounds are too often only enjoyed by campers from within the state—and we think it is fair to say that it has one of the most underrated state park systems in the country. Pennsylvania also has national forest camping, which many other states in the East do not have, and they have excellent U.S. Army Corps of Engineers camping, which is also almost completely lacking in other eastern states. There are also a lot of budget priced mom-and-pop campgrounds in the state of Pennsylvania. These are places where you can get full hook-up sites along with amenities like pools and playgrounds for a very reasonable price. If you want to camp in Pennsylvania and not spend a lot of money doing it, you have plenty of amazing options without the overcrowding issues that are so predominant in the American West.

BEST IN STATE

Seven Points Recreation Area/Raystown Lake

▷ Hesston, Pennsylvania

▷ recreation.gov

▷ RV and Tent Sites

▷ $

We wish there were more U.S. Army Corps of Engineers campgrounds in the Northeast. Lots more. Because these campgrounds are almost always nice, and they are almost always in picturesque locations on the water. The sites also often have hookups, and the pricing is dirt cheap. There are six different "camps" here—basically different loops that are not directly connected. Ridge and Meadow camp are better if you have a big rig. The other "camps" are closer to the lake (which is absolutely lovely), but the roads are a bit tighter and windier, therefore they favor smaller RVs or tent-camping setups. Most of the sites have electric, but there are some tent-only non-electric sites that cost a few bucks less. Each of the camps has a playground, which makes this COE park a bit more kid friendly than others. Options for water-based recreation are abundant here, and there is a full-blown marina on property. Mountain bikers will rejoice when camping here. The Allegrippis Trails and mountain biking skills park by the visitor center are totally epic.

French Creek State Park

▷ Elverson, Pennsylvania

▷ dcnr.pa.gov

▷ RV and Tent Sites, Cabins, Cottages, Yurts

▷ $

French Creek State Park is right next door to the Hopewell Furnace National Historical Site, which preserves an early American iron plantation and is more fascinating than it sounds. So, camping here is a pretty cool two-for-one deal—you get a terrific state park right next door to an underappreciated NPS site. The main day-use area at French Creek is situated alongside Hopewell Lake, and there are places to picnic and to rent canoes and kayaks. There is also a fishing pier here. Swimming is not allowed at either of the lakes in French Creek State Park, but there is a pool. The campground is not located directly on the lake, but it is nearby, and it is lovely. More than sixty of the sites have electric, and many also have full hookups, so this is a popular park for RV owners. There are plenty of great sites for tent campers too, with plenty of shade and privacy. Many of the sites here are slightly sloped, so bring leveling gear if you are RVing. If you are tent camping just pay attention during set up, so you are comfortable when bedtime rolls around.

Promised Land State Park

▷   **Greentown, Pennsylvania**
▷   **dcnr.pa.gov**
▷   **RV and Tent Sites, Cabins**
▷   **$**

Promised Land State Park is absolutely massive, and it is probably the best overall state park for camping in the great state of Pennsylvania. This is because it has six campgrounds within its borders—and each of them is very good. Pickerel Point Campground may be our favorite because of its combination of excellent RV sites with hookups, cute camping cottages, and wonderful waterfront walk-in sites for tent campers. If you are pitching a tent and can't get one of these sites, try to get a site at Deerfield Campground as your next option. Deerfield has large, primitive sites without hookups and is another favorite among tent campers. The Lower Lake Campground has three different areas within it (Beechwood, Northwoods, or Rhododendron) that are considered to be separate sub-campgrounds that fly under the "Lower Lake" name. There is yet another rustic campground on the northwestern side of the lake called The Pines Campground, which is also loved by tent campers. All these campgrounds are lovely options at Promised Land State

Park. There is so much wild space to explore at this world-class state park. You can swim on unguarded beaches, hike to a waterfall, and fish to your heart's content. Whether you own an RV, tent camp, or cabin camp—this is where you should camp next.

> ----- **Budget-Camping Hack: Eat Lunch Out, Not Dinner** -----
>
> If you want to splurge and enjoy a meal out at a nice restaurant (in Lancaster County, Pennsylvania, or anywhere else) grab lunch and skip dinner. Lunch is often half the price of dinner, and it is much less crowded. We have made a habit of eating out for lunch instead of dinner, and we have easily saved thousands of dollars doing so. We get to sample some amazing local restaurants this way, but at a fraction of the price.

Old Mill Stream Campground/Dutch Wonderland

▷ Lancaster, Pennsylvania

▷ dutchwonderland.com

▷ RV and Tent Sites, Cabins, Park Models

▷ $$$

Old Mill Stream is an adorable campground in an unlikely location. Located just a short distance from Lincoln Highway and right next to Dutch Wonderland (a really good family-friendly theme park), this campground has no business being quiet and peaceful. But somehow it is. The setting along the stream (with farmland on the other side) is bucolic even though the highway is just steps away. The sites are nice here, and they are very affordable considering that you get full hookups. On-site amenities for the kids are fairly limited, but they do have basketball, ga-ga ball, and a playground. The operating principle here is that you spend the day at Dutch Wonderland having a blast with the kids and then come back to the campground for a quiet evening around the campfire—or at the nearby outlet stores. When you camp at Old Mill Stream you also get discounted admission to the theme park, so you can have an all-in-one family vacation at a very reasonable price. Dutch Wonderland isn't Disney World, and Old Mill Stream isn't Fort Wilderness—but they aren't trying to be. Set your expectations accordingly, and you will have an amazing time here with your family.

ALSO GREAT

Willow Bay Campground/Allegheny National Forest

▷ Bradford, Pennsylvania

▷ recreation.gov

▷ RV and Tent Sites

▷ $

Willow Bay Campground is one of the best camping options in Alleghany National Forest. There are just over one hundred sites here, and thirty-eight of them have electric. Tent campers will want to get a site in the tent-only Deer Grove Camping Area where waterfront premium sites only cost two bucks more per night—which must be the single best camping upgrade in the country. RV owners will want to grab waterfront sites on the Hemlock or Oak loops, though not all of them have electric (which only costs five bucks more.) The cabins here with heat and electric are also an absolute bargain. Overall, this is as good as budget camping gets, and the best sites are not incredibly difficult to get, even in peak season.

Clear Creek State Park

▷ Sigel, Pennsylvania

▷ dcnr.pa.gov

▷ RV and Tent Sites, Kayak Campsites, Yurts, Cabins

▷ $

Clear Creek State Park may be the prettiest state park in Pennsylvania. The campground has only fifty-two sites, and most of them have electric. The campsites along Clear Creek and the Clarion River are the best, so get one if you can. There are also twenty-two Civilian Conservation Corps rustic cabins nestled along the river, and they are about as charming and affordable as cabin camping can get. If you are looking for something a bit more adventurous and you have the gumption and the gear, there are two campsites at Clear Creek that are only accessible by canoe or kayak.

Country Acres Campground

▷ Gordonville, Pennsylvania
▷ bird-in-hand.com/country-acres-campground/
▷ RV and Tent Sites, Cabins
▷ $$

Country Acres is as cute as a button and as clean as a whistle. The price is also nice for a campground in Lancaster County with full hook-up sites. RVers love and recommend this place wholeheartedly, but there are some cute and semi-private tent and cabin sites here as well. The pool is excellent and surprisingly large for a smaller campground, but the playground is pretty basic. Make sure you head over to Bird-in-Hand for the Smorgasbord while camping here, and bring some treats home from the bakery to enjoy around the campfire at night. There are a lot of camping options in Lancaster County. This is clearly one of the best.

Five Great Hikes in Promised Land State Park

1. **Snow Shanty Trail** (0.5 miles)—This is great for a short morning walk if you are camping at Pickerel Point Campground.

2. **Conservation Island Loop** (1.01 miles)—This hike is short but memorable. The trail loops around the island with many wide-open water views along the way.

3. **Little Falls Trail** (1.02 miles)—This easy hike has charming foot-bridges and a gently rolling creek that leads to a small waterfall that is picturesque nonetheless.

4. **Boundary Trail** (5.8 miles)—If you are looking for a longer hike on a quiet trail, this one is very good. It was created as a boundary marker between Promised Land State Park and Delaware State Forest.

5. **Bruce Lake Trail** (7.3 miles)—A great hike if you head out to the lake, take in the view, and turn back. Parts of the loop around the south side of the lake have not been maintained and are wildly overgrown at the time of this writing.

THE SOUTH

RECOMMENDED CAMPGROUNDS

★ BEST IN STATE   ○ ALSO GREAT

Lake Guntersville State Park Campground
Guntersville, Alabama

Clear Creek Recreation Area in Bankhead National Forest
Jasper, Alabama

Gunter Hill Campground
Montgomery, Alabama

Oak Mountain State Park Campground
Pelham, Alabama

Jellystone Park of the Alabama Gulf Coast
Elberta, Alabama

Gulf State Park
Gulf Shores, Alabama

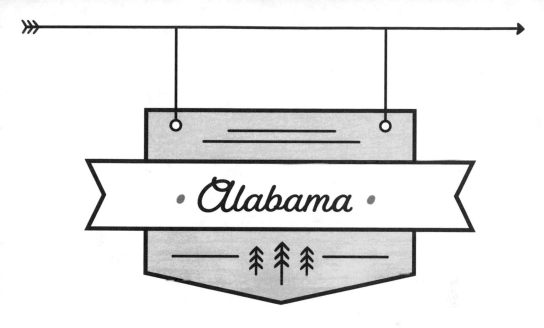

Alabama

When it comes to budget camping, Alabama delivers the goods. Its state park system is excellent and has modern recreational opportunities that you will not see in many other states—think golf, zip-lining, Segway rentals, and so much more. Classic activities like hiking and fishing also abound. There are also beautiful and affordable U.S. Army Corps of Engineers campgrounds in Alabama with campsites that will take your breath away. If that is not enough, make sure you check out the national forest camping in the state—there are many off-the-beaten-track gems to be found there. Alabama's natural landscape is stunning in so many ways. The state is filled with mountains, rivers, streams, and pristine white sand beaches. Thankfully, there are great campgrounds near all those natural wonders. So, what are you waiting for? It's time to pack up your tent or hitch up your RV and head down south to Alabama where the skies are so blue—and the campsites are available and affordable.

BEST IN STATE

Lake Guntersville State Park

▷ Guntersville, Alabama

▷ alapark.com/parks/lake-guntersville-state-park

▷ RV and Tent Sites, Cabins, Chalets, Lodge Rooms

▷ $

Lake Guntersville State Park was devastated by a tornado in April 2011. The park's superintendent called the damage "sheer devastation." The park has been completely rebuilt since then and has now become one of the best places to camp in Alabama. There are almost 300 sites at the main campground (there is also a second campground with primitive sites); most of them have water and electric, and some have full hookups. Please note that many of the sites lack shade and privacy since that the mature trees were lost during the tornado. Modern recreational opportunities abound inside this completely reimagined state park. There is a golf course, a zip line, a nature center, and an impressive beach complex. There are also cabins, lodge rooms, and stunning chalet rentals for glampers who want to splurge a little. In general, the facilities here are world class.

For just one example, consider the on-site general stores at the campground. They have all the necessities, lots and lots of tasty snacks, and even sell beer. Because who doesn't get the munchies when they go camping?

------- **Budget-Camping Hack: Go Splitsies on a Cabin** -------
Consider splitting the cost of a cabin rental with another family—of course, making this work will depend on the size of the cabin and the size of your families. Just make sure no one is sleeping on the floor!

Clear Creek Recreation Area/Bankhead National Forest

▷ Jasper, Alabama

▷ recreation.gov

▷ RV and Tent Sites

▷ $

If you camp with a canoe or kayaks, you will love Clear Creek Recreation Area. It does get busy with motorized boats on summer weekends, but it is lovely during the week. There are also lots of quiet coves to explore and plenty of refreshing places to take a dip in the clear water. There are more than one hundred sites at this campground with electric and water, and most are private and incredibly spacious—get one right on the water if you can, and you will be camping in your own private paradise. Thirty-two of the sites here are also double "buddy" sites that are terrific if you want to camp with friends. If you choose to venture out further into Bankhead National Forest, you will discover great hiking, biking, and fishing. This area is known as the land of a thousand waterfalls, so you will find a few of those too.

Gulf State Park

▷ Gulf Shores, Alabama

▷ alapark.com/parks/gulf-state-park

▷ Cottages and Cabins, RV and Tent Sites, Lodge Rooms

▷ $

Gulf State Park is an absolute favorite among Alabama's legions of campers and outdoor recreation lovers, and it is one of the finest state parks in the country. Almost two million visitors come here each year to swim and play on the sugary sand beaches and fish on the spacious pier. The campground on Lake Shelby has many of the qualities of a first-class RV resort at a fraction of the price. There are almost 500 campsites here, and almost all of them have concrete pads and full hookups. Campers with kids love the huge pool and splash pad area, which is for the exclusive use of registered campground and cabin guests. The cottages and cabins here are an absolute delight and put to shame many of the state park lodging offerings in other parts of the country. The campground at Gulf State Park should serve as a model for other state parks that want to improve their facilities in the decades to come. We would love to see state park offerings like this in New Jersey where we live—but for now we will have to hitch up and head down south to Alabama to experience public camping like this.

ALSO GREAT

Gunter Hill Campground/Alabama River Lakes

▷ Montgomery, Alabama

▷ recreation.gov

▷ RV and Tent Sites

▷ $

When people camp at Gunter Hill for the first time, they fall head over heels in love with the super long sites and the setting on Catoma Creek, and they immediately start plotting a return trip. There are almost 150 sites here with electric hookups, and about half of them have been recently improved and have full hookups. The campground is great for relaxing but also has a basketball court and

playground for the kids. Make sure you visit the Rosa Parks Museum in downtown Montgomery during your stay. Her arrest in Montgomery in December 1955 for refusing to move from her seat on a bus was a pivotal moment in the history of the Civil Rights Movement in America.

Oak Mountain State Park

▷ Pelham, Alabama

▷ alapark.com/parks/oak-mountain-state-park

▷ RV and Tent Sites, Cabins

▷ $

Oak Mountain is yet another example of a stunningly beautiful state park in the south that is also jam-packed with modern features and amenities. Oak Mountain has an eighteen-hole golf course, a BMX track, cable skiing, and horseback riding facilities—and much, much more. The campground is bordered by Beaver Lake and has a terrific mix of full hook-up, partial hook-up, and primitive sites, so there is something for everyone. The cabins here are also well-equipped with linens, utensils, cookware, and heat and air conditioning.

Jellystone Park of the Alabama Gulf Coast

▷ Elberta, Alabama

▷ jellystonegulfcoast.com

▷ Cabins, RV and Tent Sites

▷ $$

Yogi and his friends strike a perfect balance at this Jellystone Park. Campers can find peace and quiet alongside off-the-hook family fun and amenities. Many private campgrounds with lots of amenities pack campers in like sardines—but not here. Many of the RV sites look like state park sites, with plenty of elbow room and lots of shade. The cabins are also cute and offer lots of privacy and shade. BooBoo cabins are basic without bathrooms, and Cindy Bear and Yogi Bear cabins offer more space and bathrooms and kitchens. There are so many fun activities here that it is hard to know where to start.

Top Eight Things to Do in and around Gulf Shores State Park

1. Grab the shrimp and crab omelet for breakfast or the shrimp and grits for lunch at **The Ugly Diner**. The food is tasty, and the service is fast and friendly.

2. Book a guided Segway tour through a backcountry trail in Gulf State Park with **Coastal Segway Adventures**. Keep your eyes peeled for alligators and foxes.

3. Foil boards are motorized surfboards that look like they fly across the water. Get a two-hour lesson from **Foil Gulf Coast**—no previous experience necessary.

4. The **Gulf State Park Pier** is a terrific spot for fishing or for a romantic sunset stroll. Dolphins often love to swim by and say hello, so keep your eyes peeled.

5. Rent a free bike at **Gulf Shores State Park** using the park's bike-share program. Fifty bikes are available and can be checked out for up to three hours.

6. The **Gulf State Park Nature Center** is free and is home to many living examples of the area's animals and plants.

7. There are many great spots for mini golf around Gulf Shores State Park, but the pros play at **Beachside Mini Golf**, which has a fun coastal theme.

8. Let your pup run wild (and get wet) at **The Dog Pond at Lake Shelby** in the park. Hours are from 8:00 a.m. to sunset.

RECOMMENDED CAMPGROUNDS

★ BEST IN STATE   ○ ALSO GREAT

Charlton Recreation Area Campground/ Ouachita National Forest

Royal, Arkansas

Shady Oaks Campground & RV Park

Harrison, Arkansas

Petit Jean State Park

Morrilton, Arkansas

Gulpha Gorge Campground

Hot Springs National Park, Arkansas

Crater of Diamonds State Park

Murfreesboro, Arkansas

Lake Catherine State Park Campground

Hot Springs, Arkansas

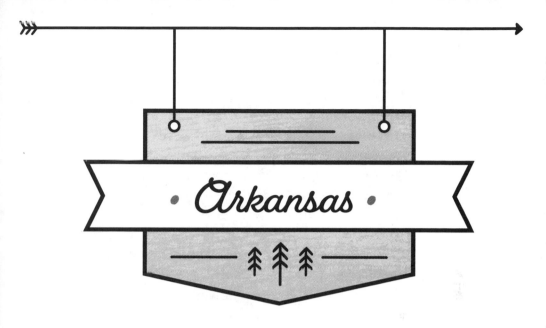

Arkansas

Arkansas has to be one of the most underrated states in the country for camping—at least for campers from the East and West coasts who rarely put a trip to the "Natural State" on their bucket lists, even though they definitely should. The state is hard to fully grasp as a camping destination when you are looking from the outside in. Arkansans know that their state is filled with dozens of terrific hidden gems, but sometimes they can be hard to find. There isn't much information out there about the many national forest and U.S. Army Corps of Engineers campgrounds that can be found here, so most people gravitate toward state park camping. Thankfully, the state park system here is very good. And don't forget to check out Hot Springs National Park—it may be the country's smallest national park, but there is a terrific budget camping option inside of the park and many great options nearby.

BEST IN STATE

Lake Catherine State Park

▷   Hot Springs, Arkansas

▷   arkansasstateparks.com

▷   RV and Tent Sites, Cabins

▷ $

Lake Catherine State Park is a destination unto itself, but it can also serve as a base camp for exploring Little Rock (which is an hour away) and Hot Springs (which is twenty minutes away). The twenty Civilian Conservation Corps cabin rentals are the star of the show here when it comes to overnight accommodations. These cabins are pretty as a picture, and they come fully equipped with linens, towels, coffee makers, and all of the necessary kitchen items to walk right in and cook—the only thing not included are the ingredients for a cozy cabin meal. One of the cabins even has its own private fishing pier. The campground here is also great. There are seventy campsites here in a parklike setting right by the lake, and more than half of them have full hookups. The waterfront sites here are magnificent, so catch one if you can. If you can't get

one of them, don't pout—the sites right across the street from them still have great water views. There are a handful of primitive tent-camping sites here and one yurt with bunk beds and a wraparound porch. There is no bathroom in the yurt, but there is one nearby. The lake is also just steps away.

Crater of Diamonds State Park

▷ Murfreesboro, Arkansas
▷ arkansasstateparks.com
▷ RV and Tent Sites
▷ $

Crater of Diamonds State Park has to be one of the most unique state parks in the country. You can actually search for diamonds in a plowed field here, and while your chances of finding a real diamond are slim, you will probably walk away with some really cool minerals and gemstones. The campground has forty-seven full hook-up sites that are shady and spacious and easy to back into—and they also have a handful of walk-in sites just for tent campers. Both of the bathhouses at the campground were recently updated and made to be more environmentally efficient. Kudos to the state of Arkansas for investing in its camping facilities.

Petit Jean State Park

▷ Morrilton, Arkansas
▷ arkansasstateparks.com
▷ RV and Tent Sites, Cabins, Lodge
▷ $

Petit Jean was the first state park in Arkansas, and it certainly set the gold standard for the rest of the beloved park system. It is located on Petit Jean Mountain, adjacent to the Arkansas River and situated between the Ouachita Mountains and the Ozark Plateaus.

Many features in the park were built by the Civilian Conservation

Corps, so Petit Jean showcases lots of the classic architecture of the New Deal. Visitors love the rustic lodges and structures built from native stone and timber. The campground is located at the northern end of the state park and is made up of four loops in total. There are a total of 125 campsites (twenty-seven of which are pull-throughs), and all have water and electric hookups. A few have full hookups, a notable state park accomplishment. Petit Jean State Park also has lodge accommodations, cabins, and yurts.

------------------ **Budget-Camping Hack:** ------------------
Don't Spend a Fortune on Firewood

Buying firewood at the campground is often very expensive. You can usually buy firewood right outside of the campground from local merchants (or in front of people's homes) for much less. Just don't transport firewood from home unless you live locally. The consequences can be devastating. Learn more about the environmental risks of transporting firewood at www.dontmove firewood.org.

ALSO GREAT

Charlton Recreation Area Campground/ Ouachita National Forest

▷ Royal, Arkansas
▷ recreation.gov
▷ RV and Tent Sites
▷ $

The campground at the Charlton Recreation Area offers up another base camp option for camping near Hot Springs, but once you are here you may never want to leave. The campground is nestled into a peaceful forest and offers shady sites with water and electric hookups in two of the three loops. Campers can swim in the day-use area if they want to cool off on a hot summer day. The water is fed by a mountain creek, so it is quite cold, but also quite refreshing. Cell phone reception is non-existent, so plan on checking out for a while if you camp here.

Shady Oaks Campground & RV Park

▷ Harrison, Arkansas

▷ camptheoaks.com

▷ RV and Tent Sites, Cabins, Glamping Tents

▷ $$

Pride of ownership is on display at this delightful family-owned campground near the Buffalo National River in the middle of the Ozarks. Every inch of this campground is super clean, and the customer service is excellent. There is a rec room for rainy days, and the park offers activities and potluck dinners on weekends. The full hook-up sites are nice, and we also recommend the cute-as-a-button cabin rentals. Glamping tents were recently added and offer guests a rare chance to try glamping without breaking the bank

Gulpha Gorge Campground/Hot Springs National Park

▷ Hot Springs National Park, Arkansas

▷ nps.gov

▷ RV and Tent Sites

▷ $

Gulpha Gorge Campground is the only campground inside Hot Springs National Park, and it is an absolute gem. This park is particularly great for RV owners, because every site offers full hookups and most of them can accommodate larger rigs. How many NPS campgrounds can you say that about?

Many of the sites are also located on Gulpha Creek, and those are the best and hardest to get. Tent campers may feel a distinct lack of privacy here, but for the price and considering there are no other campground options inside the park, we still think it is a very good option.

Eight Things to Do in and around Hot Springs, Arkansas

1. Camp at **Gulpha Gorge Campground** inside the national park. RV owners love it because it has full hookups. Tent campers will have little privacy.

2. Stop in at the **Fordyce Bathhouse Visitor Center** in Hot Springs National Park to get situated and learn about the history of Bathhouse Row—but don't plan on taking a soak here because you can't.

3. We recommend heading to **Buckstaff Bathhouse** for a Whirlpool Mineral Bath—the price is surprisingly affordable.

4. Hike the 3.3-mile **Hot Springs Mountain Trail** for scenic views of the area. Start the hike right at the Gulpha Gorge Campground.

5. **The Gangster Museum of America** tells the stories of the gangsters and reprobates that visited Hot Springs in the 1920s, '30s, and '40s.

6. The **Mid-America Science Museum** is affordable and makes for a great rainy-day activity. Permanent exhibits like The Light Bridge and The Marvelous Motion Gallery are fun and educational.

7. **Garvan Woodland Gardens** is operated by the University of Arkansas and has a lovely setting surrounded by the Ouachita Mountains. You can bring your dog, but you have to pay a small fee for them to enter. Admission for humans is also reasonably priced.

8. The **Superior Bathhouse Brewery** is the only brewery located inside a National Park in America. It uses thermal spring water as the main ingredient in the eighteen beers it keeps on tap.

RECOMMENDED CAMPGROUNDS

★ BEST IN STATE   ○ ALSO GREAT

Anastasia State Park
St. Augustine, Florida

Henderson Beach State Park
Destin, Florida

Alexander Springs Recreation Area
Altoona, Florida

Salt Springs Recreation Area in Ocala National Forest
Fort McCoy, Florida

Lake Kissimmee State Park
Lake Wales, Florida

W.P. Franklin Lock Campground
Alva, Florida

Jonathan Dickinson State Park
Hobe Sound, Florida

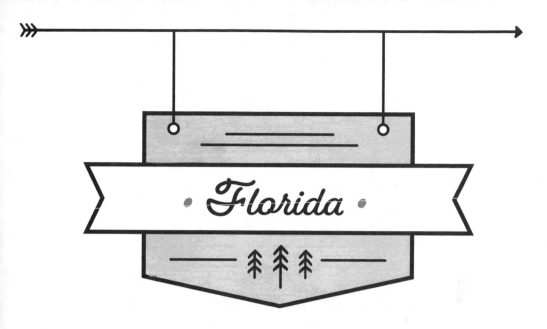

Florida

Trying to choose the best campgrounds in the state of Florida is something of a fool's errand. There are so many incredible camping options in the state that it can seem unfair to those of us who are not Floridians. So, take these picks with a grain of salt, because we know there are many other wonderful options. The state park system is legendary for having great campgrounds right on the beach and throughout the state. These state park campgrounds alone would make Florida a contender for the best camping state in the country—but of course there is so much more. The Sunshine State has wonderful national forest campgrounds and excellent waterfront U.S. Army Corps of Engineers campgrounds. There are also many excellent private mom-and-pop campgrounds—and RV resorts—but those get expensive fast. The main problem with camping in Florida, especially in the winter, is that getting sites is incredibly difficult. There are even rumors on the dark web about RV owners paying hackers to break into the state park reservation system to get sites. Yeah—it is that competitive. Because the camping here really is that beautiful.

BEST IN STATE

Henderson Beach State Park

- ▷ Destin, Florida
- ▷ floridastateparks.org
- ▷ RV and Tent Sites
- ▷ $

Henderson Beach State Park in Destin is a little slice of heaven in the Florida panhandle. The white sand beaches and warm emerald waters directly in front of the campground are downright seductive. The sixty campsites here are carved into the landscape and most are spacious, shaded, and private—and all of them have water and electric. These sites are perfect for tents or larger motorhomes and fifth wheels—they are awesome for every kind of camping experience. Amenities here are limited but natural wonders abound. The park is good for biking and great for fishing and swimming and spending time relaxing in the sand, however you want to do it. The clock slows down when you camp here. Everything about this place is peaceful and relaxing, but all the madcap fun in Destin is just a short drive away. There are amazing options for seafood nearby and a gigantic Bass Pro Shops (along with dozens of other stores) is just five minutes away. The only imperfection here is that this campground is incredibly difficult to book—but someone has to get a site, and we think it might as well be you.

Anastasia State Park

- ▷ St. Augustine, Florida
- ▷ floridastateparks.org
- ▷ RV and Tent Sites
- ▷ $

If you are a beach lover, the location of Anastasia State Park is completely epic. The campground is nestled right next to Salt Run (a 3-mile lagoon next to the beach), which is great for fishing and peaceful kayaking. There is a concessionaire right on the water that rents kayaks, canoes, and paddleboards at an affordable price, and its customer service is very friendly. A beautiful sandy beach right on the Atlantic Ocean is also just a short walk or bike ride away. Some of the best surfing in the state of Florida happens right here—so plan on waxing up your surfboards and hitting the water if the swell is good. After a long day at the beach, there isn't anything much better than chilling out and grilling out at one of the campground's 139 sites with electric and water. These sites, like so many Florida state park sites, are spacious and private and absolutely beautiful. Downtown St. Augustine, which is known for its Spanish Colonial architecture and great food and drink, is less than 3 miles away. Plan on spending some time in town even though you may never want to leave this sandy and sun-drenched campground.

Salt Springs Recreation Area/Ocala National Forest

▷ Fort McCoy, Florida

▷ recreation.gov

▷ RV and Tent Sites

▷ $

When most people think of camping in Florida, they often think of amazing oceanfront campgrounds like Henderson Beach State Park, Topsail Hill Preserve State Park, and many other spots along the coast. But there is so much more to Florida camping than those famous state parks. Case in point is the campground at Salt Springs Recreation Area in Ocala National Forest, which is an absolute gem and has some unique features. It actually almost functions as two campgrounds wrapped into one. There is a primitive tent-camping loop with fifty-four sites, and a separate loop with 106 full hook-up RV sites. The tent-camping sites are spacious, and many are private and shaded by pines and palms, while the RV sites are mostly out in the open in more of a parklike setting. Visitors love both of these campgrounds, but they love the springs even more. If you love to swim and snorkel, this is yet another slice of paradise in the Sunshine State.

ALSO GREAT

Lake Kissimmee State Park

▷   Lake Wales, Florida

▷   floridastateparks.org

▷   RV and Tent Sites, Glamping Tents

▷ $

Florida's state parks have some of the prettiest campsites in the country. In park after park, you will find sites that are carved into the landscape in an almost magical way. These sites offer privacy and seclusion and make you feel like you are living in paradise...because you are, at least for a little while. Lake Kissimmee State Park has a wonderful campground with sixty wonderful water and eclectic sites. The campground also has glamping tents and a few primitive campsites that can only be accessed by foot. There are 13 miles of trails here, and they are packed with wildlife viewing opportunities including deer and wild turkeys. The bird-watching is also great, so bring your binoculars.

W.P. Franklin Lock Campground

▷   Alva, Florida

▷   recreation.gov

▷   RV and Tent Sites

▷ $

This U.S. Army Corps of Engineers campground, which is located about 30 miles from Fort Myers, is small but magnificent. Or at least the sites directly on the water are. Each site is nicely paved and comes with a covered picnic table to provide some shade on hot summer days. There are twenty-nine RV sites here, but we wish there were a hundred more. W. P. Franklin also has boat-in sites. You can dock your boat for the night and enjoy all the campground facilities. How cool is that?

Alexander Springs Recreation Area

▷ Altoona, Florida

▷ recreation.gov

▷ RV and Tent Sites

▷ $

Like Salt Springs Recreation Area (page 109), Alexander Springs Recreation Area is located in Ocala National Forest. They are located less than 30 miles from each other. Alexander Springs also has a wonderful campground and an excellent swimming area. Kayak rentals are available, and the water is crystal clear and fun to explore. There are sixty-seven campsites here, and none of them have hookups. These sites are huge and shaded with lots of room to kick back and relax.

Jonathan Dickinson State Park

▷ Hobe Sound, Florida

▷ floridastateparks.org

▷ RV and Tent Sites, Cabins

▷ $

Another Florida state park campground with a spectacular location and spacious sites with hookups? It just doesn't seem fair to us non-Floridians, does it? There are actually two campgrounds at Jonathan Dickinson, which is located along the Sunshine State's southeast coast. Pine Grove has ninety sites, and the River Campground has fifty-two sites near the scenic and winding waters of the Loxahatchee. While you are camping here, make sure to check out the park's concessionaire. It offers an excellent boat tour of the river along with canoe and kayak rentals.

Nineteen Tips for Beach Camping in Florida

1. Always pack separate beach and bath towels to avoid bringing sand into the RV or tent.

2. Do not allow any shoes in the RV or tent. Find a place to store them outside the front door.

3. Keep a small tub of water by the door to rinse feet before coming inside the tent or RV.

4. Invest in a nice outdoor rug and broom. Sweep off the rug daily.

5. A small handheld vacuum is great for getting sand out of beds and sleeping bags—because sand *will* get in them both!

6. Use the outdoor shower if your RV has one. If not, bring a splitter and attach an extra hose to the water spigot at your campsite for a quick rinse.

7. Bring separate beach and camping chairs. Once you are showered and changed, you will want to sit around the fire without getting sandy again.

8. Always pack at least two swimsuits. No one likes putting on a wet suit for an afternoon swim.

9. Invest in quality rash guards that will protect you from the sun. They will also ease the sting while you practice your professional body surfing moves.

10. If you have younger children, pack an inflatable baby pool. Often the surf may be too rough or the water too cold for the little ones. Splashing in a baby pool on the beach will keep them happy for hours.

11. Sunscreen will be much more affordable when you buy it at home rather than in an expensive tourist shop. Make sure you get a water-resistant, high SPF.

12. Make sure everyone in the family has comfortable, breathable hats that can be worn all day.

13. Bring an umbrella or two for shaded breaks while hanging out on the beach. Never set up your beach umbrella without a handy-dandy anchors!

14. Never leave your RV awning extended while camping at the beach. We have seen many RVs lose their awnings in a single, sudden gust of wind.

15. If you are tent camping, purchase extra-long stakes to secure your tent in the sand.

16. Pin everything down. Stake those outdoor carpets, clip on the tablecloth, and put the napkins in a caddy.

17. Bring extra water and stay hydrated on the beach!

18. Don't leave food out around your campsite. You may not be in the mountains, but you can still endanger wildlife.

19. Bring fun outdoor games like Frisbee, paddle ball, and Wiffle ball for the beach!

RECOMMENDED CAMPGROUNDS

📍 **BEST IN STATE** ○ **ALSO GREAT**

Vogel State Park
Blairsville, Georgia

Jenny's Creek Family Campground
Cleveland, Georgia

Paynes Creek Campground at Hartwell Lake
Hartwell, Georgia

Duckett Mill Campground at Lake Sidney Lanier
Gainesville, Georgia

Skidaway Island State Park
Savannah Georgia

F.D. Roosevelt State Park
Pine Mountain, Georgia

Cumberland Island National Seashore
Saint Marys, Georgia

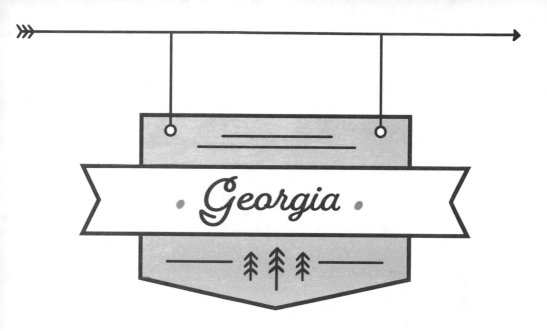

· Georgia ·

When it comes to camping, Georgia has it all. The state has invested heavily in its state park campgrounds, and it shows. RVers, tent campers, and cabin campers speak of places like Skidaway Island State Park and Cloudland Canyon State Park in hushed and reverent tones. There is also incredible National Forest Service camping here for those who want to drop off the map for a while and find some hidden gems near creeks, waterfalls, and pristine lakes—and there are U.S. Army Corps of Engineer campgrounds with some of the best waterfront sites in the country. Cumberland Island National Seashore has some of the best coastal tent camping in America, and the state still has privately owned mom-and-pop campgrounds with full hookups that offer a great value for family vacations. This is just scratching the service when it comes to camping in Georgia, because there is great camping in seemingly every nook and cranny of the Peach State—and much of it is budget friendly.

BEST IN STATE

Cumberland Island National Seashore

▷ Saint Marys, Georgia

▷ nps.gov

▷ Tent Sites

▷ $

Cumberland Island can only be reached by boat—but that is, of course, a big part of the fun. A concessionaire-run ferry (which is reasonably priced) departs from downtown Saint Marys and takes forty-five minutes to reach the island. All your tent-camping equipment needs to come with you on the boat. If you are camping at the Sea Camp campground, you can bring a cart to help transport your gear or rent one at the Sea Camp dock. If you bring your own cart, it needs to fit through a standard door frame so you can get it on and off the ferry. The Sea Camp campground is located just half a mile away, and because it is easiest to reach, it is the most popular option for camping on the island. The Stafford Beach campground is 3.5 miles from the dock, and you have to hike in to get there. The three "wilderness" campgrounds farther north (Hickory Hill, Yankee Paradise, and Brickhill Bluff) are also hike-in only. Getting here may be challenging, but once you are here it is a beach lover's paradise. The island is 17.5 miles long and filled with natural wonders. Keep your eyes open for wild horses and sea turtles—they are among the park's most popular residents.

Vogel State Park

▷ Blairsville, Georgia

▷ gastateparks.org

▷ RV and Tent Sites, Cottages

▷ $$

At the time of this writing, Vogel State Park was wrapping up some much-needed renovations to its immensely popular and beloved campground. The park was upgrading the water and electric hookups and even adding sewer to fifty of the sites. Soon RV owners will be able to enjoy full hookups in one of Georgia's oldest and most lovely state parks. Tent campers need not worry, as the gorgeous primitive sites will remain. The campground here is absolutely beautiful, just as pretty as the much more famous NPS campgrounds inside Great Smoky Mountains National Park—especially if you can get a creek-side site. The cottages near Lake Trahlyta are also excellent bargains. Some have water views and lots of private space outside, but the interiors are far from glampy. There is some amazing hiking nearby—the 4-mile Bear Hair Gap Loop that leads to Trahlyta Falls is excellent. The museum inside the park dedicated to telling the story of the young men of the Civilian Conservation Corps (CCC) is open seasonally and well worth visiting. We should all thank the young men of the CCC for building so many of the state park campgrounds that are featured in this book—and countless others.

Skidaway Island State Park

▷ Savannah, Georgia

▷ gastateparks.org

▷ RV and Tent Sites, Cabins

▷ $$

Everything about the campground at Skidaway Island State Park, located 15 miles from downtown Savannah, is spectacular—even the Spanish moss-covered road that leads you to the entrance. The sites here are spacious and shady, and the roads are easy to navigate. There are eighty-seven sites here with water and electric—and some of them even have full hookups. Because of the small size of this park, the quality of its sites, and its proximity to Savannah, this park is very difficult to book, so try to reserve a site far in advance and check back for cancelations if at first you don't succeed. The stress of trying to get a site here will fade away once you arrive and set up camp—most visitors immediately head out for a walk on the park's lovely trails. The cabins with screened-in porches and air conditioning are also quite comfortable—just don't forget to bring your own towels, sheets and blankets, dishes, and cookware.

ALSO GREAT

Jenny's Creek Family Campground

▷ Cleveland, Georgia

▷ jennyscreek.com

▷ RV and Tent Sites, Yurts, RV Rental

▷ $$

The family that owns Jenny's Creek Family Campground takes pride in offering a budget-friendly camping experience in a lovely natural setting with lots of fun activities and all the basic amenities that you need. The full hook-up sites here are very nice, and their location on Jenny's Creek in the North Georgia Mountains is excellent. There is hiking, mountain biking, and fishing nearby.

F.D. Roosevelt State Park

▷ Pine Mountain, Georgia

▷ gastateparks.org

▷ RV and Tent Sites, Cottages

▷ $$

This picturesque state park is located in lovely rolling hills just an hour and a half south of Atlanta. It flies under the radar of out-of-state campers, but it is much beloved by native Georgians who take great pride in their incredible state park system. There are more than one hundred sites here with water and electric, and they are all situated just steps away from Lake Delanor, which is great for fishing. There are also twenty-one Civilian Conservation Corps stone cottages that are absolutely adorable and also close to the lake.

Duckett Mill Campground/Lake Sidney Lanier

▷ Gainesville, Georgia

▷ recreation.gov

▷ RV and Tent Sites

▷ $

When hardworking people consider hitting the road in an RV, they often dream about ending up at places with magnificent waterfront campsites like those at Duckett Mill. Does anyone in the country do waterfront campsites better than the U.S. Army Corps of Engineers? Some of the best sites here are back-ins that slope down toward Lake Lanier—if you reserve one of these, just take your time backing in and make sure you chock up your rig. This place is also amazing for tent campers—the sites are wooded and private, and you certainly don't need an RV to enjoy them. Fourteen of the sites here are actually tent only, while the other ninety-seven sites have water and electric.

Paynes Creek Campground/Hartwell Lake

▷ Hartwell, Georgia

▷ hartcountyga.gov

▷ RV and Tent Sites

▷ $

Paynes Creek Campground was built by the U.S. Army Corps of Engineers but is currently leased and managed by Hart County, Georgia. The facilities here (especially the bathrooms) could use some updating, but besides that this place is an absolute gem. Most of the water and electric sites here are directly on Hartwell Lake, and there are some nice little sandy beaches for swimming spread throughout the campground. Some of those little beaches are right in front of the sites, allowing campers to have their own little private slice of paradise.

More Budget Camping in Chattahoochee and Oconee National Forests

These two national forests have more than thirty campgrounds between them—though most of them are in Chattahoochee in far northern Georgia. Here are four National Forest Service gems that are definitely worth checking out. Sites can be booked through recreation.gov.

1. **Lake Rabun Beach Campground** near Clarksville, Georgia, has eighty sites, many of which are near a peaceful lake with a small beach.
2. **Morganton Point Campground** near Blue Ridge, Georgia, has water and electric hookups and has great hiking and fishing nearby.
3. You can hike to two waterfalls near **Desoto Falls Campground**, which is near Cleveland, Georgia.
4. There is a small but beautiful waterfall near **Sarah's Creek Campground** near Clayton, Georgia, and the trout fishing in the creek is excellent.

RECOMMENDED CAMPGROUNDS

★ BEST IN STATE   ○ ALSO GREAT

Carter Caves State Resort Park
Olive Hill, Kentucky

Kentucky Horse Park Campground
Lexington, Kentucky

Hillman Ferry Campground at Land Between the Lakes
Grand Rivers, Kentucky

Holly Bay Campground in Daniel Boone National Forest
London, Kentucky

Natural Bridge State Resort Park
Slade, Kentucky

Bailey's Point Campground
Scottsville, Kentucky

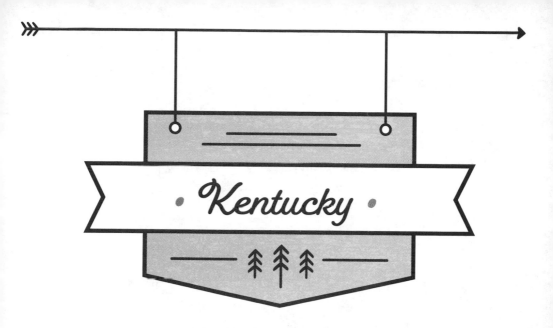

Kentucky

When campgrounds across the country (both public and private) began to raise their rates during the pandemic, the campgrounds in Kentucky gleefully ignored the message. Camping in Kentucky is just downright affordable—whether you choose to stay in a public or private campground, you will not have to break the bank. The resort camping trend that has taken root in other southern states has also been slow to gather any momentum here. That may also be because there are so many lovely camping options at public campgrounds that those considering building high-end private campgrounds might feel like they can't compete. When it comes to public campgrounds, Kentucky has it all. Great state park campgrounds, NPS campgrounds, national forest campgrounds, and some real gems from the U.S. Army Corps of Engineers. Kentucky may be known for its horse racing and bourbon, but it is also well-known for its great camping, at least by its residents and neighboring states. The rest of the country should pay more attention. There is bucket-list camping all over this great state.

BEST IN STATE

Holly Bay Campground/Daniel Boone National Forest

▷ London, Kentucky

▷ fs.usda.gov

▷ RV and Tent Sites

▷ $

Holly Bay Campground has to be one of the best National Forest Service campgrounds in the country. The seventy-five deeply wooded RV sites here have water and electric hookups, and you will feel like you have your own private slice of the forest when you are staying in one. It would be very difficult to find a bad campsite here, but those near Laurel River Lake are the most desirable— especially the two-tiered sites with an upper level for your tent or camper and a lower level for your picnic table. There are also nineteen walk-in sites for those who love to tent camp and want even more privacy and seclusion. Most of the action at Holly Bay happens on and around the water. There is a swimming beach near the campground, a boat ramp, and even a marina. Laurel Lake is one of the clearest, cleanest, and most beautiful lakes in all of Kentucky, and its wooded shoreline is filled with quiet nooks that are wonderful for exploring by boat. There are other campgrounds on this lake as well, and two of them are commonly accessed by boat, though you can also hike in.

Kentucky Horse Park Campground

▷ Lexington, Kentucky

▷ kyhorsepark.com

▷ RV and Tent Sites

▷ $

This publicly owned campground has the look and feel of a private RV resort, but it costs a fraction of the price. One of the only visible differences between this and a true resort is that the sites have water and electric, but not sewer. This is a more RV-centric campground, as most of the more than 260 sites have hookups—but there are some primitive campsites available. Big rigs are welcome here, and all of the water and electric sites are advertised as being fifty-five feet long. Families will enjoy the pool and playgrounds, and those with older kids will be happy to see basketball, volleyball, and tennis courts. The entire campground is also nicely paved and great for biking. You will be doing a lot of walking if you don't bring a bike, so consider bringing them along for the ride. Campers who want to visit the amazing Kentucky Horse Park will also be pleased to know that they can purchase discounted tickets at the camp store—and their parking will also be free.

------------ **Four Awesome Kentucky Attractions** ------------
with Nearby Camping Options

1. **The Louisville Slugger Museum and Factory** and the **Mohammed Ali Center** in downtown Louisville are both excellent whether you love those respective sports or not—and the Louisville South KOA is very popular and within striking distance.

2. **Mammoth Cave National Park** is the state's most-visited attraction with many great campgrounds nearby including the Wax Campground by the U.S. Army Corps of Engineers (for those on a budget) and a great Jellystone Park (for those who want to splurge).

3. **The Bluegrass Music Hall of Fame and Museum** is a great place to learn about the history of this uniquely American music, and it's also a great place to check out a live show. The Diamond Lake Resort is nearby and offers tent sites, RV sites, cabins, and motel rooms.

4. **The National Corvette Museum** is a must for sports car nuts, and the guided tours, which run seven days a week, are highly recommended. Campers of all kinds love the Bowling Green KOA less than fifteen minutes away.

Hillman Ferry Campground/Land Between the Lakes

▷ Grand Rivers, Kentucky

▷ landbetweenthelakes.us/seendo/camping/hillman-ferry-campground

▷ RV and Tent Sites, Cabins

▷ $

Land Between the Lakes National Recreation Area is exactly what it says it is and more. The peninsula between Lake Barkley and Kentucky Lake is partly in the state of Kentucky and partly in the state of Tennessee—but all of it is beautiful. The entire peninsula is packed with wonderful opportunities for all kinds of outdoor recreation. The Hillman Ferry Campground is one of the best camping options for exploring this underrated region for a whole variety of reasons. The first reason is, quite simply, that it has great sites (and lots of them!) for tent campers, RV owners of every kind, and cabin campers. If you want a snapshot of the entire American camping scene, just come to Hillman Ferry on a Friday night in the summer and you will see a little bit of every kind of camping. There are almost 400 sites here—both wooded and lakefront— and the quality of the sites is very good across the board. The cabins are cute, and they have electric and air conditioning (but no bathrooms), and they can sleep up to eight people. Make sure you head over to Patti's 1880 Settlement for a meal while you are camping here—the two-inch-thick pork chop is the house specialty—but one of them will cost you more than a 50-amp electric site back at Hillman Ferry.

ALSO GREAT

Natural Bridge State Resort Park

▷ Slade, Kentucky

▷ parks.ky.gov/

▷ RV and Tent Sites, Cottages, Lodge

▷ $

There are two good campgrounds at Natural Bridge—one is called Whittleton and one is called Middle Fork, and in a general sense, both are better for those with tents or smaller RVs. There are sites that will accommodate the big rigs, but turning and backing in can be challenging. The lodge rooms in the Hemlock are nice for those without tents or RVs, and the one- and two-bedroom cottages are also very cozy. While the accommodations in this state park are very good, the outdoor activities are absolutely awesome. You can hike to the Natural Bridge or take the Skylift—either option is memorable.

Bailey's Point Campground

▷ Scottsville, Kentucky

▷ recreation.gov

▷ RV and Tent Sites

▷ $

Bailey's Point Campground is a great place to kick back, relax, and chill or grill and enjoy the camping life. With 215 sites (most with water and electric), this is much larger than a typical U.S. Army Corps of Engineers campground, but it still manages to feel small and cozy. This is because the campground is split into five loops that each have a different vibe. Obviously, the waterfront sites are the best, though some are a bit unlevel, so bring the necessary gear to level your rig if you are in an RV. Mammoth Cave National Park is just about an hour north—so you could use Bailey's Point as your base camp if you don't mind the drive.

Carter Caves State Resort Park

▷ Olive Hill, Kentucky

▷ parks.ky.gov

▷ RV and Tent Sites, Cottages, Lodge

▷ $

This campground takes some visitors by surprise because it looks more like a privately owned RV park than a typical state park campground. The sites are mostly out in the open and easy to navigate for larger RVs, so this is not exactly a tent-centric place to camp. However, there are options for back-country camping within the park. There are some fun amenities for kids here like swings and ga-ga ball, but the star of the show is the state park itself. Campers and day-trippers love the amazing cave tours, especially the Cascade Cave tour, which includes a 30-foot underground waterfall and a reflecting pool. Carter Caves State Park also offers lodge rooms and cottages, and the food at Tierney's Cavern Restaurant is excellent.

RECOMMENDED CAMPGROUNDS

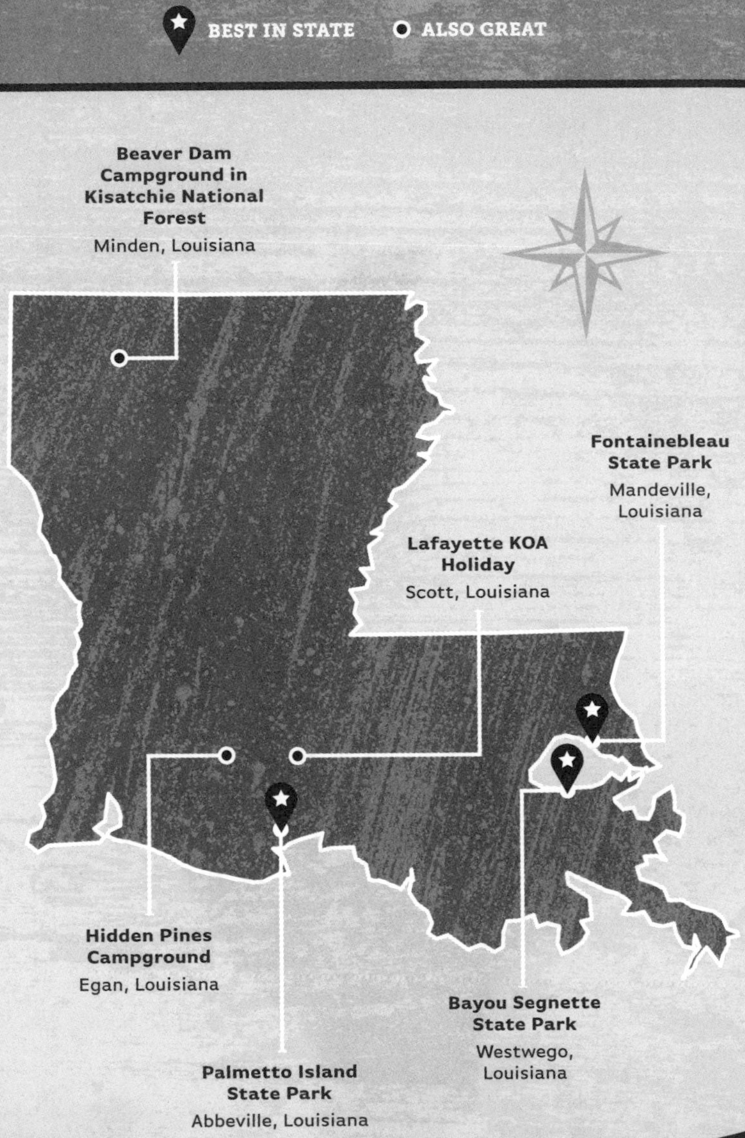

★ BEST IN STATE   ○ ALSO GREAT

**Beaver Dam
Campground in
Kisatchie National
Forest**
Minden, Louisiana

**Fontainebleau
State Park**
Mandeville,
Louisiana

**Lafayette KOA
Holiday**
Scott, Louisiana

**Hidden Pines
Campground**
Egan, Louisiana

**Bayou Segnette
State Park**
Westwego,
Louisiana

**Palmetto Island
State Park**
Abbeville, Louisiana

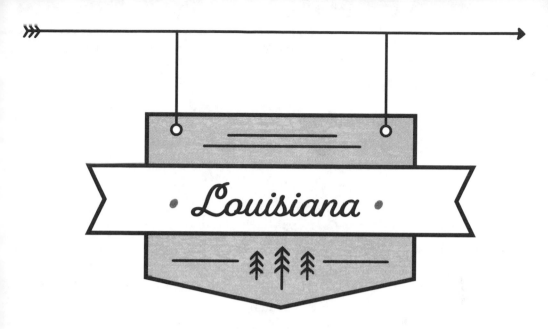

The state of Louisiana is working hard to bring tent campers, glampers, and RV owners into its great state for a vacation. It has invested in many of their state parks in recent years, especially when it comes to the area of unique accommodations like lakefront cabins and glamping tents. The state park system's public/private partnership with Tentrr should serve as an example to other states that want to improve their camping offerings to those without their own camping gear—or just those who want a unique experience for the weekend. Tentrr is a privately owned company that is partnering with a handful of state parks to bring canvas safari tent rentals to consumers. Like so many other states in the south, there is also great U.S. Army Corps of Engineers and national forest camping here. But the real surprise for some budget campers may be that many of the private campgrounds in the state are also quite affordable—and they pack a punch when it comes to family fun.

BEST IN STATE

Palmetto Island State Park

▷ Abbeville, Louisiana

▷ lastateparks.com/parks-preserves/palmetto-island-state-park

▷ RV and Tent Sites, Cabins

▷ $

The shady campsites here are spacious and private, and they are surprisingly big rig friendly. In fact, this may just be one of the most big rig friendly state parks in the country. There are ninety-six sites here with hookups, and twenty of them have full hookups at a bargain-basement price. Some of the RV sites even have a nice tent pad on them if you want to pitch a tent for your kids right near your rig. A primitive campground is also available, and there is also backcountry camping that is walk-in only. The playground at the campground is comically small, so bring some fun outdoor games for the kids to use at your site. Also make sure to check out the super fun water playground within the park, but be forewarned—it is closed on Mondays for cleaning. The campground offers free use of washers and dryers for laundry, and it has a robust lending library with dozens of options for those who need a book to read back at their awesome campsite. There is also a boat launch here and very good kayaking for those who love to paddle.

Bayou Segnette State Park

▷ Westwego, Louisiana

▷ lastateparks.com

▷ RV and Tent Sites, Cabins

▷ $

The campground at Bayou Segnette State Park is grassy and parklike with big, back-in sites and wide-open spaces that are great for games of catch or Wiffle ball. Everything about this place is peaceful and relaxing. Dog owners love the mile-long walking trail winding through a pretty swamp area that is wooded and filled with shade, making it a perfect place to take your pooch for a stroll on a hot summer day. Campers also love the laundry room with free washers and dryers—so kudos to the Louisiana state park system for doing this. It's a pretty unique amenity! The newly built waterfront cabins are also pretty awesome and have sweeping bayou views from their spacious front decks. These units have full kitchens and bunk beds that make them a great choice for families without RVs. The location of Bayou Segnette State Park is also convenient. Downtown New Orleans is only about thirty minutes away, depending on traffic. If you don't want to "camp" in the city at the French Quarter RV Resort, then this is an obvious and excellent choice.

------ **Budget-Camping Hack: Bring Your Own Ice Cream** ------

Camping can get hot in Louisiana—especially during the summer—but ice cream can help. Unfortunately, camp store ice cream can be expensive, especially if you are buying it for a bunch of kids. So why not bring your own ice cream instead? Just make sure you bring a variety of individually wrapped ice-cream-truck-style brands and flavors like chipwiches, ice cream sandwiches, chocolate eclairs, or creamsicles so your kids can pick and it still feels special. Also make sure that your kids don't eat them while you are not looking since they won't be under lock and key inside the camp store!

Fontainebleau State Park

▷ Mandeville, Louisiana

▷ lastateparks.com

▷ RV and Tent Sites, Lakefront Cabins, Lodge Rooms, Tentrr, Safari Tents

▷ $

Fountainebleau State Park is an awesome place to camp when it is warm and dry. But be forewarned—it can get soggy and swamp-like after a good rain. The sites are large and private here, and the campground has direct access to the north shore of Lake Pontchartrain. Lovely walking trails can be found throughout the park, and lodge and cabin options are excellent and affordable for those without tents and RVs. The campground is also one of several Louisiana State Parks to partner with Tentrr to provide glamping tent rentals at a reasonable price. Twelve tents are available for rent, and one of them is only reachable by canoe or kayak, so if you are looking for a memorable glamping adventure, then look no further. This has to be one of the best public/private partnerships we have seen in American state parks in recent years—kudos to the Louisiana State Park System for thinking outside of the box when it comes to accommodations. New Orleans is within striking distance for a day trip if you feel like having some gumbo or tapping your toes to some of the best music in the world.

ALSO GREAT

Beaver Dam Campground/Kisatchie National Forest

▷ Minden, Louisiana

▷ recreation.gov

▷ RV and Tent Sites

▷ $

All of the sites at Beaver Dam Campground are good, and some of them (especially those with water views and paths down to the water) are truly exceptional. The sites here are all large and shaded and offer space and privacy from one's camping neighbors. Water and electric hookups are available at each site. The location of the campground in Kisatchie National Forest places you in prime position for hiking, biking, and fishing. This is back-to-nature camping at its best. So come here to escape the cares and worries of everyday life and seek out a classic camping experience compliments of the National Forest Service.

Hidden Pines Campground

▷ Egan, Louisiana

▷ hiddenpinesllc.com

▷ RV and Tent Sites

▷ $$

Hidden Pines Campground gets universally good reviews for being clean, fun, and friendly in every way. The owner is on-site here, and the customer service is excellent. The setting of the park is lovely and shady, and the RV sites (both pull-through and back-in) are spacious and level. The pool complex is very nice, and there is live music every Friday night, while every Saturday night there is a cornhole tournament that is very popular among guests. So, brush up your A game and get ready for old-school mom-and-pop family-owned camping at its best. Everybody who visits loves it here—and so will you.

Lafayette KOA Holiday

▷ Scott, Louisiana

▷ koa.com

▷ RV and Tent Sites

▷ $$$

If you are looking for a clean and friendly campground with full hookups during your Louisiana road trip, it is definitely worth taking a look at the KOAs in the state. We think the Lafayette KOA Holiday may be one of the best of them. There are two pools and good fishing on the lake. Make sure you grab a cup of coffee in the morning before heading out—it's from a local roaster and it is very, very good. The cabins here are cozy, and KOAs can pretty much always handle the big rigs.

RECOMMENDED CAMPGROUNDS

📍 BEST IN STATE   ◯ ALSO GREAT

Wall Doxey State Park
Holly Springs, Mississippi

Tishomingo State Park
Tishomingo, Mississippi

Persimmon Hill Campground at Enid Lake
Enid, Mississippi

Clarkco State Park
Quitman, Mississippi

Paul B. Johnson State Park
Hattiesburg, Mississippi

Buccaneer State Park
Waveland, Mississippi

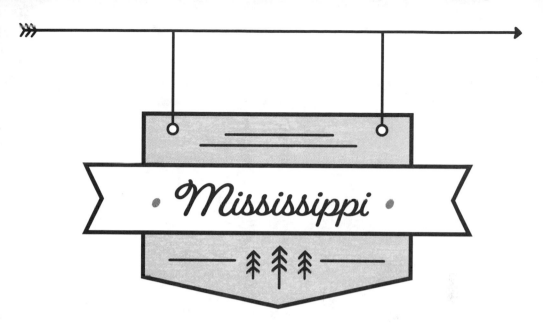

Mississippi

Mississippi has plenty of budget-friendly campgrounds across the state, but most of the best options are in its state park system. There are so many beautiful campgrounds in Mississippi's state parks that it is hard to choose which ones to feature here. Many are on the water and have excellent recreational opportunities such as hiking, biking, swimming, and boating. While these parks are beautiful, it must also be noted that many of them have been sadly neglected by the state and are woefully underfunded. The backlog for maintenance and repairs in the state park system is absolutely massive. There has been some updating throughout the system, but campers in Mississippi would certainly like to see more. Many of these state parks and their campgrounds were built by the young men of the Civilian Conservation Corps (CCC) almost one hundred years ago, and it is sad to hear so many campers complain about outdated facilities and natural landscapes that are overgrown and untended. As Americans who love the great outdoors, we should all want to honor the legacy of the CCC by pushing our state representatives to fund repairs in our great state parks—in Mississippi and elsewhere. Americans have enjoyed many of these parks for almost one hundred years, and we certainly hope that our children and grandchildren will enjoy them for the next one hundred years. But it will take more than hope to save these magnificent places for future generations.

BEST IN STATE

Tishomingo State Park

▷ Tishomingo, Mississippi

▷ mdwfp.com/parks-destinations/state-parks/tishomingo

▷ RV and Tent Sites, Cabins, Glamping Tents

▷ $

Tishomingo State Park, which is nestled among the foothills of the Appalachian Mountains on the edge of Haynes Lake, offers a classic camping experience that has been much beloved by generations of Mississippians. We are making the claim here: this is Mississippi's prettiest state park, and it is a great place to park your RV or pitch your tent. It's also a great place to rent a glamping tent through the state park system's public/private partnership with Tentrr. The most exciting thing to note about Tishomingo is that the state is investing resources into updating some of the campground's older facilities. In recent years it has even added delightful full hook-up sites that are very popular with RV owners. Many of the best sites here are perched right along the lake and offer excellent views of the water. The hiking and fishing are very good here, and you can go rock climbing with a permit. The park also has a nice swimming pool (in season) for campers and day-trippers.

Paul B. Johnson State Park

▷ Hattiesburg, Mississippi

▷ mdwfp.com/parks-destinations/state-parks/paul-b-johnson/

▷ RV and Tent Sites, Cabins, Cottages

▷ $

The campground and cabins at Paul B. Johnson State Park wrap around the calm and reflective waters of Geiger Lake, and there are views of the water from many of the individual campsites. This 225-acre freshwater lake is great for fishing and boating, and campers love to stroll around at night and simply take in the views. There are 125 RV sites here that are located on a shady hill, and they all have full hookups. We love the fact that the campground has its own private beach and swimming area that are separate from the rest of the state park. Cabin and cottage rentals are also popular at Paul B. Johnson, partly because they all have direct access to the lake and views of the water. These cabins are close to the RV sites, but they are in their own separate row. There is also an excellent area set aside for primitive tent camping. The sites in the primitive section are spacious, wooded, and private, but they do not have views of the lake. However, the lake is just a short walk away. This is one of the rare state parks that seems to treat cabin campers, tent campers, and RV owners equally, which is an approach to campground design that we fully appreciate.

Buccaneer State Park

▷   Waveland, Mississippi

▷   mdwfp.com/parks-destinations/state-parks/buccaneer

▷   RV and Tent Sites, Glamping Tents

▷ $

The name may make this sound like a cheesy third-rate theme park, but this top-notch state park is anything but cheesy. It is rich in history (think smugglers, pirates, and Andrew Jackson) and has a magnificent waterfront setting and modern amenities throughout. Buccaneer State Park's structures and facilities were completely destroyed by Hurricane Katrina in 2005, but by November 2013 the park had been completely rebuilt. The campground now offers more than 200 spacious and level sites with full hookups. There are just under fifty recently renovated sites available with stunning views of the Gulf of Mexico. Campers have been giving these newly renovated sites rave reviews. These premier sites are not the only exciting new thing at Buccaneer. This is yet another Mississippi State Park that offers glamping tents through Tentrr that are comfortable and reasonably priced. Recreational options abound inside the state park proper. Families love cooling off at the Buccaneer Bay Water Park, which is available to all campers for an additional fee. The wave pool is a blast, and the two giant water slides will keep the kids occupied for hours at a time. Make sure you bring your bikes so you can right ride up to the beach from your campsite.

> ------------------- **Budget-Camping Hack:** -------------------
> **Purchase an Annual Tentrr State Park Pass**
>
> If you live in Mississippi, Louisiana, West Virginia, New York, or Nebraska and you love camping but don't have a tent or RV, then consider getting an annual pass from Tentrr. The price may not look budget friendly at first glance, but if you feel inspired to camp a lot, the yearly fee will definitely save you money. There is also a weekday-only option that is even more affordable. If you have a non-traditional work schedule, then this could be your jam.

ALSO GREAT

Clarkco State Park

- ▷ Quitman, Mississippi
- ▷ mdwfp.com/parks-destinations/state-parks/clarkco/
- ▷ RV and Tent Sites, Cabins, Cottages, Glamping Tents
- ▷ $

Clarkco State Park is yet another example of a magnificent state park built by the Civilian Conservation Corps (CCC) during the Great Depression.

The park was built by the young men of the CCC from 1934 to 1938, and it is still being enjoyed every single day almost one hundred years later. The campground at Clarkco is wooded and shady, and some sites can fit the big rigs, but the roads can be a little tight. The sites by the lake are great if you can get one, but all the other sites are just a short walk away. Cabin and Tentrr rentals are also available, and they are nicely situated within the park.

Wall Doxey State Park

- ▷ Holly Springs, Mississippi
- ▷ mdwfp.com/parks-destinations/state-parks/wall-doxey
- ▷ RV and Tent Sites, Cabins, Cottages, Glamping Tents
- ▷ $

This is a beautiful state park campground that could use a little TLC and support from the state. Despite the fact that the park is clearly underfunded and not in its prime, it is still a lovely place to camp. The campground has sites with hookups and primitive sites for tent camping. The cabins have so much potential to be great but need some freshening up. If you want to have a glamping experience, skip the cabins and rent one of the canvas tents from Tentrr—they are getting rave reviews from visitors.

Persimmon Hill Campground/Enid Lake

- ▷ Enid, Mississippi
- ▷ recreation.gov
- ▷ RV and Tent Sites
- ▷ $

Like so many U.S. Army Corps of Engineers parks, this one is clean and has large, level sites with water views. Campers love the cute little beach area for swimming, and outdoor enthusiasts love the Persimmon Hill Multi-Purpose Trail for walking, jogging, and biking. The park tends to be packed with RVers, but tent campers are also welcome here. A nice playground will keep the little ones occupied and parents with teenagers should remember to pack a basketball. Campers with kayaks and canoes love it here. There is a boat ramp located right inside the campground.

Camping on the Mississippi Side of Gulf Islands National Seashore

We are huge fans of our national seashores (like Cape Hatteras) and national lakeshores (like Sleeping Bear Dunes) and think that they are too often over-looked in favor of NPS units with national park designations. Gulf Islands National Seashore stretches out across 150-plus miles along the northern coast of the Gulf of Mexico in Florida and Mississippi with a wide variety of coastal and marine habitats. It also has some of the coolest camping options in America.

Ever tried "boat-in" backcountry camping? Well, neither have we, but it is an awesome option for boat owners with adventurous spirits. **Primitive beach camping** is available on the following islands in Mississippi: Petit Bois, West Petit Bois, Horn Island, and part of Cat Island. Visit nps.gov to find out rules and regulations for camping in those places.

Tent and RV owners also have an excellent option for camping the **Davis Bayou Campground.** It is clean and well kept and has spacious shady sites surrounded by live oaks and pine trees. The campground is adjacent to a saltwater marsh and is in a great spot for those who love bird-watching. Downtown Ocean Springs is a short bike ride away and has good eats and fun and funky coastal shopping.

RECOMMENDED CAMPGROUNDS

★ BEST IN STATE   ○ ALSO GREAT

Bandits Roost Campground
Wilkesboro, North Carolina

Lake Powhatan Recreation Area and Campground
Asheville, North Carolina

Hanging Rock State Park
Danbury, North Carolina

Ocracoke Campground
Ocracoke, North Carolina

Deep Creek Campground
Bryson City, North Carolina

Lake James State Park
Nebo, North Carolina

Carolina Beach State Park
Carolina Beach, North Carolina

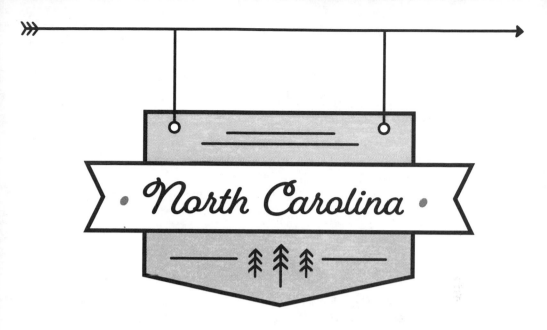

North Carolina

You could write a whole book about camping in North Carolina. Whether you are a tent camper, a cabin camper, a glamper, or an RV owner, there is an absolute embarrassment of riches for you in the Tar Heel State. The landscape in this great camping state is also incredibly varied, from the sparkling sand beaches of the Outer Banks to the rushing rivers of Great Smoky Mountains National Park. There is almost every conceivable type of campground in North Carolina: the state has RV resorts, National Park Service campgrounds, National Forest Service campgrounds, U.S. Army Corps of Engineers campgrounds, state parks, county parks, and more. We have had several epic camping vacations in North Carolina that started along the beach on the east coast and ended in the western part of the state in the Blue Ridge Mountains. It is also worth noting that the vast middle of the state is filled with great camping experiences as well. When you plan a camping trip to North Carolina, you get to choose your own adventure—from surfing in Cape Hatteras to hiking in America's most visited national park.

BEST IN STATE

Hanging Rock State Park

▷ Danbury, North Carolina

▷ ncparks.gov

▷ RV and Tent Sites, Cabins

▷ $

Hanging Rock State Park is yet another example of the profound and lasting influence that the Civilian Conservation Corps (CCC) has had on outdoor recreation in America. This state park, like so many others in the south and across the country, was largely brought into being by the hardworking young men of the CCC almost one hundred years ago. Hanging Rock State Park is magnificent in almost every way. Here you will find easy hikes to waterfalls, and strenuous hikes to epic views of the Blue Ridge Mountains. The options for biking, fishing, swimming, and kayaking are also excellent here. The campground has an upper and a lower loop filled with shaded and semi-private sites. There are no hookups at any of the sites, and the campground favors tent campers and those with smaller RVs, though there are certainly some sites that can accommodate larger rigs. There is also a lovely row of family-friendly cabins that feature spacious screened-in porches, small kitchens, heat, and electric. Hanging Rock State Park is in the middle of nowhere, so make sure you bring everything you need. There is a small country store just outside of the park for basics, but there isn't much else nearby.

Deep Creek Campground/Great Smoky Mountains National Park

▷ Bryson City, North Carolina

▷ nps.gov

▷ RV and Tent Sites

▷ $

When it comes to camping in Great Smoky Mountains National Park, Deep Creek Campground, near Bryson City, is pretty far off the beaten track. Pigeon Forge and Townsend are about an hour and a half to two hours away. But this is an absolutely magical campground that is well worth visiting. Even if you don't camp here during your Smokies trip, you should consider it for a day trip. This is one of the most beautiful places to go tubing in the country, and the campground is nestled right alongside the tubing run. The sites here are nicely shaded, but many of them offer little in the way of privacy, especially the tenting sites right along the creek—so prepare yourself for a busy, bustling campground with neighbors all around. There are three waterfalls at Deep Creek (Indian Creek Falls, Juney Whank Falls, and Tom Branch Falls), and you can see all of them in one easy 2.4-mile hike aptly named the Waterfall Loop. Tubers float right past Tom Branch Falls in one of the most beautiful little spots in the entire park. Nearby Bryson City has good food, good coffee, good beer, and whatever supplies you may have forgotten for your Deep Creek adventure. There are no hookups at this campground.

Ocracoke Campground/Cape Hatteras National Seashore

▷ **Ocracoke, North Carolina**

▷ **nps.gov**

▷ **RV and Tent Sites**

▷ **$**

It takes a bit of effort to get to Ocracoke Island, because it is only reachable by ferry, but that effort is rewarded with one of the best beach camping experiences on the East Coast—if the weather, and the mosquitoes, cooperate.

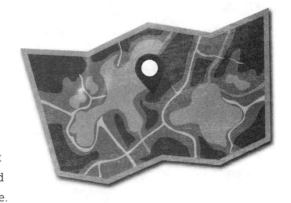

It can be very windy here (and everywhere along the Outer Banks), so get extra-long tent stakes if you are a tent camper, and if you are an RV owner, do not leave your awning unattended. Also make sure to bring lots of sunscreen and bug spray, especially in the summer. So yes, conditions can be challenging here to say the least, but there is so much to love when you are prepared, and the weather is good—including a pristine stretch of uncrowded coastline with clear water that is warm and lovely in the summer and perfect for surfing, swimming, fishing, and sunbathing. Ocracoke has more than one hundred spacious dry-camping sites that have no shade, but all are just a short walk away from the beach. The charming little town of Ocracoke is just a few minutes away for good food, charming shopping, and basic supplies.

ALSO GREAT

Carolina Beach State Park

▷   Carolina Beach, North Carolina

▷   ncparks.gov

▷   RV and Tent Sites, Cabins

▷ $

Despite not being directly on an ocean beach, and having hungry mosquitoes during the warmest months, Carolina Beach State Park, which is situated along the shores of the Cape Fear River and Snow's Cut, is a little slice of heaven that is often overlooked by non-locals. This state park is home to the Venus flytrap and a very good campground with a small selection of full hookups sites. What other state park can you say that about? Most of the seventy-nine sites do not have hookups—but the family cabins (which sleep six comfortably) do have electric, heat, and air conditioning.

Bandits Roost Campground

▷ Wilkesboro, North Carolina

▷ recreation.gov

▷ RV and Tent Sites

▷ $

You may read some negative reviews complaining about the size of the sites at Bandits Roost, but you should ignore them. Considering the price, and the natural beauty of the setting, the sites here are quite all right. Bandits Roost has seventeen tent sites that are nice and flat and eighty-five sites with water and electric—and many of them are actually quite spacious. There are two camping areas here that are both excellent. Many of the sites in camping area A have partial water views, and a handful offer spectacular water views. Camping area B is tucked away in the woods a bit more, but the trees and the shade are absolutely lovely.

---------- **Budget-Camping Gear: Intex River Tubes** ----------

Deep Creek is one of the best places for tubing in America, but renting tubes day after day can get expensive. So why not buy your own, save a few bucks, and have them for your next trip? The Intex River Run Sport Lounge has over 12,000 five-star ratings on Amazon—and the price is very reasonable. These river tubes are also comfortable and built to last, so you will get a good return on your investment.

Lake Powhatan Recreation Area

▷ Asheville, North Carolina

▷ adventurepisgah.com/lake-powhatan

▷ RV and Tent Sites, Glamping Tents

▷ $$

Lake Powhatan is the best budget-friendly camping option near Asheville, which is only about ten minutes away. The North Carolina Arboretum is also just a few minutes away, and it is absolutely lovely. The campground has four loops and each of them is within walking distance of the lake, which is good for fishing and swimming. Some of the sites here have electric—but most do not. New to the campground are twelve fully furnished glamping tents. They are not as posh as the glamping tents at Under Canvas or Collective Retreats, but they cost a fraction of the price. Is budget glamping even a thing? It definitely is at Lake Powhatan!

Lake James State Park

▷   **Nebo, North Carolina**

▷   **ncparks.gov**

▷   **Tent Sites**

▷   **$**

Lake James State Park is a tent camper's paradise. There are three different options for tent camping here, and no designated sites for RV owners. Paddy's Creek Campground has thirty-three sites that are accessible by car—the sites here are spacious and come with level pads. There are also twenty walk-in sites along the Catawba River with excellent views. If you want a more epic adventure, you can paddle out to Long Arm Peninsula to one of the thirty tent sites there—just make sure you have a reservation first.

Free and Low-Cost Activities in and around Asheville, North Carolina

Asheville, North Carolina, has become more and more expensive over the last ten years, but there are still tons of free and low-cost activities for those on a budget.

▷ **The North Carolina Arboretum** is a lovely place to spend a quiet afternoon after a morning in the city.

▷ **The WNC Nature Center** is home to more than sixty species of animals—most of which have been injured and cannot survive in the wild.

▷ **The Shindig on the Green Festival** brings free bluegrass music to downtown Asheville on Saturday evenings all summer long. Bring a lawn chair or blanket, and bring your own dinner if you want to save even more money.

▷ If you want to eat out while visiting downtown Asheville, order up a grilled cheese and a bowl of tomato soup at **Tupelo Honey**—the price is terrific, but it gets very crowded on weekends.

▷ Check out **Sliding Rock** for oodles of family fun in Pisgah National Forest. It only costs a few bucks per person to slide down this waterfall into a natural pool at the bottom. And you can go as many times as you want.

RECOMMENDED CAMPGROUNDS

★ BEST IN STATE   ○ ALSO GREAT

Robbers Cave State Park
Wilburton, Oklahoma

Big Bend Campground at Canton Lake
Canton, Oklahoma

Natural Falls State Park
Colcord, Oklahoma

Stafford Air & Space Museum (Harvest Hosts Location)
Weatherford Oklahoma

Lake Thunderbird State Park
Norman, Oklahoma

Beavers Bend State Park
Broken Bow, Oklahoma

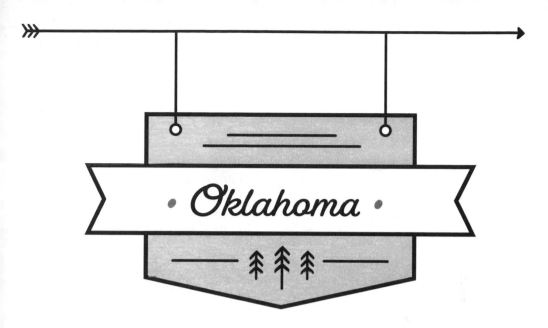

Oklahoma

Oklahoma takes pride in its state park campgrounds, and it is easy to see why. There are many updated facilities throughout the state, and the marketing for all its properties is detailed and fun. Whether you are a tent camper, a cabin camper, or an RVer, you will delight in Oklahoma's state park accommodations. There are other excellent budget camping options in the state in Ouachita National Forest, and there are also many excellent U.S. Army Corps of Engineers campgrounds. Camping at private campgrounds in Oklahoma also tends to be quite reasonably priced— though we do not feature any private campgrounds in this chapter because of the sheer abundance of great public options. That being said, we do encourage you to check out the private campgrounds in the state—there are many good KOAs and Good Sam Parks here that have kept their prices low. Oklahoma is an incredible place for an extended family vacation. It is sad that so many people never make it here or race by too quickly as they are passing through.

BEST IN STATE

Robbers Cave State Park

▷ Wilburton, Oklahoma

▷ travelok.com/robberscave

▷ RV and Tent Sites, Cabins, Yurts, Covered Wagon, Lodge Rooms

▷ $

Robbers Cave State Park offers up a robust and almost unmatched collection of accommodations for campers and glampers of every kind. The campground has full and partial hook-up sites for RVers and offers adventurous primitive sites located along quiet trails for tent campers who love seclusion. The cabins are cute and cozy with excellent views of the park, and some of them even have fireplaces. But the recently remodeled lodge is really the star of the show here. It has the look and feel of a stunning national park lodge. In fact, it is better than many of the national park lodges we have visited in recent years. The family suites at either end of this lodge can sleep ten comfortably and have two sets of bunk beds in the loft. Your kids will love it—and so will you. Even if you are tent camping or RVing during your stay at Robbers Cave, you will want to spend some time in the lodge hanging out in the lobby and relaxing. You will probably end up cheating on your tent or RV and booking a room for a family vacation or romantic couple's getaway without the kids.

Lake Thunderbird State Park

▷ Norman, Oklahoma

▷ travelok.com/state-parks/lake-thunderbird-state-park

▷ RV and Tent Sites

▷ $

Lake Thunderbird State Park has a very cool name, and it has a collection of very cool campgrounds—several on the north side of the lake and several on the south side. It's also a cool place to be in the summer when you want to swim or spend time boating on the lake during a hot summer day, and Oklahoma gets plenty of those. The park has two swim beaches, two marinas, and nine boat ramps, so it is easy to get wet here. Locals like to joke and call it Lake Dirtybird, but take that with a huge grain of salt—those same locals also love the park. Part of the problem is that Lake Thunderbird gets absolutely packed in the summer and unfortunately not everyone picks up their trash. We don't think the entire park should be downgraded because of the bad behavior of just a few. Visit during the shoulder seasons if you want to avoid the crowds—and if you see trash, pick it up. There is so much to do and enjoy here, including hiking and biking, and there are more than 200 campsites with a variety of hookups. Oklahoma City is just thirty minutes away, and this serves as a terrific base camp for driving in and enjoying all that OKC has to offer.

Natural Falls State Park

▷ Colcord, Oklahoma
▷ travelok.com/state-parks/5293
▷ Yurts, RV and Tent Sites
▷ $

Most of the RV sites at Natural Falls State Park are huge and could easily fit two RVs on them. Seven of the forty-four sites even have full hookups. Camp here on a warm summer night and you will hear the sound of kids playing catch and burgers and dogs sizzling over charcoal grills. The sites are big enough to set up a game of bocce ball or invite a bunch of friends over for a campfire. This Oklahoma gem also features a 77-foot waterfall that can be viewed by hikers from a railed observation platform and a second observation deck that has seats so you can kick back and enjoy the relaxing sound of water cascading down across the rocks. There is also a basketball court and a volleyball court for the older kids and a playground for the little ones. Glampers will also love the spacious and well-equipped yurts. They come with microwaves, small fridges, air conditioning and heat, electrical outlets, and a coffee maker. Make sure to spend some time in the forest here—it is packed with dense trees and wildflowers and makes for a perfect place for a quiet summer stroll.

------ **Four Budget-Friendly Activities in Oklahoma City** ------

1. **The American Banjo Museum** in downtown OKC has more than 400 instruments in its historic collection. The best exhibit is the Learning Lounge where you can pick up a banjo and watch instructional videos that will teach you to play.
2. Catch an affordable **Oklahoma City Dodgers** minor league baseball game at the beautiful ballpark on Mickey Mantle Drive in the super fun Bricktown district of downtown OKC.
3. After the ballgame is over, take a relaxing stroll along the **Riverwalk in Bricktown**—or for a reasonable price, take the narrated forty-minute water taxi tour. If you spend a ton of money in the shops while you are there, that's on you!
4. If you have an aesthete in the family, take them to the **Oklahoma City Museum of Art**—it has rotating exhibits and a delightful permanent collection. Admission is free for children seventeen and under.

ALSO GREAT

Big Bend Campground/Canton Lake

- ▷ Canton, Oklahoma
- ▷ recreation.gov
- ▷ RV and Tent Sites
- ▷ $

If you love to fish, then this U.S. Army Corp of Engineers campground might be your jam. Canton Lake is known for its walleye fishing, and there is even a walleye fishing derby held here once a year. Good luck getting a campsite during the event. Otherwise, this waterfront campground is fairly easy to book—but be forewarned, it can be incredibly hot here during the summer, so try the shoulder seasons. There are more than one hundred sites with water and electric, and many of them have panoramic water views.

Beavers Bend State Park

▷   Broken Bow, Oklahoma

▷   www.travelok.com/state-parks/beavers-bend-state-park

▷   Rustic and Modern Cabins, RV and Tent Sites, Lakeview Lodge

▷ $

This is a delightful place for those who love to glamp at a reasonable price. There are almost fifty comfortable cabins with kitchenettes here, and the park's location on a prime spot right along the Mountain Fork River is excellent. Some of them are even pet friendly. The forty-room Lakeview Lodge is also a glamper's delight. It is nestled along the shores of Broken Bow Lake, and every single room has a view of the water. So how about the campground? It's pretty darn special too. It has more than 400 sites (many with hookups), and it is an easy walk down to the water from most of them.

-- **Budget-Camping Hack: Anyone Can Camp with the Corps** --

You don't have to be active duty or retired military to camp at a U.S. Army Corps of Engineers campground. Many of those wonderful campgrounds, like Big Bend Campground at Canton Lake, are reviewed right here in this book. These campgrounds are all on the water, and many have striking views and spacious sites with hookups at a bargain-basement price. They may be the best-kept secret in American camping.

Stafford Air & Space Museum (Harvest Hosts)

▷ **Weatherford, Oklahoma**

▷ **harvesthosts.com**

▷ **Self-enclosed RVs Only**

▷ **$**

This Harvest Hosts location has an excellent permanent collection of aerospace artifacts and interactive exhibits that is appealing to anyone who is interested in the history of flight and space exploration—and who isn't interested in flight and space? There are four parking spots here for self-contained RVs, and they are level and easy to navigate. The staff here is also very helpful, and they respond quickly to requests for reservations.

RECOMMENDED CAMPGROUNDS

★ BEST IN STATE   ○ ALSO GREAT

Longleaf Campground in Congaree National Park

Hopkins, South Carolina

Lakewood Camping Resort

Myrtle Beach, South Carolina

Oconee Point Campground at Lake Hartwell

Seneca, South Carolina

Calhoun Falls State Park

Calhoun Falls, South Carolina

Tideland Brewing (Harvest Hosts Location)

Charleston, South Carolina

Edisto Beach State Park

Edisto Island, South Carolina

James Island County Park

Charleston, South Carolina

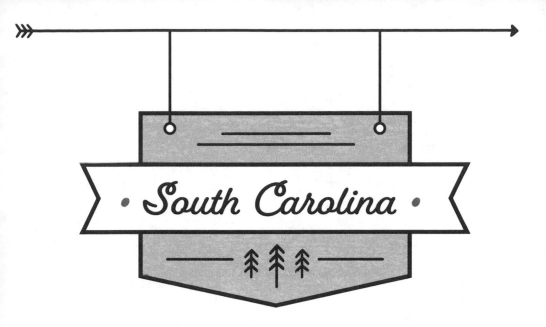

South Carolina

South Carolina is home to one of the most popular RV destinations in the country. Tampa may be home to the nation's biggest RV show, but we consider Myrtle Beach to be the capital of RVing on the East Coast. The entire area is packed with great public and private campgrounds, and many of them are directly on the ocean. State parks like Huntington Beach State Park and Myrtle Beach State Park (and Edisto further south) recently raised their prices and now are among the most expensive state park campgrounds in the country. Even so, they are still a good bargain. Ironically, there are so many good resort campgrounds in the area that those prices have remained relatively affordable when compared to recent prices in other parts of the country. But enough about Myrtle. The rest of the state also has amazing options for budget camping. Further down the coast you will find great options for affordable camping near Charleston, a city that is one of the great gems of the south. There are also affordable camping options around the popular city of Greenville in the western part of the state. Many campers do not even know that South Carolina has its own national park in Congaree—there is great budget camping there too.

BEST IN STATE

Edisto Beach State Park

▷ Edisto Island, South Carolina

▷ southcarolinaparks.com/edisto-beach

▷ RV and Tent Sites, Cabins

▷ $$

There are actually two campgrounds at Edisto Beach State Park—one is called Beach Campground and one is called Live Oak Campground. Beach is just steps away from the ocean, so it is much harder to book than Live Oak, which is a short drive or bike ride away from the beach. So, make Beach your first choice, but don't feel sad if you can only book Live Oak, which is also very pretty and deeply shaded and great for hot summer days. The sites at both campgrounds have electric hookups, and they can accommodate a wide variety of RV sizes. Most of the sites in both campgrounds are really good for tent camping because they do offer some privacy. Looking at the pictures of each site before booking will help you pick a site that is right for you. There are also seven cabins for rent here—they are not Instagram cute, but they are comfortable and very practical. Camping at Edisto Beach is much quieter and slower paced than camping in Charleston or Myrtle Beach, so if you want a super chill southern beach vacation, this is where you should camp next.

Calhoun Falls State Park

▷ Calhoun Falls, South Carolina

▷ southcarolinaparks.com/calhoun-falls

▷ RV and Tent Sites

▷ $

Calhoun Falls has two separate campgrounds (known as Campground One and Campground Two) that are also sometimes referred to as separate loops. All the sites in these two campgrounds have water and electricity except for a separate section of walk-in tent sites that are near section two. The campsites here are absolutely wonderful. They are large, private, and lovingly designed to flow into the landscape. Many of the sites on the outer loops of both campgrounds have stunning water views, so catch one of those if you can. The sites here are so large and lovely that they may spoil you and make it hard to ever camp at a private campground again. Outdoor recreation at Calhoun Falls is also excellent—there is fishing (with a license) and great kayaking and canoeing. There is an unprotected swimming area as well. You may not want to leave the park during your stay, but if you do, head to Regina's Savannah Grill for the country-fried steak with onion gravy—it is budget priced, and every bite is delicious.

James Island County Park

▷ Charleston, South Carolina

▷ ccprc.com/68/James-Island-County-Park

▷ RV and Tent Sites, Vacation Cottages

▷ $$

James Island County Park may just be the best county park in the country. It also has one of the most beloved campgrounds in the south—especially for RV owners—because many of its spacious sites have full hookups for a reasonable price. Tent campers also love the sites here, especially the walk-ins with fire rings, picnic tables, and hammock posts. These sites are in a separate area away from the main section of the campground. There are also ten charming vacation cottages for rent that are situated along the Stono River Marsh. James Island County Park encompasses 643 acres, and it is filled with excellent opportunities for outdoor recreation. Many of these are a short drive or bike ride away from the campground. The playground here is pretty epic, and so are the climbing wall and the splash zone water park. The dog park (which is the size of a small campground) is also a community hub that gets quite busy after work hours during the week. The location of James Island County Park, just minutes from downtown Charleston depending on traffic, is hard to beat when you are visiting The Holy City. We have never met someone who did not love their stay at James Island County Park. We have also never met someone who didn't want to go back...and soon. This place is that good.

ALSO GREAT

Oconee Point Campground/Lake Hartwell

▷ Seneca, South Carolina

▷ recreation.gov

▷ RV and Tent Sites

▷ $

The U.S. Army Corps of Engineers operates some of the most beautiful waterfront campgrounds in the country, and Oconee Point is clearly one of the crown jewels in its system. There are seventy sites here with water and electric—and many of them have excellent views of Hartwell Lake. There are great options for swimming, boating, and fishing here, and downtown Clemson and Clemson University are both about fifteen minutes away.

Lakewood Camping Resort

▷ Myrtle Beach, South Carolina

▷ lakewoodcampground.com

▷ RV and Tent Sites, Vacation Rentals

▷ $$$

There are so many great options for oceanfront camping in Myrtle Beach, but when it comes to budget camping, we think that Lakewood Camping Resort rises to the top. The prices here are reasonable (with full hook-up sites), and the entire campground is clean and family friendly. This place, like so many of the campgrounds in Myrtle, is like a city by the sea—but it is a city filled with RVs. The sites here are not huge, but the fun is. So, get ready to socialize with your camping neighbors and spend a few days beachside, or poolside, or both.

Longleaf Campground/Congaree National Park

▷ Hopkins, South Carolina

▷ nps.gov

▷ Walk-in Tent Sites

▷ $

The bugs are really bad here in the summer, but in the winter and shoulder seasons this is a fascinating place for adventurous campers who don't mind hauling gear to their campsites—because the sites here are walk-in only. Congaree National Park has over 26,000 acres of old-growth bottomland hardwood forest and the waters that sweep through its floodplain. There is incredible hiking, bird-watching, fishing, and kayaking in this underrated national park—and this campground puts you just half a mile away from the visitor center.

---- **More South Carolina State Park Beachfront Camping** ----

✧ **Edisto Beach State Park** is just one of four state park campgrounds with oceanfront camping in South Carolina. The other three are also excellent and could easily be "Best in State" picks in this chapter.

✧ **Myrtle Beach State Park** is less than 7 miles away from the boardwalk and promenade, but it feels like it is a world away. This classic state park is beloved by tent campers and RV owners, and there are also cabins for rent just 200 yards from the beach.

✧ **Huntington Beach State Park** is about 15 miles further south than Myrtle Beach State Park, and it is a quieter option further away from the madness of the crowd. Campsites here have hookups and shade, and there is also a walk-in tent camping area.

✧ **Hunting Island State Park** is the most-visited state park in South Carolina—it receives over one million visitors a year. Despite that fact, camping here is quiet and peaceful. There are actually two campgrounds here—one with hookups and one without.

Tideland Brewing (Harvest Hosts)

▷ Charleston, South Carolina

▷ harvesthosts.com

▷ Self-enclosed RVs Only

▷ $

This delightful brewery in North Charleston has a large, flat parking area for self-contained RVs that is easy to navigate, so getting in and out is a cinch. It has a nice outdoor seating area that is dog friendly and plenty of seating inside as well. There are twenty-five beers on tap with something for every taste, and the burgers and sandwiches are very good. Make sure you order the fried pickles with house sauce as an appetizer to go with your first brew.

RECOMMENDED CAMPGROUNDS

📍 BEST IN STATE   ○ ALSO GREAT

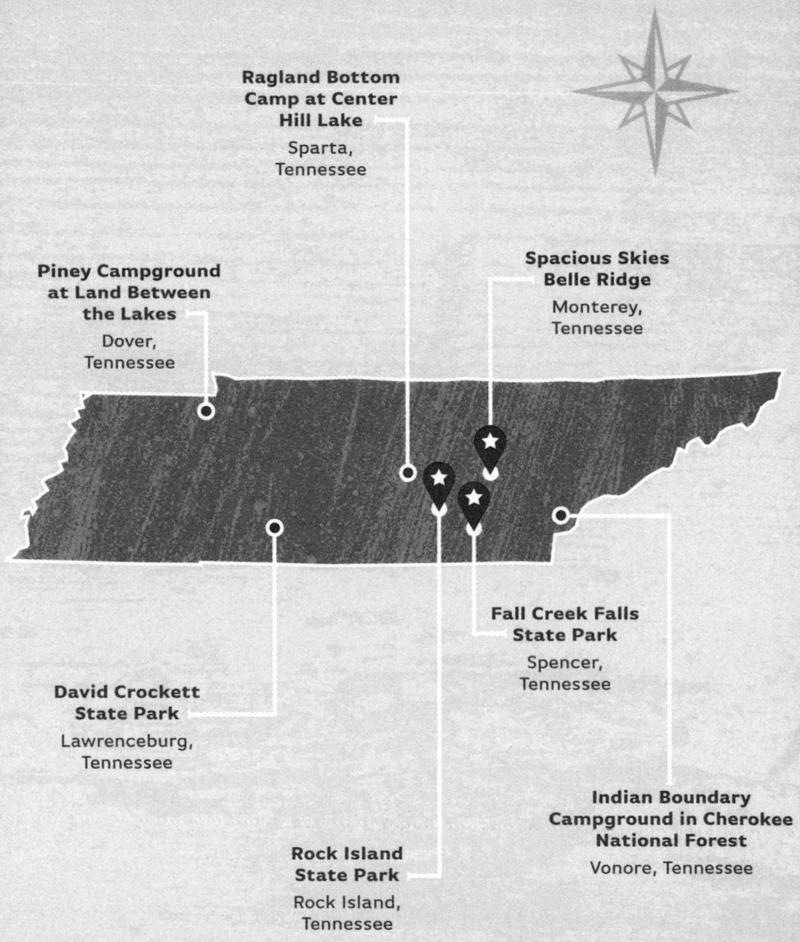

Ragland Bottom Camp at Center Hill Lake

Sparta, Tennessee

Spacious Skies Belle Ridge

Monterey, Tennessee

Piney Campground at Land Between the Lakes

Dover, Tennessee

Fall Creek Falls State Park

Spencer, Tennessee

David Crockett State Park

Lawrenceburg, Tennessee

Indian Boundary Campground in Cherokee National Forest

Vonore, Tennessee

Rock Island State Park

Rock Island, Tennessee

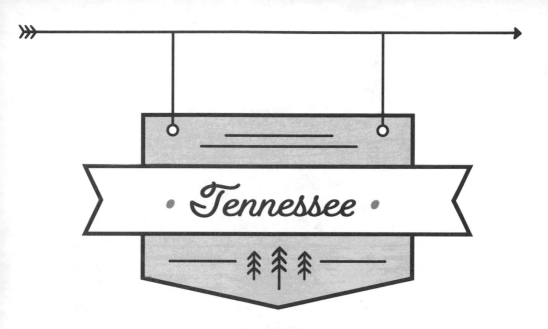

Tennessee

Much like neighboring state North Carolina, Tennessee is a camping wonderland that is packed with budget-friendly options in nearly every corner of the state. While many other state park systems have neglected their campgrounds for too long, the Tennessee state park system has invested heavily in its campgrounds, cabins, and alternate lodging. Many of the state park campgrounds here have upgraded their campsites and facilities to accommodate today's larger RVs, while simultaneously protecting and upgrading tent-camping sites across their system. You might want to take a good look at Tennessee's state parks for your next great camping trip, because they are truly amazing, but don't forget to check out its national forest campgrounds, its U.S. Army Corps of Engineers campgrounds, and its affordable private campgrounds. There are excellent options for budget camping in each of those categories as well.

BEST IN STATE

Fall Creek Falls State Park

▷ Spencer, Tennessee

▷ tnstateparks.com/parks/fall-creek-falls

▷ RV and Tent Sites, Cabins, Lodge

▷ $

Fall Creek Falls State Park is absolutely magnificent. It is one of those state parks, like Custer State Park in South Dakota, that is every bit as epic as a national park—so plan accordingly. A weekend here might not be enough—give this place some time, and let it sink into your bones. The park is packed with water features including its namesake waterfall (and many others) and countless other cascades and swimming holes. There is also rock climbing, hiking, biking, boating, fishing, birding, and much more. The park even has an excellent eighteen-hole golf course, for goodness' sake. When it comes to lodging within the park, the Fisherman Cabins on Fall Creek Lake deserve a special shout-out because they are absolutely stunning. You can even fish directly from your own private

porch when you rent one. If you can't book one of these, there are other cabins available and there is an excellent waterfront lodge. The campground here is also terrific, with 222 shady and spacious sites spread out across five different areas. They can handle the big rigs here, and many of the sites even have full hookups. It's no wonder campers come from many states away to spend their precious vacation days enjoying the wonders of Fall Creek Falls State Park. If you live anywhere near the Volunteer State, then this is where you could camp next.

------- **Budget-Camping Gear: Lodge Cast-Iron Skillets** -------

Lodge's 10-inch and 12-inch American-made cast-iron skillets may win the prize for all-time best budget camping gear. These skillets will last a lifetime, but they only cost a few bucks. They come pre-seasoned and ready for scrambled eggs or seared steaks—and basically anything you can throw at them. Make sure you visit the Lodge Museum of Cast Iron in the company's hometown of South Pittsburg, Tennessee—admission is reasonably priced, and the interactive exhibits will make you want to fire up your camp stove and get cooking.

Rock Island State Park

▷ Rock Island, Tennessee
▷ tnstateparks.com/parks/rock-island
▷ RV and Tent Sites, Cabins
▷ $

Rock Island State Park is perfect for families and great for everyone else. The amenities within the campground look more like the amenities you would find in a classic private campground. There is a modern playground, covered outdoor Ping-Pong table, really nice basketball and volleyball courts, and a nature center. There are also two hiking trails that can be accessed directly from the campground—both are good, but they are far from the best hiking trails in this park that is known for its lovely waterfalls. But more on those in a second. The campground has fifty sites all with water and electric, and a handful of them even have a place to drain the septic. These sites are almost universally shady, semi-private, and spacious. As good as this campground is, it is not even the star of the show at Rock Island State Park. Hikers come from far and wide to experience the park's excellent hiking trails—there are nine of them and several lead to waterfalls.

Spacious Skies Belle Ridge

▷ Monterey, Tennessee

▷ spaciousskiescampgrounds.com

▷ RV and Tent Sites, Cabins, House Rental

▷ $$

Because Great Smoky Mountains National Park is under two hours away, the Cumberland Plateau region is often overlooked by campers from out of state. But it shouldn't be, because this area is a natural wonderland. If you are looking for a peaceful retreat with gorgeous views, look no further than Spacious Skies Belle Ridge, a private campground that has something for just about everyone. Most of the full hook-up RV sites are out in the open without privacy—but the views are spectacular, and the sites are spacious. The cabins and lodging options here are also quite charming and very reasonably priced. Tent sites are also available in a separate loop away from the RV sites. The amenities here, including the playground, swimming hole, and jumping pillow, are very good considering the reasonable price—and there is great hiking all around the campground. Themed weekends are offered from April to November, so weekends are lots of fun, and weekdays are peaceful and quiet. This campground also earns bonus points for being incredibly clean and well-manicured—almost every inch of the property is lovely.

ALSO GREAT

David Crockett State Park

▷ Lawrenceburg, Tennessee

▷ tnstateparks.com/parks/david-crockett

▷ RV and Tent Sites, Cabins

▷ $

When it comes to state park camping, two campgrounds are always better than one. Campground #1 at David Crockett has forty-five water and electric sites and ten walk-in sites for tent campers. Campground #2 was recently renovated and has freshly paved sites with 50-amp hookups. Many of the sites in #2 can easily accommodate the big rigs. There are also stunning, modern, and energy-efficient cabins for rent right next to Lake Lindsey. While you are here, make sure to check out the museum dedicated to David Crockett, who lived nearby for a time. The museum is excellent and separates fact from fiction when it comes to this American icon. The park also has a pool, excellent hiking and biking, and much more.

Piney Campground/Land Between the Lakes

▷ Dover, Tennessee

▷ landbetweenthelakes.us/seendo/camping/piney-campground

▷ RV and Tent Sites, Cabins

▷ $

The Land Between the Lakes is a 170,000-acre natural wonderland situated between Kentucky Lake to the west and Lake Barkley to the east. Piney Campground serves as a great base camp for exploring this region, and there is plenty to do right at the campground as well, including swimming, fishing, and archery. There are almost 400 campsites here: 283 of them have electric and 44 have full hookups. The pricing for these sites is one of the best bargains in American camping.

Ragland Bottom Camp/Center Hill Lake

▷ **Sparta, Tennessee**

▷ **recreation.gov**

▷ **RV and Tent Sites**

▷ **$**

This campground, which is 15 miles west of Sparta, Tennessee, provides yet another example of beautiful and affordable waterfront camping compliments of the U.S. Army Corps of Engineers. This lush green park is situated along the shores of Center Hill Lake, which is great for boating and fishing. There are forty sites here with water and electric, and there are also sixteen primitive tent sites. Older kids will enjoy the basketball and volleyball courts, and the littles will enjoy the playground.

Indian Boundary Campground/Cherokee National Forest

▷ **Vonore, Tennessee**

▷ **recreation.gov**

▷ **RV and Tent Sites**

▷ **$**

This exquisite national forest campground is nestled along the shores of Indian Boundary Lake, and many campers consider it to be one of the prettiest campgrounds in the South. It is hard to book on summer weekends, but nabbing a site during the week or during the shoulder season is far from impossible. There are eighty-seven campsites here with electric hookups that are split up into three loops. Loops A and B are closer to the water (and the wonderful Lakeshore Trail), but Loop C is also plenty good, so take what you can get.

Tennessee Mixtape—Your Ultimate Playlist for a Road Trip to the Volunteer State

▷ Arrested Development: "Tennessee"

▷ Solomon Burke: "That's How I Got to Memphis"

▷ Chris Stapleton: "Tennessee Whiskey"

▷ Dolly Parton: "My Tennessee Mountain Home"

▷ The Osborne Brothers: "Rocky Top"

▷ Grateful Dead: "Tennessee Jed"

▷ Elvis Presley: "Memphis Tennessee"

▷ Carl Perkins: "Tennessee"

▷ Drive By Truckers: "Carl Perkins Cadillac"

▷ Bob Dylan: "Stuck Inside of Mobile with the Memphis Blues Again"

▷ Waylon Jennings: "Nashville Bum"

▷ Paul Simon: "Graceland"

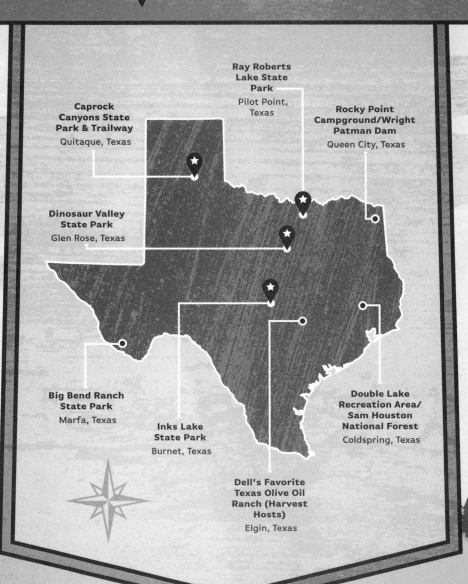

RECOMMENDED CAMPGROUNDS

 BEST IN STATE   ○ ALSO GREAT

Ray Roberts Lake State Park
Pilot Point, Texas

Caprock Canyons State Park & Trailway
Quitaque, Texas

Rocky Point Campground/Wright Patman Dam
Queen City, Texas

Dinosaur Valley State Park
Glen Rose, Texas

Big Bend Ranch State Park
Marfa, Texas

Inks Lake State Park
Burnet, Texas

Double Lake Recreation Area/ Sam Houston National Forest
Coldspring, Texas

Dell's Favorite Texas Olive Oil Ranch (Harvest Hosts)
Elgin, Texas

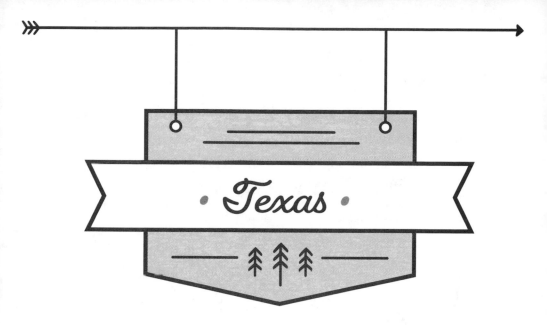

Texas

Texas is packed with high-end luxury RV resorts for the high rollers in the big rigs, but the state is also incredible for budget camping. When it comes to camping in Texas, there is truly something for everyone. It is also very possible that Texas has the best state park system for RV owners in the country. The sheer number of Texas state park campgrounds that offer full hookups for bargain-basement prices is astonishing. That is not to say that the state is not great for tent campers—because it is. Options for tent camping abound in the state park system and beyond. Texas also has a huge network of U.S. Army Corps of Engineers campgrounds and its fair share of national forest campgrounds. To the far west, Big Bend National Park and Big Bend Ranch State Park offer options for adventurous campers who want to leave the crowds behind. Everything really is bigger in Texas, and that might be especially true when it comes to camping. It's hard to even find another state to compare Texas to when you ponder its vast options for camping. California does come to mind. Just don't tell anyone from Texas that we said so.

BEST IN STATE

Ray Roberts Lake State Park

▷ Pilot Point, Texas

▷ tpwd.texas.gov/state-parks/ray-roberts-lake

▷ RV and Tent Sites, Lodge

▷ $

The campground at Ray Roberts Lake State Park is a terrific natural escape for campers who live in the Dallas/Fort Worth area. For many citizens of the DFW metroplex, the campground is just about an hour away. There are beach areas here for swimming, and the clear waters of the lake are also great for kayaking and fishing. The park has nine units and two of them have campgrounds—one is called Johnson Branch and one is called Isle du Bois. Both campgrounds have great sites with hookups. Texas campers are known to debate which campground is better, but the results of those arguments are inconclusive. Your best bet is to try both campgrounds on separate trips because they are both excellent. Primitive camping sites are also available at both campgrounds. Because this park is so close to Dallas/Fort Worth, it does get crowded on the weekends and is filled with the sounds of laughter and children playing. If that's not your jam, then camp here during the week. Don't forget to check out the lodge and marina in the Johnson Unit if you don't have an RV or tent. The lodge has charming Western decor and wonderful views of the lake. The pricing is also reasonable.

Caprock Canyons State Park & Trailway

▷ Quitaque, Texas

▷ tpwd.texas.gov/state-parks/caprock-canyons

▷ RV and Tent Sites, Lodge

▷ $

The panoramic views of the rough and rugged canyons at this state park are nothing short of spectacular. When visiting here you might feel like you are in one of our great national parks. Some of Texas's state parks have a way of doing that. Caprock Canyons State Park is located about 100 miles southeast of Amarillo in a quiet part of the state that is filled with wildlife (think bison, bats, woodpeckers, prairie dogs, pronghorn, and mule deer just to name a few) and wonderful views of dark skies at night. The campground offers large, mostly private, RV sites with electric and water and plenty of options for tent camping, including walk-in and backcountry options. Hiking and mountain biking opportunities abound in this park, and there is no-wake boating available on Lake Theo, where you will also find a modern lodge. The rooms there are not necessarily Insta-worthy, but they are practical and comfortable. This is the third largest state park in Texas, and it may be the most magnificent. Texans love to debate which state park is best, but the state is so big that few of its citizens have visited all of them. But many Texas campers will die trying—and love every second of it.

Inks Lake State Park

- ▷ **Burnet, Texas**
- ▷ **tpwd.texas.gov/state-parks/inks-lake**
- ▷ **RV and Tent Sites, Cabins**
- ▷ **$**

Texas Hill Country has to be one of the most underrated camping destinations in the country. Inks Lake State Park is located just over an hour southwest of Austin—and it is not only one of the best places to camp in Hill Country, it is one of the best places to camp in all of Texas. It's also one of the best places to beat the heat in the entire state. The lake here is great for swimming and fishing, and the park store rents paddle boats, kayaks, canoes, and more at a very reasonable price. This park is nice for biking, but watch out for grass burrs that are known to pop bicycle tires. The campground here is quite large, and there are some sections that can accommodate big rigs, but in a general sense smaller campers like pop-ups will have an easier time. There are spacious campsites all over the place, but the roads can be tight and windy in places. Inks Lake State Park also works as a great jumping-off point for day trips to Enchanted Rock State Natural Area and Colorado Bend State Park, so you could easily justify spending a week's vacation camping here. But be forewarned—it gets mighty hot in the summertime!

Dinosaur Valley State Park

- ▷ Glen Rose, Texas
- ▷ tpwd.texas.gov/state-parks/dinosaur-valley
- ▷ RV and Tent Sites
- ▷ $

Dinosaur Valley State Park in Glen Rose is unique among state parks. Where else can you search for dinosaur footprints just steps away from your campsite? The park is also a terrific place to cool off on hot summer days. The Paluxy River winds its way through this park and offers up several perfect swimming holes for cooling off on a hot Texas day. Well-marked hiking and biking trails abound for those who love nonstop outdoor adventure. This is a great place to chill or a great place to break a sweat. The campground here is small and popular, so it can be difficult to nab a site—but it is well worth the effort if you can get one. Sites are shady and private, and the facilities are clean and well maintained. Big rigs might take caution as some of the turns are tight and there are low-hanging trees. Tent campers and small RV owners love it here, though—and not just because sites have electric hookups so you can run the AC in the summer. Downtown Glen Rose is nearby and has a handful of really good restaurants and tons of Texas charm.

ALSO GREAT

Big Bend Ranch State Park

- ▷ Marfa, Texas
- ▷ tpwd.texas.gov/state-parks/big-bend-ranch

> ▷ RV and Tent Sites, Single-Bed Lodging
> ▷ $

Big Bend Ranch State Park, which is positioned along the Rio Grande in West Texas, offers a stunning alternative to Big Bend National Park for those look- ing for rugged, remote, and adventurous camping. There are a variety of options for camping here; some are drive-in and some are walk-in. All are primitive without hookups. Some people think that Big Bend Ranch only offers tent camping, but there are sites that will fit the big rigs. The night skies here are amazing. Prepare to be wowed.

-------------------- **Budget-Camping Hack:** --------------------
Get an RTIC Cooler Instead of a Yeti

We like Austin, Texas—based Yeti products, but they are definitely expensive. If you want a high-end rotomolded cooler that will keep your food and drinks cold for days but you don't want to bust the budget, check out the coolers made by Houston-based RTIC. They do a great job of keeping your beverages cold, but they cost quite a bit less than a comparably sized Yeti. RTIC coolers are not exactly cheap—but you can buy a whole lot of ice with the money you save if you skip the Yeti.

Rocky Point Campground/Wright Patman Dam

> ▷ Queen City, Texas
> ▷ recreation.gov
> ▷ RV and Tent Sites
> ▷ $

Texas has more than its fair share of excellent U.S. Army Corps of Engineers campgrounds, and the Rocky Point Campground at Wright Patman Dam is definitely one of the best. Like so many parks built by the corps, the sites are spacious and level, and many have great views of the water. Boaters and anglers love the easy-to-use boat ramp, and kids love the playground. All 124 sites have water and electric hookups.

Double Lake Recreation Area/Sam Houston National Forest

▷ **Coldspring, Texas**

▷ **recreation.gov**

▷ **RV and Tent Sites**

▷ **$**

Double Lake Recreation Area is located just outside of Coldspring, and it is a wonderful place to kick back, relax, and enjoy nature. Weekends get very busy here, so if you want peace and quiet try to come during the week. This is a national forest campground, but once again, the facilities were built by the young men of the Civilian Conservation Corps (CCC) almost one hundred years ago. Some of the sites here are just magnificent. The best sites are spacious and shady, and also offer full hookups.

Dell's Favorite Texas Olive Oil Ranch (Harvest Hosts)

▷ Elgin, Texas

▷ harvesthosts.com

▷ Self-enclosed RVs Only

▷ $

This is a really fun Harvest Hosts location just 30 miles east of Austin. It even offers 30-amp hookups for a small fee and allow for two-night stays if you purchase at least $60 worth of goods. The owner often gives a great tour of the ranch, and the olive oil here is fantastic. You can sample it before you make a purchase.

Ten Texas State Parks with Full Hookups

You could spend your entire life exploring the Texas state park system—and some tent campers and RV owners do just that. Those traveling by RV give Texas state park campgrounds especially high marks for the sheer number of campgrounds that have full hook-up sites—which is almost definitely more than any other state park system in the country. This is not a complete list of Texas state park campgrounds with full hookups, but the campgrounds at these ten parks are much beloved by Texans and definitely worth checking out.

1. Lake Corpus Christi State Park in Mathis
2. Davis Mountains State Park in Fort Davis
3. Lake Whitney State Park in Whitney
4. Palmetto State Park in Gonzales
5. Eisenhower State Park in Denison
6. Lake Casa Blanca International State Park in Laredo
7. Kickapoo Cavern State Park in Brackettville
8. Mother Neff State Park in Moody
9. Falcon State Park in Falcon Heights
10. Lake Tawakoni State Park in Wills Point

Texas Road Trip Mixtape—Your Ultimate Playlist for a Road Trip to the Lone Star State

▷ Gene Autry: "Deep in the Heart of Texas"

▷ Marty Robbins: "El Paso"

▷ Bob Dylan: "Brownsville Girl"

▷ George Strait: "All My Ex's Live in Texas"

▷ Old 97's: "A State of Texas"

▷ Elvis Presley: "The Yellow Rose of Texas"

▷ Turnpike Troubadours: "Every Girl"

▷ Willie Nelson: "Beautiful Texas"

▷ Tanya Tucker: "Texas (When I Die)"

▷ Ernest Tubb: "Waltz across Texas"

▷ Johnny Cash: "'T' For Texas"

▷ Alabama: "If You're Gonna Play in Texas (You Gotta Have a Fiddle in the Band)"

RECOMMENDED CAMPGROUNDS

 BEST IN STATE   ○ **ALSO GREAT**

**Spacious Skies
Shenandoah Views**
Luray, Virginia

**Sherando Lake
Recreation Area
Family Campground**
Lyndhurst, Virginia

**Stony Fork
Campground**
Wytheville, Virginia

**Hungry Mother
State Park
Campground**
Marion, Virginia

**Goose Point
Park at
Philpott Lake**
Bassett, Virginia

**First Landing
State Park
Campground**
Virginia Beach,
Virginia

**North Bend Park
at John H. Kerr
Reservoir**
Boydton, Virginia

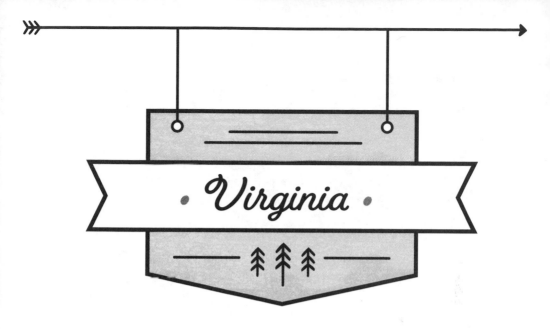

Virginia has a plethora of options for budget camping and plenty of places where you can find sites—even on popular summer weekends. Virginians take great pride in their state park campgrounds, and for good reason. They have excellent and well-maintained state park campgrounds near the coast and in the mountains. Many of them also have great options for cabins and alternative lodging for those who don't tent or RV. The state also has many beautiful national forest campgrounds that are, unfortunately, not as well maintained as its state park campgrounds. Many of them are still worth taking a good look at, especially if you have an RV with its own bathroom and shower. The excellent U.S. Army Corps of Engineers campgrounds in Virginia take the state over the top when it comes to budget camping. Virginia is for campers—no matter how they camp.

BEST IN STATE

Hungry Mother State Park

▷   Marion, Virginia

▷   dcr.virginia.gov/state-parks/hungry-mother

▷   RV and Tent Sites, Cabins, Lodge, Yurts

▷ $

The legacy of the Civilian Conservation Corps (CCC) runs strong at this beautiful state park, which first opened in 1936. There are three lovely campgrounds at Hungry Mother (Camp Burson, Creekside Campground, and Royal Oak Campground) that have excellent sites for tent campers and RV owners. There are also yurts, CCC-era cabins, and a lodge within the park—making this a truly great place for any kind of camper. Camp Burson is located about 1 mile away from the entrance to the state park, and campers will have to drive in to enjoy all that the park has to offer. RV owners love it here because they get full hook-up sites at state park prices. Creekside Campground is located within the park proper and offers water and electric in a cozy setting with less than twenty sites and—you guessed it—the creek is nearby. Royal Oak campground is delightful for tent camping. The sites here are super cool. Each one has parking and a large wooden deck. A private campground would call this a deluxe site and charge you twice as much. All roads here lead to Hungry Mother Lake, which has great fishing and a guarded swimming area in season.

First Landing State Park

▷   Virginia Beach, Virginia

▷   dcr.virginia.gov/state-parks/first-landing

▷   RV and Tent Sites, Cabins, Yurts

▷ $

First Landing State Park is an oasis of quiet and calm in the midst of busy and bustling Virginia Beach—at least it is during the shoulder seasons. The park is very popular with the denizens of Virginia Beach in the summertime. The campsites here are right over the dunes from an excellent stretch of Chesapeake Bay Beach that stretches for 1.5 miles and is terrific for swimming and kayaking. The dunes protect the campground, but they also cut off any real views of the water from the individual campsites. But most of the sites here are just awesome. They are spacious and shaded, and many of them have water and electric. Most coastal campgrounds in the East have no shade and no privacy—so the fact that these sites are shaded is a major score for campers. The beach gets mighty hot here in the summer, and it is very nice to take a break from the sun and retreat to a cool campsite just a short walk away. Downtown Virginia Beach is nearby for food, shopping, and nightlife, but some campers love to spend an entire week here without leaving the park. The camping magic is strong at First Landing—so we totally understand why.

Sherando Lake Recreation Area

▷ Lyndhurst, Virginia

▷ recreation.gov

▷ RV and Tent Sites

▷ $

Sherando Lake Recreation area offers up a little slice of heaven in the Blue Ridge Mountains. There are two lakes here (Lower Sherando Lake and Upper Sherando Lake), which both have lovely settings. The Upper Lake is stocked with fish in the spring and fall, so make sure you bring your gear when you camp here, and make sure you have the required fishing license. Swimming is not allowed at the upper lake, but thankfully a swimming area and bathhouses are available in the lower lake. You can also fish and use non-motorized boats in the lower lake, so it is the more popular of the two. The campground is situated between these two lakes, and the sites flow into the landscape and are absolutely lovely. Campers love that the individual sites are all quite different, so regulars return to their favorites year after year. Loop A has no hookups and is best for tent campers and those who like to dry camp in small RVs. Loops B and C have electric hookups and can accommodate larger RVs. This is one of the best campgrounds in Virginia, and it flies under the radar of many campers from out of state. So, getting a good site here should be quite doable—even in prime season.

> ‑‑‑‑‑‑‑‑ **Budget-Camping Gear: Let's Go Surfing Now!** ‑‑‑‑‑‑‑‑
>
> If your kids fall in love with surfing while camping in Virginia Beach, consider buying them a foam (a.k.a. soft-top) surfboard instead of a fiberglass surf-board for their first board. A new foam surfboard can easily be half the price of a new fiberglass surfboard, and they are also safer. Check out boards by Wave Bandit or Surftech for very good quality at a reasonable price.

ALSO GREAT

Stony Fork Campground/Jefferson National Forest

- ▷ Wytheville, Virginia
- ▷ recreation.gov
- ▷ RV and Tent Sites
- ▷ $

Do you like woodsy camping in a deeply forested setting with private sites that still have electric hookups? Then Stony Fork Campground in Jefferson National Forest might be your jam. This is a great place for kicking back, relaxing, and reconnecting with nature. The creek and the nature trails are fun and family friendly, and the paved loop road is great for riding bikes.

Goose Point Park/Philpott Lake

▷ **Bassett, Virginia**

▷ **recreation.gov**

▷ **RV and Tent Sites**

▷ **$**

This campground has some tight and winding roads that make it challenging for larger rigs, but besides that, this lakefront gem is just about perfect. Most of the sites here have water and electric—and like most U.S. Army Corps of Engineers campgrounds, the price is dirt cheap. This is a terrific campground for swimming and kayaking, and the facilities are clean and very well maintained. The waterfront sites here are the bee's knees, so catch one if you can.

North Bend Park/John H. Kerr Reservoir

▷ **Boydton, Virginia**

▷ **recreation.gov**

▷ **RV and Tent Sites**

▷ **$**

When the U.S. Army Corps of Engineers builds campgrounds, they don't mess around. This is yet another waterfront masterpiece of campground design situated directly on the John H. Kerr Reservoir. There are four different camping areas, and each one has its own swimming beach. There are more than 200 spacious and private sites—some with electric and some without. Each loop has water views and its own

swimming area. It would be very difficult to find a single bad site at this excellent campground.

------- Free and Low-Cost Activities in Virginia Beach -------

✦ Book a surf lesson with **WRV Surf Camp.** The prices are reasonable, and they offer a solid discount for each additional child or adult.

✦ Spend a day enjoying the surf and sand at **Oceanfront Resort Beach**, **Chesapeake Bay Beach**, or **Sandbridge Beach**, which are all free and open to the public.

✦ Grab an oven-baked sub at **Zero's Subs Oceanfront**. Prices are great and portions are substantial. We highly recommend the Jersey Italian Monster.

✦ Support local farms by stocking up on fresh fruits, veggies, and meats at the **Old Beach Farmers Market** located just six blocks from the ocean. Please bring reusable shopping bags when you go.

✦ **The Virginia Beach Surf and Rescue Museum** is packed with artifacts and exhibits that preserve the maritime heritage and history of one of the South's most popular beaches. Hours and availability are variable, so call before you go.

Spacious Skies Shenandoah Views

▷ Luray, Virginia

▷ spaciousskiescampgrounds.com

▷ RV and Tent Sites, Cabins and Yurts

▷ $$$

Some of the high-end RV sites at this campground do not fit the price criteria of this book. But the entry-level RV sites do—and they are quite nice and have full hookups. Cabin and yurt prices here are also reasonable considering how nice they are. This campground is situated in beautiful countryside just a short drive away from Shenandoah National Park, and the setting is relaxing and peaceful. There is plenty for the kids to do after a day of exploring the national park, including two pools, a playground, a jumping pillow, and much more.

RECOMMENDED CAMPGROUNDS

 BEST IN STATE   ○ ALSO GREAT

North Bend State Park
Cairo, West Virginia

Audra State Park
Buckhannon, West Virginia

Big Bend Campground at Monongahela National Forest
Cabins, West Virginia

Holly River State Park
Hacker Valley, West Virginia

Battle Run Campground
Summersville, West Virginia

Brushcreek Falls RV Resort
Princeton, West Virginia

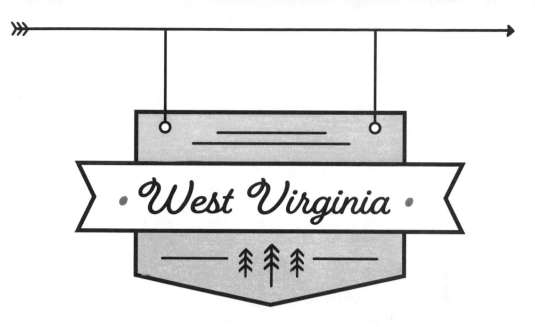

·West Virginia·

When it comes to budget camping, West Virginia is wild and wonderful and among the best states in the country. This is not just because of its incredible state park system that offers natural beauty and modern facilities in spades, it is also because the state has excellent national forest camping and U.S. Army Corps of Engineers camping—along with some surprisingly budget-friendly private campgrounds. RV owners love the number of campsites that offer hookups here, tent campers love the number of private, wooded sites along rivers and lakes, and cabin campers love the classic look and modern amenities of this state's fleet of alternative camping options.

Great campgrounds in West Virginia are also not impossible to book. The state does, in many ways, fly off the radar of many campers from the West and the Northeast. The recent addition of New River Gorge to our country's magnificent list of national parks has served to put that part of the state on the map for many outdoor adventurers. But the rest of the state is waiting for those campers who love to escape the crowds and those who celebrate when their cell phone signal drops off the map. Budget campers should move West Virginia to the top of their bucket lists.

BEST IN STATE

Holly River State Park

▷ Hacker Valley, West Virginia

▷ wvstateparks.com/park/holly-river-state-park/

▷ RV and Tent Sites, Cabins

▷ $

A camping trip to Holly River State Park in Hacker Valley really can feel like it's "Almost Heaven." Whether you are hiking to a waterfall or fly fishing on the Left Fork of the Holly River, this is a natural wonderland. The campground is absolutely delightful. It has eighty-eight sites with electric hookups and nine supercozy Works Progress Administration stone cabins from the 1930s. There is also one two-bedroom "vacation cabin." All these cabins are well-equipped and offer electricity, hot water, and heating options—and the pricing is bargain-basement considering what you get with them. The campsites are spacious and shady with varying degrees of privacy. For a state park, this place is packed with amenities like basketball, volleyball, and tennis courts, and it has a robust schedule of activities in the summer that range from ranger-led nature hikes to marshmallow roasts. There is even a pool here—a real rarity for a state park—and a welcome spot to cool off on a hot summer day.

Audra State Park

▷ Buckhannon, West Virginia

▷ wvstateparks.com/park/audra-state-park

▷ RV and Tent Sites

▷ $

This lovely campground is nestled along the Middle Fork River, which is heavily stocked with golden and brook trout, making this an excellent destination for those who love to fish. Just make sure to have a current West

Virginia fishing license and a trout stamp. If you don't like to fish, the river is also lovely for swimming. There are a few great spots along the river, but make sure you bring water shoes and step carefully. There are sixty-five sites here, and more than half of them have electricity—and most of them are quite spacious and shaded. The sound of the rushing river fills this campground with delightful music, especially if you book a site right along the edge of the water. Make sure to do the Alum Creek and Cave Trail while you are here—the boardwalk under the cave's overhang is really cool. Also make sure to grab a biscuit breakfast sandwich at the nearby Tudor's Biscuit World—this is a chain restaurant, but the food tastes almost as good as Grandma's home cooking.

Brushcreek Falls RV Resort

▷ **Princeton, West Virginia**
▷ **brushcreekfalls.com**
▷ **RV and Tent Sites, Cabins and Luxury Suites**
▷ **$$$**

You might be shocked to see an RV resort in the pages of this budget camping book, but Brushcreek Falls RV Resort meets our price criteria. It may just be one of the best value-priced RV resorts in the country. The sites here are not large and not private, but they are clean and well-manicured and can fit the biggest of the big rigs. The amenities and facilities here are excellent. Families love the gem mining, mini golf, playgrounds, and the pool with mountain views. The cabins and luxury suites with electric, AC, and heat here are also excellent for those who don't tent or RV. They are cozy, clean, and comfortable, and they come pretty darn close to a glamping experience in a state that is not exactly packed with opportunities for luxurious camping. Brushcreek Falls also has wonderful customer service that makes its guests feel like they are at home. Downtown Princeton is only fifteen minutes away for charming shopping and lots of good eats.

North Bend State Park

▷   Cairo, West Virginia

▷   wvstateparks.com/park/north-bend-state-park

▷   RV and Tent Sites, Cabins, Lodge

▷ $

North Bend State Park has two campgrounds (River Run and Cokeley), a lodge, and a separate cabin area nestled atop a wooded ridge. In other words, there is something for everyone here. River Run is the older campground, and it has forty-nine sites, twenty-six of which offer 50-amp service and water hook-ups. This campground is located near an entrance for the popular 72-mile North Bend Rail Trail, which is terrific for biking. Cokeley is a smaller, much newer campground that was specifically designed with larger RVs in mind. The sites here have water and electric and they are spacious, but they lack shade and privacy. The cedar cabins at North Bend are especially lovely, and they offer water and electric and linen service at a bargain price. The lodge is also lovely and has been recently updated. The park has a full-service restaurant and an Olympic-sized pool along with boat rentals and a nature center.

ALSO GREAT

Big Bend Campground/Monongahela National Forest

▷   Cabins, West Virginia

▷   fs.usda.gov

▷   RV and Tent Sites

▷ $

This peaceful and somewhat remote National Forest Service campground in the Monongahela National Forest has forty-six sites without hookups. About a dozen of those sites are right on the river—so catch one if you can. The South Branch of the Potomac River offers excellent opportunities for fishing, hiking, and tubing right around the campground, and there are excellent hiking and mountain biking trails nearby. Cell reception is non-existent here, so plan on disconnecting for a while and reconnecting with wild and wonderful West Virginia.

Battle Run Campground/Summersville Lake

▷ Summersville, West Virginia

▷ recreation.gov

▷ RV and Tent Sites

▷ $

Battle Run Campground has a spectacular location right on the shores of Summersville Lake, the largest lake in the state. Not every site has a water view, but many of them do, and getting one is attainable if you plan ahead. There are 110 sites here with electric hookups, and seven primitive walk-in sites for tent campers only. The lake is excellent for fishing, swimming, boating, and even cliff jumping. New River Gorge National Park (and world-class whitewater rafting) is only twenty minutes away as well—so if you love outdoor adventure, then this is where you should camp next.

Visit the Capital! Free and Low-Cost Activities in Charleston, West Virginia

▷ No road trip through West Virginia is complete without making a visit to its riverfront capital city. **Charleston** is a lovely town that also has excellent free and low-priced activities.

▷ If you want to camp really close to the city, we recommend **Kanawha State Forest**, which is just 7 miles away. It may not be one of the elite campgrounds in the state, but it is very good for tent campers and those with small RVs. Its proximity to the capital is also hard to beat.

▷ **The West Virginia State Museum** walks you through the history of the state in a dynamic and interactive fashion. This place is fantastic for kids and adults, and not just on a rainy day. Admission is always free for kids and adults.

▷ **The Capitol Market** is an indoor/outdoor food lover's paradise located in what was once the freight station of the Kanawha and Michigan Railroad. Today it is a beloved community hub serving everything from sushi to craft-roasted coffee. Most merchants have very reasonable prices.

▷ If you love minor league baseball, catch a **Charleston Dirty Birds game at the GoMart Ballpark**. Check the schedule for games with free fireworks and dollar beer nights. Or better yet, head to the ballpark on a night with free postgame glow party yoga!

▷ **Haddad Riverfront Park** hosts a free concert series on Friday nights at 6:30 p.m. from Memorial Day to Labor Day. The mix of performances is eclectic and can include anything from jazz to swing to Motown to an all-female Led Zeppelin cover band, so check the schedule before you go.

THE MIDWEST

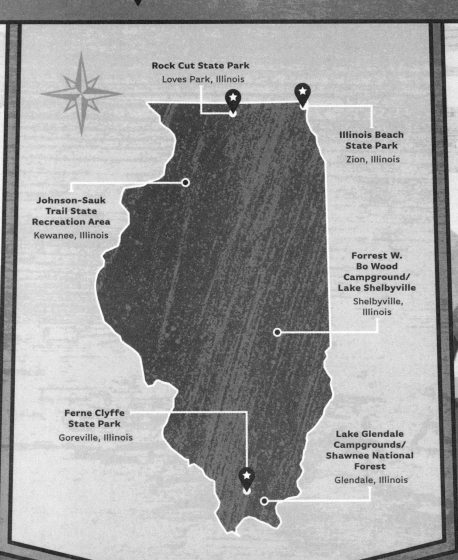

RECOMMENDED CAMPGROUNDS

★ BEST IN STATE   ○ ALSO GREAT

Rock Cut State Park
Loves Park, Illinois

Illinois Beach State Park
Zion, Illinois

Johnson-Sauk Trail State Recreation Area
Kewanee, Illinois

Forrest W. Bo Wood Campground/ Lake Shelbyville
Shelbyville, Illinois

Ferne Clyffe State Park
Goreville, Illinois

Lake Glendale Campgrounds/ Shawnee National Forest
Glendale, Illinois

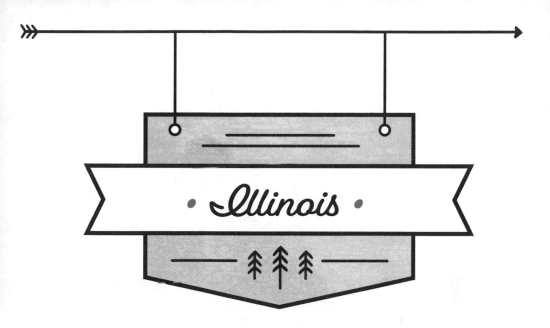

· Illinois ·

It's a shame that so many RV owners barrel through the Midwest for points farther east and points further west. The Midwest offers budget camping options galore, and state after state offers excellent public campground options. Illinois certainly gets overlooked as a camping destination nationally, but it also gets overlooked within the context of the Midwest. This is probably because Michigan and Wisconsin are truly spectacular states for camping, and they are both right next door. But it is not like Illinois has an inferiority complex about its camping culture—it is just busy doing other things. All of that being said, many campers who live within the state love their state park campgrounds for a wide variety of reasons. Campers who live in the Chicago area seem to have the most to be happy about it. There are a bunch of great campgrounds within a few hours' drive from the Windy City, making it quite easy to escape into nature after a long week at work.

BEST IN STATE

Ferne Clyffe State Park

▷ Goreville, Illinois

▷ dnr.illinois.gov/parks/camp/park.ferneclyffe

▷ RV and Tent Sites

▷ $

Ferne Clyffe State Park has both ferns and cliffs—so it delivers on that essential promise in its name. It also delivers in every other way imaginable. There are several nice hikes within the park (such as Big Rock Hollow Trail and Round Nature Preserve Trail) that lead to lovely waterfalls and others that lead to excellent views. Other hikes also lead to caves and rock climbing and scrambling opportunities—just be careful any time you are hiking in this park in wet weather because it can get quite slippery. The hiking here often takes newcomers by surprise when they visit for the first time, and so does the quality of the camping experience. There are actually two campgrounds within the park that cater to different customers. Deer Ridge Campground is more suitable for RV owners and has a parklike setting with shady trees and large sites with little privacy between most of them. This campground is fairly easy to navigate and can accommodate larger RVs. Turkey Hollow offers primitive campsites with spacious, private, and deeply wooded sites. These campgrounds are popular with tent campers who must self-register and pay on the honor system upon arrival. The price here is almost ridiculously low for such a great tent-camping experience. Ferne Clyffe is something of an undiscovered state park gem in Illinois—at least for those who don't live in the Prairie State.

Rock Cut State Park

▷ Loves Park, Illinois

▷ dnr.illinois.gov/parks/camp/park.rockcut.html

▷ RV and Tent Sites, Cabin

▷ $

Rock Cut State Park is just 80 miles northwest of Chicago, close to the border of Wisconsin. Campers who live close to the Windy City often find themselves here for quick weekend getaways. This peaceful park has two lovely lakes and offers a great combination of back-to-nature experiences and easy-to-access local activities. A hiking trail circumnavigates Lake Pierce (the larger lake) and makes for a lovely stroll, particularly when the leaves are red and gold in the fall. The lake is also excellent for kayaking and fishing, and there is a sandy beach for swimming that has concessions and picnic areas. RV owners and tent campers love the campground, which has almost 300 electric sites and single cabins with electric. Some are wooded and private, and some are out in the open with a few shady trees, but all of them are spacious and relatively level. The campground is open year-round for those hearty souls who love winter camping. We also love taking in a minor league sports game when we are traveling, and there are two options near Rock Cut. The Rockford IceHogs hockey team are a few minutes away, and the Beloit Snappers baseball team plays just over the border in Wisconsin, just fifteen minutes away from the campground.

Illinois Beach State Park

▷ **Zion, Illinois**

▷ **stateparks.com/illinois_beach_state_park_in_illinois.html**

▷ **RV and Tent Sites, Lodge Rooms**

▷ **$**

Illinois Beach State Park is a source of great pride for campers and nature lovers in Illinois. This park is located along a sandy stretch of shoreline just an hour north of Chicago, so it serves as a super fun camping getaway for residents of the Windy City. The campground fills up regularly during the summer months, but it is much quieter in the fall. You can even do some early winter camping here because the campground closes on the last day of December. There are almost 250 sites here with electric hookups, and most of them are large and private and somewhat scruffy—but scruffy in a good way that is common for beach camping. Campers who escape from the city to come here in the summer mainly do so for the sandy beach and the swimming, but the hiking and fishing are also good. If you are a dog owner, please be aware that your precious pup is allowed at the campground, but is not allowed on the beach or in the nature preserve.

-------------------- **Budget-Camping Gear:** --------------------
Estwing Fireside Friend Splitting Tool

The Estwing family has been making high-quality American-made goods in the northern Illinois city of Rockford for more than one hundred years. The Estwing Fireside Friend Splitting Tool is one of our all-time favorite pieces of camping gear. It has a heavier head than a traditional camping ax, so it makes splitting firewood much easier—and firewood that is split into smaller pieces burns better. When you consider the fact that Estwing's tools will last multiple lifetimes and can be handed down to your children, their pricing is incredibly budget friendly. Go get yourself a Fireside Friend today! Because who doesn't need another friend around the campfire? Especially if they don't say much and are only there to help.

ALSO GREAT

Forrest W. Bo Wood Campground/Lake Shelbyville

▷   Shelbyville, Illinois

▷   recreation.gov

▷   RV and Tent Sites

▷ $

The consistent excellence of U.S. Army Corps of Engineers campgrounds is quite astonishing. The sites are almost always level and spacious, electric hookups are provided way more often than they are not—and every single one of their campgrounds is on the water. This means lots and lots of waterfront sites. Bo Wood Campground in central Illinois has all these qualities and more. The entire park is shaded by oak and hickory trees and is a peaceful and calming place for a morning or evening stroll. The fishing is also good, and there are catfish, crappie, bass, and much more. Bo Wood is also well managed and always seems to have the nicest camp hosts.

Lake Glendale Campground/Shawnee National Forest

▷   Glendale, Illinois

▷   fs.usda.gov

▷   RV and Tent Sites

▷ $

This National Forest Service campground in southern Illinois is an absolute gem. Lake Glendale is terrific for kayaking and swimming, and the campground is a neat and tidy masterpiece nestled in a forest right by the lake. There are about sixty shady and spacious campsites here, and more than half of them have electric hookups. The only bummer about this otherwise near-perfect location is that it does not accept reservations. This is first-come, first-served camping only. This policy favors the locals and keeps many travelers from out of state from ever trying to camp here.

Johnson-Sauk Trail State Recreation Area

▷   Kewanee, Illinois

▷   dnr.illinois.gov/parks/park.johnsonsauktrail.html

▷   RV and Tent Sites, Cabin

▷ $

The RV and tent sites set among the tall pine trees at the Chief Keokuk Campground are stunning, and when the wind starts to blow through them the sound is calming and borderline mesmerizing. Located in the rolling hills of north-central Illinois, this state park is packed with options for outdoor adventure. There is also a single cabin for rent overlooking Johnson Lake. Make sure to bring your own bedding—if you can get a reservation!

Four More Illinois State Park Campgrounds Worth Visiting

When it comes to great state park camping in Illinois, the campgrounds reviewed in this chapter really just skim the surface. Illinois's state park campground system has a deep bench with lots of wonderful options for campers of every kind. Here are four more Illinois State Parks worth considering for a camping trip:

1. **Kankakee River State Park** in Bourbonnais is a great place for fly fishing and for photographers who love to dabble with long exposures of the flowing water. The campground has large, shaded sites.

2. **Chain O' Lakes State Park** in Spring Grove is heavenly for lake lovers who also like to camp. There are several camping areas within the park and all of them are clean, tidy, and family friendly.

3. **Starved Rock State Park** in Oglesby is one of the prettiest state parks in the country. The hiking here is great and so is the campground. The park's stone-and-log lodge is a historic structure built by the Civilian Conservation Corps in the 1930s. Today it offers cozy rooms and great amenities like saunas and a hot tub.

4. **Mississippi Palisades State Park** in Savanna is excellent for fishing, boating, and hiking—and it has a popular campground with almost 250 sites. The Palisades are steep limestone cliffs that are very popular with rock climbers.

RECOMMENDED CAMPGROUNDS

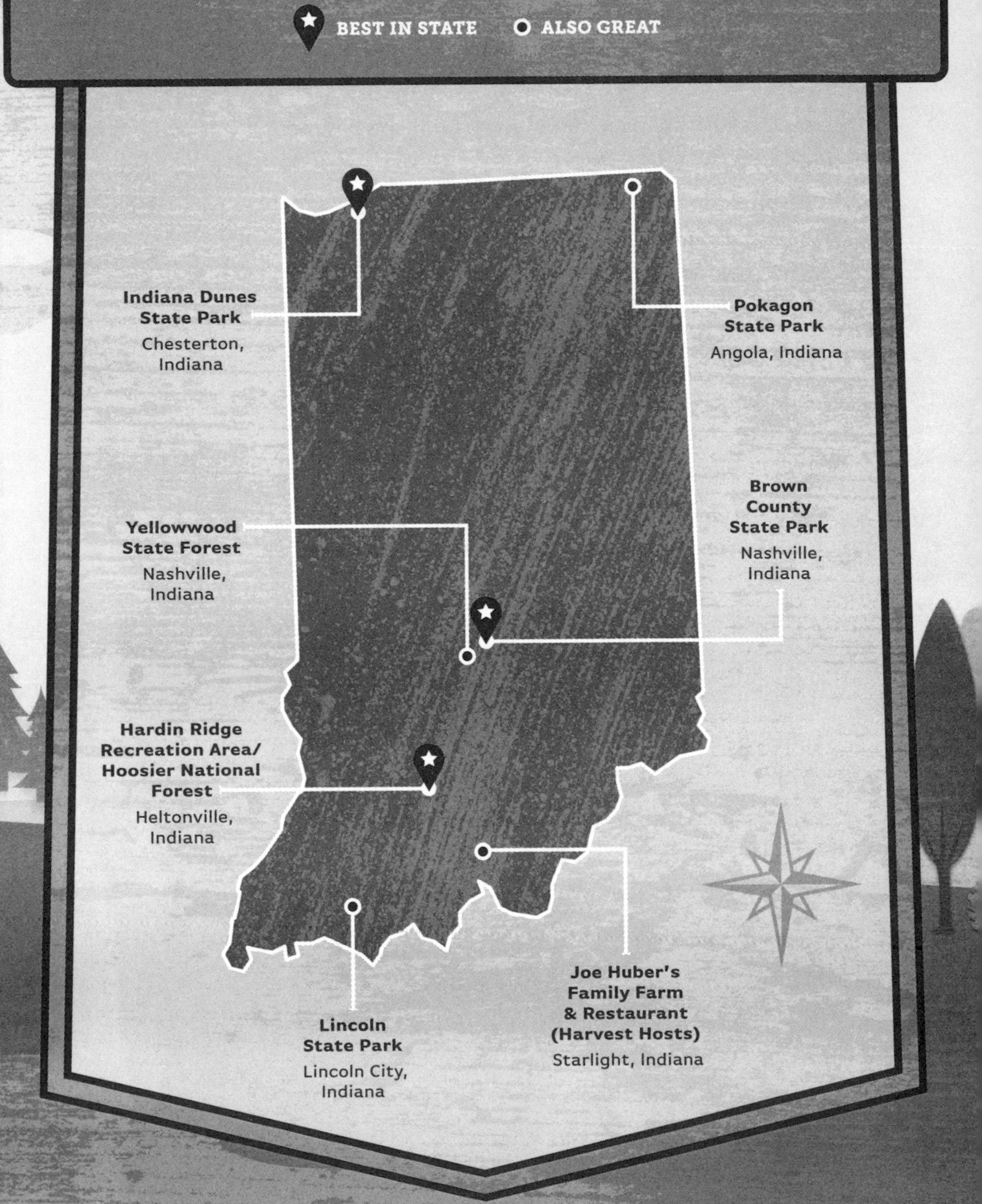

⚲ BEST IN STATE　○ ALSO GREAT

Indiana Dunes State Park

Chesterton, Indiana

Pokagon State Park

Angola, Indiana

Yellowwood State Forest

Nashville, Indiana

Brown County State Park

Nashville, Indiana

Hardin Ridge Recreation Area/ Hoosier National Forest

Heltonville, Indiana

Lincoln State Park

Lincoln City, Indiana

Joe Huber's Family Farm & Restaurant (Harvest Hosts)

Starlight, Indiana

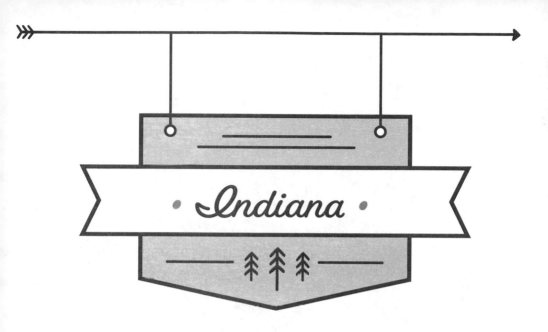

Indiana

Indiana is known as the Crossroads of America for good reason. Many RVers visit the state on their way out West or on the way back home to the East. Those quick visits usually involve a stopover in Elkhart, Indiana, to visit the RV capital of the world and maybe a one-day stop to visit Indiana Dunes National Park. But that is an absolute shame. The southern portion of the state is an absolute wonderland when it comes to good camping, and most people never get there. The state parks in southern Indiana are surprisingly beautiful, and many of them have terrific campgrounds. There are also good private campgrounds in this region that are well worth investigating, even if they do not meet our criteria for budget camping. This chapter also features excellent camping in Hoosier National Forest— yet another location in Indiana that is beloved by locals but flies far under the radar for out-of-state campers. If Indiana is not on your bucket list, it should be.

BEST IN STATE

Brown County State Park

▷ Nashville, Indiana

▷ in.gov

▷ RV and Tent Sites

▷ $

If you dropped off most Americans in the middle of this wonderful park and asked them what state they were in, very few would guess Indiana. There's a reason why this part of the state is nicknamed "Little Smokies." The rolling hills and pristine waters of Strahl and Ogle Lakes will make you feel like you are rambling around in Tennessee. There are actually three campgrounds in Brown County State Park: Buffalo Ridge, Raccoon Ridge, and Taylor Ridge— and they are all excellent. Combined, these campgrounds have more than 400 sites, and most of them have electric hookups. The park even has equestrian sites with both primitive and electric options. The Abe Martin Lodge inside the park also offers lodging, cabins, dining, and even an indoor water park. There is excellent hiking throughout the park, and the entire region becomes magical in the fall when colorful foliage bursts into view. During your visit, make sure you climb the 90-foot fire tower on Weed Patch Hill for panoramic views that will fill you with awe and wonder.

Hardin Ridge Recreation Area/Hoosier National Forest

▷ Heltonville, Indiana

▷ recreation.gov

▷ RV and Tent Sites, Cabins

▷ $

Hardin Ridge is much beloved by campers in the Hoosier state, but it flies under the radar for everyone else. This campground and recreation area, which is located on the largest lake in the state, is an absolute gem. RV owners and tent campers love the large, shaded, private sites carved into the landscape. There are six loops with a mix of electric and primitive campsites, and they also offer two cabin rentals. These cabins are rustic and basic, but they have bunk beds, so they are popular with families. While the cabins are on the lake, the campsites are not—so plan on walking or riding your bike to get to the water for a swim. Some sites here are reservable and some are not, so those who live nearby sometimes come and crash the gates for last-second sites—and they usually get them. With more than 200 sites, the campground only fills up on the busiest summer weekends. Fishing is popular here—just make sure you have a permit if you want to wet a line.

Indiana Dunes State Park

▷ Chesterton, Indiana

▷ in.gov

▷ RV and Tent Sites

▷ $

Indiana Dunes State Park may be the most beloved campground in the state. Campers in the Hoosier state love it because it is a world-class destination with excellent beaches and dunes and an RV-friendly campground with more 140 sites with electric hookups. Neighboring campers from the Chicago area also love it because it is only about an hour away and offers up a great escape from the crowds and congestion of the Windy City. The sites are spacious and many are shady. Most have a concrete pad for your rig or tent and an additional driveway area that can easily park two cars. This state park has robust programming and plenty of outdoor activities for campers of all ages, but a huge part of the appeal here is that Indiana Dunes National Park is right next door. So, make sure you head over to the NPS visitor center during your state park stay and see what is going on over there as well. When you combine the offerings of the state and national parks, you end up with Indiana's most magnificent tourist attraction and an incredible place for campers of all kinds. The national park also has a very good campground called Dunewood that is rustic, shady, and pretty—especially when the fall colors come in. But we give the campground at the state park the edge—and not just because it has electric hookups. The sites and location are also just a little bit better in every single way.

ALSO GREAT

Pokagon State Park

▷   Angola, Indiana

▷   in.gov

▷   RV and Tent Sites, Lodge, Cabins

▷ $

Pokagon State Park, which is nestled along the shores of Lake James, is another great Indiana state park for hiking, biking, and fishing. There are almost 300 sites here and most of them have electric, making this a popular spot for RVers. Some of the sites are not level and some are a bit hard for big rigs to navigate, but overall, the campground is very good. The Potawatomi Inn and Cabins within the park are excellent—so much so that you might want to consider ditching your tent or RV for the weekend and booking accommodations. They have an indoor pool, hot tub, sauna, and several cozy fireplaces that are just perfect for relaxing with a good book.

Lincoln State Park

▷   Lincoln City, Indiana

▷   in.gov

▷   RV and Tent Sites, Cabins

▷ $

If you are a United States history buff, you will love camping at this state park located in the rolling hills and thick forests where Abraham Lincoln grew up.

You can even take a short hike from the campground to the Lincoln Boyhood National Memorial, which is just across the street. In fact, the park is filled with good hiking, and there are two lakes within its boundaries that offer fishing, boating, and swimming in a designated area. The campground has more than 200 sites, most with electric. Be forewarned—it can get loud here on summer weekends.

----- **Budget-Camping Gear: Rockwood Pop-Up Campers** -----

Looking to buy your first RV? On a budget and don't know where to start? Check out Rockwood's excellent and affordable line of pop-up campers (a.k.a. camping trailers or tent trailers). The roof lifts up and the beds extend out on these types of RVs, so they are incredibly compact when not in use. While other manufacturers have shut down their production lines for pop-up campers, Rockwood, which is headquartered in Millersburg, Indiana, seems to have doubled down on making them. If you look at pictures of campgrounds in the 1960s and 70s, they were filled with pop-ups—and pop-ups are still popular today among first-time RV owners. When compared to fifth wheels and motorhomes, the price also looks downright reasonable.

Yellowwood State Forest

▷ Nashville, Indiana

▷ in.gov

▷ RV and Tent Sites

▷ $

Yellowwood State Forest is located near the immensely popular Brown County State Park and is often overlooked for that reason, but it shouldn't be. It has one of the prettiest campgrounds in the state of Indiana. The campground is nestled alongside a gorgeous 133-acre lake in a deeply wooded and natural setting. The seventy-four campsites here do not have hookups, so many RV owners don't bother coming here. This is an excellent spot for old-school tent camping—and for hiking and fishing in a peaceful, relaxing, and uncrowded environment.

Joe Huber's Family Farm & Restaurant (Harvest Hosts)

▷   Starlight, Indiana

▷   harvesthosts.com

▷   Self-enclosed RVs Only

▷ $

Located in southern Indiana, not too far from Louisville, Joe Huber's Family Farm & Restaurant is an excellent Harvest Hosts location. Plan your stay so you can grab a meal during your time here. The fried chicken is excellent, and so are the burgers and sandwiches. It also offers pick-your-own produce and an excellent farm market so you can stock up your RV fridge with goodies for the road.

Six Great Things to Do in Southern Indiana

1. Visit **Holiday World** and **Splashin' Safari** in Santa Claus, Indiana. The rides and water slides are fast paced and fun for kids of all ages, and admission is reasonably priced.

2. **Visit downtown Jeffersonville, Indiana,** for terrific pubs and coffee shops and a robust public art program that has made this town a cultural center for the entire region.

3. Indiana's Blue River is an enchanting place for a long paddle. **Rent kayaks or canoes from family-owned Cave Country Canoes—** its customer service is great, and its prices won't break the bank.

4. Take a **Haunted Indiana Road Trip** as detailed by onlyinyourstate .com. Start your tour at the stunning Willard Library in Evansville—just watch out for the fabled "Grey Lady," because she is known to haunt the stacks even during daylight hours.

5. Dip down into Louisville to visit the **Louisville Slugger Museum and Factory** and get a bat with your name engraved in it. While you are there, make sure to visit the **Muhammad Ali Center** right across the street.

6. Try **Nellie's Restaurant in Newburgh, Indiana,** for an amazing breakfast that will stick to your ribs. Its country-fried steak breakfast comes with hash browns, eggs, and your choice of toast or pancakes!

RECOMMENDED CAMPGROUNDS

★ BEST IN STATE   ○ ALSO GREAT

Cherry Glen Campground/ Saylorville Lake
Polk City, Iowa

Lazy H Campground
Akron, Iowa

Pikes Peak State Park
McGregor, Iowa

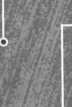

Viking Lake State Park
Stanton, Iowa

Sugar Bottom Campground/ Coralville Lake
Solon, Iowa

A camping trip to Iowa will surprise and delight you—and it definitely won't break the bank. There are public camping options galore in this state. The Iowa state park system is very good and offers electric hookups at many sites throughout the state. Full hook-up campsites are also starting to pop up at some locations. These state parks offer a superabundance of hiking, biking, fishing, and boating opportunities that many out-of-state campers do not even know exist. The good people of Iowa love to get outdoors, and they love to visit their state parks. The Hawkeye State also has a robust list of U.S. Army Corps of Engineers campgrounds, and as most camping aficionados know, those are almost always incredibly good. The state also has wonderful family-owned campgrounds—some of which fall nicely into the RV resort category. Those coming from out of state will be incredibly pleased with the affordability of some of these delightful RV resorts.

BEST IN STATE

Pikes Peak State Park

▷ McGregor, Iowa

▷ iowadnr.gov

▷ RV and Tent Sites

▷ $

Pikes Peak State Park is definitely one of the prettiest places to visit in Iowa, and it is also one of the most photographed locations in the entire state. The views of the Mississippi River from the park's scenic bluffs are nothing short of breathtaking. This is also a great park for those who love to hike and bike. There are easy trails for short rambles and more challenging trails that lead to views of the mighty river. The campground here has sixty-two sites, and most of them have electric hookups. A small handful of sites also have water, electric, and sewer—but those can be hard to book. Many of the spots are spacious and offer lots of shade and privacy. Fall is the best time to visit Pikes Peak, as it is the area's peak foliage season. The leaves usually burst into full color during the first two weeks of October, and they light up the campground and hiking trails with rich shades of red, yellow, and gold.

------------------- Budget-Camping Hack: -------------------

Stir-Fry Dinners on the Blackstone Griddle

We love making huge stir-fry dinners on our 22-inch Blackstone griddle and then heating up leftovers throughout the rest of the camping trip. We can easily make several versions to please the picky eaters in our camping crew. If you have vegetarians and meat eaters in your crew, it is also very easy to make everyone happy. The best part about stir fry is that the ingredients are cheap, and you can easily feed a hungry army at the campground.

Sugar Bottom Campground/Coralville Lake

▷ Solon, Iowa

▷ recreation.gov

▷ RV and Tent Sites

▷ $

Iowa is blessed to have more than its fair share of terrific U.S. Army Corps of Engineers campgrounds, and Sugar Bottom is one of the best in the state. With more than 200 sites, this is definitely one of the largest Army Corps of Engineers campgrounds we have encountered. The sheer size of this place gives it more of a state-park feel and less of the cozy and intimate feel that can be found at many other campgrounds that were built by the corps. This is an excellent location nevertheless—and it has robust options for fishing, boating, biking, and swimming, all just steps away from your campsite.

Lazy H Campground

▷   Akron, Iowa

▷   lazyhcampground.com

▷   RV and Tent Sites, Cabins

▷ $$$

This private resort campground opened in 2020 and has been earning non-stop rave reviews ever since. Two things strike you immediately when you pull in. The first thing most guests notice is that this place is Disney World clean. The second thing is that the sites are absolutely gigantic. They have level concrete pads with almost seventy feet of nicely manicured lawn in between each site. Bring your baseball gloves—you can have a game of catch right in front of your RV. Many of the sites have views of Little Pearle Lake, which is stocked with a wide variety of fish including bass, catfish, and rainbow trout, so grab a breakfast burrito and a cup of coffee at the Lazy Susan Food Truck before you head to the beach to catch some fish. This on-site food truck is named after the owner's mother, and the food is mighty good. The cabins here are also cute as a button and include linens and towels and cookware. This may just be the best family-owned campground in the state, and they are just getting started. The prices may be higher than other privates in the state, but it still fits into the upper level of our pricing criteria for this book. We think Lazy H is well worth the splurge, and we are certain that you will too.

ALSO GREAT

Cherry Glen Campground/Saylorville Lake

▷ Polk City, Iowa

▷ recreation.gov

▷ RV and Tent Sites

▷ $

Cherry Glen Campground is the most popular campground on Saylorville Lake, a popular recreation area just north of Des Moines. This beautiful and shady U.S. Army Corps of Engineers campground closed for the entirety of the 2023 camping season so that repairs could be made to its water and sewer line systems. This saddened local campers at the time, but the end result will make this great campground even better. There are so many opportunities for recreation here, including biking, fishing, sailing, and swimming. The upgrades will ensure that campers will enjoy this splendid spot for at least another fifty years.

Viking Lake State Park

▷ Stanton, Iowa

▷ iowadnr.gov

▷ RV and Tent Sites

▷ $

Viking Lake State Park is a little slice of camping heaven less than two hours southwest of Des Moines. This popular state park has a wide variety of sites for tents and RVs, and many of them are situated right on the lake. These large sites are perfectly angled and easy to back into, making this a top state park for larger rigs. Full hookups are available, and so are a handful of buddy sites that are perfect for group camping. Those who travel with kayaks and SUPs will love it here—especially in the summertime.

Budget-Friendly Food and Attractions in Des Moines, Iowa

▷ Start your day in Des Moines at **Smokey Row Coffee Co.** and order up a hot cup of joe and the biscuits and gravy or homemade breakfast casserole. If you feel like hanging out, there is plenty of seating in its hip and charming shop and coffee refills are free.

▷ The very fit people at *Shape* magazine anointed the **Des Moines Farmers' Market** as the second-best farmer's market in the country, and it is easy to see why. This Saturday market runs from 7:00 a.m. to 12:00 p.m. from May to October, and the sheer number of vendors is amazing. This is the place to stock up on veggies, baked goods, wine, cheese, and so much more!

▷ The public hours at the **Better Homes & Gardens Test Garden** are very limited, but this is a special place that is worth visiting if you have an interest in horticulture. Experts are available to answer questions, and the garden is located right in downtown Des Moines so you can combo a visit here with a great meal and shopping.

▷ Principal Park is not Wrigley Field, but it is still a great place to catch a ball game on a summer night. Minor league baseball team **Iowa Cubs** tickets are a bargain compared to big-league tickets, so come on out to the park and catch a rising star. You will save enough money on the ticket to get plenty of pretzels, hot dogs, and cold drinks, with money left over for a few souvenirs.

▷ Head to the **High Life Lounge** before or after the game for great food and drink. This iconic spot is just a few blocks away from the ballpark. It may sound expensive, but it is not. This is an old-school neighborhood tavern that will give you a better taste of Des Moines than just about anywhere else in town. Try the Velvet Elvis Dip for an appetizer and the Philly-style pot roast sandwich for the main course. You won't be disappointed.

RECOMMENDED CAMPGROUNDS

★ BEST IN STATE   ○ ALSO GREAT

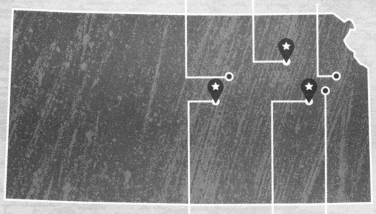

**Tuttle Creek
State Park**
Manhattan,
Kansas

**Salina KOA
Holiday**
Salina, Kansas

**Cedar Ridge and
Hickory Walnut
Campgrounds/
Bloomington
East Park**
Lawrence, Kansas

**Pomona
State Park**
Vassar, Kansas

**Kanopolis
State Park**
Marquette, Kansas

**Eisenhower
State Park**
Osage City,
Kansas

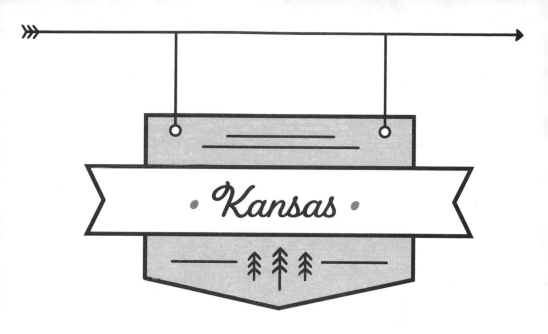

· Kansas ·

The Kansas state park system has tons of potential, but it does also seem understaffed and underfunded. There are great campsites across the state, and many of them offer full hookups for RVers and spacious primitive sites for tent campers, but the best sites and the best state park campgrounds can be hard to find. The Kansas Department of Wildlife and Parks has a difficult-to-navigate website that is desperately in need of an update. Frankly, they make it hard for someone from out of state to figure out what is offered and where they should consider going. Because of this, most campers in Kansas state parks are Kansans. Seems like a missed opportunity to capture tourism dollars if you ask us. The rest of the state offers good camping from the U.S. Army Corps of Engineers, and most private campgrounds are quite affordable. Kansas is a beautiful state that is well worth exploring by those headed farther west, but we wish that it was easier for visitors to find some of the state's best camping gems. We hope that this chapter points you in the right direction.

BEST IN STATE

Tuttle Creek State Park

▷ Manhattan, Kansas

▷ ksoutdoors.com

▷ RV and Tent Sites, Cabins

▷ $

Tuttle Creek State Park is a popular option for day-trippers and campers from all over eastern Kansas. The campground can get crowded on summer weekends, and the staff can have trouble keeping facilities and bathrooms clean. But besides that, this is a very good place for all kinds of recreation, and it is one of the best places to camp in this part of the state. Tuttle Creek has five units within the park, and each of them has campgrounds with a wide variety of sites. The River Pond and Rocky Ford Campgrounds are the best of the bunch with almost 400 sites between them that appeal to RV owners and tent campers. About half of these campgrounds have water and electric hookups, and half of them are primitive. The campgrounds at the Fancy Creek Unit have limited sites with electric hookups and more than 200 primitive sites. The Randolph Unit has a horse campground, and the Cedar Ridge Campground is primitive only. Fishing and boating are excellent at this park, as are the mountain biking and horseback riding. It's also a great place to go for a dip on a hot summer day, so don't forget your bathing suit.

-------- **Budget-Camping Gear: Coleman Camp Stoves** --------

The Coleman Company, which is headquartered in Wichita, Kansas, has been making quality camp stoves at a reasonable price for more than one hundred years. If you are looking for your first camp stove, then check out the two-burner classic propane gas camping stove—you can find it at a terrific price at many big-box stores. These stoves are built to last, but their temperature range runs from hot to nuclear. If you want a two-burner camp stove with a greater temperature range, check out the Coleman Cascade classic camping stove. Their names might sound similar, but the upgrade costs about twice as much as the entry-level model, and it is about four times as good. In the grand scheme of things, both are budget-friendly options worth considering for your ever-growing camp kitchen collection.

Eisenhower State Park

▷ Osage City, Kansas
▷ ksoutdoors.com
▷ RV and Tent Sites, Cabins
▷ $

Campers of all kinds go to Eisenhower State Park (which is less than an hour south of Topeka) to kick back, relax, and enjoy the water. There are six camping areas to choose from, and all of them are tucked along Melvern Reservoir. Blackjack Campground is farthest out on the point and closest to a beach, so those hauling kayaks or canoes around might check here first. More than 100 sites (between the six campgrounds) have water and electric hookups. There are also twenty-five full hook-up sites in the Doud Campground, which is also very nice. In a general sense, the campground is big rig friendly, and the pull-through sites are very popular with RV owners. Plenty of tent campers come to Eisenhower, but it is a bit more RV-centric because most of the sites lack privacy. There are lots of wide-open grassy spaces for kids to play in here, so bring a football or Wiffle ball set. There is also a nineteen-target archery trail, which is super fun, and a kids' fishing pond. This state park is huge and filled with nicely paved roads, so kids and adults love to ride their bikes here.

Kanopolis State Park

- ▷ **Marquette, Kansas**
- ▷ **ksoutdoors.com**
- ▷ **RV and Tent Sites, Cabins**
- ▷ **$**

The landscape at Kanopolis State Park, which is located in the Smoky Hills section of the state, is wild and varied and blows up the preconceptions that most people have about Kansas. There are caves and sandstone bluffs and miles and miles of varied hiking trails that wind through the hills in and around this otherworldly park. This is the Kansas that residents of the state know and love—and it is the Kansas that far too many people never experience. There are almost 450 campsites here in two primary camping areas called Langley Point and Horsethief. There is plenty of primitive camping for those who love to throw a tent in the back of the car and go, and there are full hookups for RV owners who want it all. There are also six deluxe cabins in the Little Bluestem Cabin Area that sleep up to five people and come equipped with full kitchens and bathrooms. These cabins, with names like Buffalo Bill and Bat Masterson, pay tribute to the area's rich history and let new campers experience the beauty of this park without having to sleep on the cold, hard ground in Kansas's oldest state park.

ALSO GREAT

Cedar Ridge and Hickory Walnut Campgrounds/Bloomington East Park

▷ Lawrence, Kansas

▷ recreation.gov

▷ RV and Tent Sites

▷ $

Another great collection of U.S. Army Corps of Engineers campgrounds can be found at Bloomington East Park on Clinton Lake. The sites here are huge and most are level, and there is a mix of electric sites and water and electric sites. Get a site as close to the water as possible if you can. You can't access the water directly from these sites, but there is a swimming beach nearby that is just a short walk or bike ride away.

Salina KOA Holiday

▷ Salina, Kansas

▷ koa.com

▷ RV and Tent Sites, Cabins

▷ $$$

This KOA wins rave reviews for getting all the little details right. The sites are level, the restrooms are clean, and they welcome you like family at the front desk. Kids love the playground and jumping pillow, and everyone loves the fresh-baked pizza and the wide variety of flavors at the ice cream parlor in the cozy camp store. Big Daddy D's all-you-can-eat pancake breakfasts are also good and very affordable. The sites are a bit small for the biggest of big rigs, but all other RVs should be fine. The cabins here are also good, but some lack privacy from other guests.

Pomona State Park

▷ Vassar, Kansas

▷ ksoutdoors.com/State-Parks/Locations/Pomona

▷ RV and Tent Sites, Cabins

▷ $

Pomona State Park (which used to be called Vassar State Park) has a lovely lake and is a great place for a summer camping retreat. There are actually nine campgrounds here. Some of them have electric and water hookups and some do not. We prefer the string of three campgrounds along the Pomona Reservoir (Cedar Wind Campground, Four Winds Campground, and Osage Campground) because their waterfront location is good, and they have water and electric sites.

The Little Apple! Five Great (and Affordable) Things to Do in Manhattan, Kansas

Several of the campgrounds that are recommended in this chapter are close to Manhattan, Kansas, which is often referred to as "The Little Apple." Manhattan, Kansas, is obviously quite a bit different from the Manhattan in New York City—but it is still well worth visiting. If you find yourself in the home of Kansas State University, here are five budget-friendly attractions you don't want to miss.

1. If you head into town early, make sure to **grab breakfast at Guilty Biscuit**, which is a self-described "dine out dive." The Risk It Biscuit comes with fried chicken, citrus almond pecan hot sauce, sliced homemade pickles, and mozzarella cheese. If you want something a bit less adventurous, try the Guilty Biscuit itself, which is a French toast biscuit with fried chicken, cream gravy, and pecan bacon.

2. The **MHK Farmer's Market** is a great place to grab fresh produce, local coffee, or sweets and treats from local vendors. It is open on Saturdays from April to October during the hours of 8:00 a.m. to 1:00 p.m. There is also a Wednesday evening market from May to September during the hours of 4:00 p.m. to 7:00 p.m.

3. **The Gardens at Kansas State University** are packed with irises, lilies, roses, peonies, and much more. There is also an insect zoo that is very popular with kids. Admission is free and so is parking.

4. Grab a couple of books for the road at **The Dusty Bookshelf** in the famous Aggieville section of Manhattan.

5. **The Midwest Dream Car Collection** has more than sixty-five cars in its permanent collection that range from 1886 to 2020. Admission is dirt cheap, the building is pleasant and attractive, and the signage for each vehicle is informative. Staff members will let you sit in some of the cars if you are well-behaved, and they may even fire up a few engines while you are there.

RECOMMENDED CAMPGROUNDS

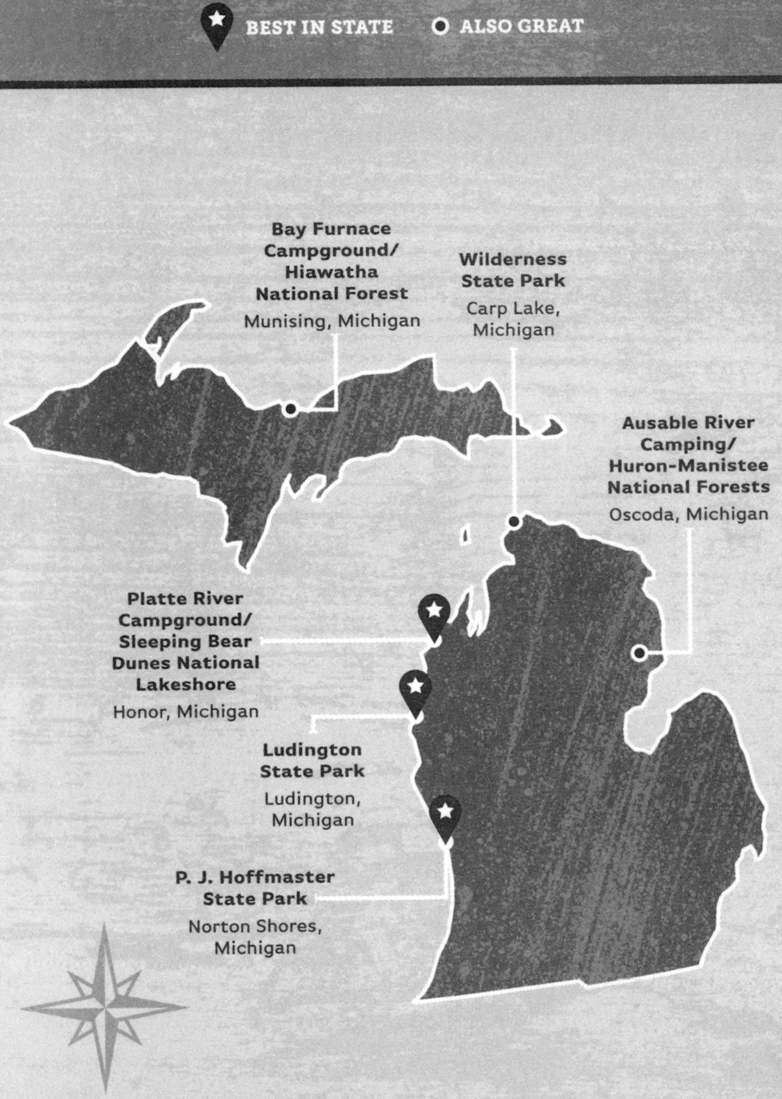

★ BEST IN STATE   ○ ALSO GREAT

Bay Furnace Campground/ Hiawatha National Forest

Munising, Michigan

Wilderness State Park

Carp Lake, Michigan

Ausable River Camping/ Huron-Manistee National Forests

Oscoda, Michigan

Platte River Campground/ Sleeping Bear Dunes National Lakeshore

Honor, Michigan

Ludington State Park

Ludington, Michigan

P. J. Hoffmaster State Park

Norton Shores, Michigan

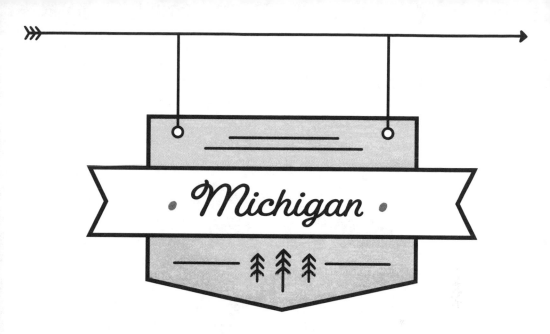

Michigan

Michigan may be the most underrated state for camping in the entire nation. We tend to think of Michigan as one of America's great camping states, along with California, Texas, Florida, and New York. There are so many great campgrounds in Michigan, both public and private, that choosing a handful of them feels like a sin. The state's best budget camping options are anchored by its magnificent state park system and supplemented by national park and national forest campgrounds in several key locations across the state. Very few RV owners across the country make plans to spend a weeklong summer vacation in Michigan—but we think more of them should. When it comes to camping, Michigan has it all. Tent campers love it here, and it seems like someone owns an RV on every single block in every single town in the entire state. If you are looking for an under-the-radar summer vacation that is not Yellowstone or Yosemite, try a couple of places called Sleeping Bear Dunes or Pictured Rocks—or any of the state parks reviewed in this section. You can thank us later—hopefully at a campground somewhere in Michigan.

BEST IN STATE

P.J. Hoffmaster State Park

▷ Norton Shores, Michigan

▷ www2.dnr.state.mi.us/parksandtrails

▷ RV and Tent Sites

▷ $

P.J. Hoffmaster State Park is named after the first commissioner of Michigan's state parks, and it is located on Lake Michigan, just forty minutes away from Grand Rapids. Day-trippers and campers absolutely love the natural beauty of the dunes and the beach here—and it certainly is one of the nicest spots in Michigan to spend a day on the sand. There are almost 300 electric sites at the campground here, and many of them are large and shaded. Despite its size, the campground usually serves as a peaceful and relaxing base camp for exploring everything that this park has to offer. Hoffmaster has excellent hiking throughout the park, and much of it is intertwined with its 3 miles of pristine shoreline. A highlight for many visitors is hiking the Dune Climb Stairway, which leads to an observation deck with spectacular views of the park and Lake Michigan. The summer may be the best time for swimming, but the fall colors here are vibrant and spark new life into the park's excellent hiking trails.

Ludington State Park

▷ Ludington, Michigan

▷ www2.dnr.state.mi.us/parksandtrails

▷ RV and Tent Sites, Cabins

▷ $

Ludington State Park, which is located between the shores of Hamlin Lake and Lake Michigan, may be the single most popular and beloved camping destination in all of Michigan. There are three different campgrounds in this magnificent state park, with a total of over 350 sites. The Ludington-Beechwood Campground has three loops near Hamlin Lake, and the sites here are large and have electric hookups. Some even have 50-amp. The Ludington-Pines Campground also has spacious sites with electrical hookups but offers more shade than Beechwood and is closer to Lake Michigan. There are more than one hundred other sites at the Ludington-Cedar Campground (which is between the other two) that are also good and offer electrical hookups. Picking a favorite campground out of the three is difficult, and sites here can be difficult to book, so take whatever you can get. Some RV owners complain that many of the sites are not level, so just bring leveling blocks and be prepared to take a few extra minutes to get your rig situated. If you are tent camping, just make sure to position your tent so that your head is on the upper end of the slope if there is one. The park has miles of pristine shoreline to explore, and the Civilian Conservation Corps–built beach house on Lake Michigan and the Big Sable Point Lighthouse are both charming and historic. No trip is complete without visiting both of them.

Platte River Campground/Sleeping Bear Dunes National Lakeshore

▷   Honor, Michigan

▷   nps.gov

▷   RV and Tent Sites

▷ $

Camping aficionados love to stroll around this magical campground and pick out their favorite sites for future trips. The campsites are lovingly carved into the landscape at this NPS gem, and each one seems to be shaped differently. Many of the best sites are nestled into the woods and have two separate spaces—one for your RV or tent, and another space behind that for your campfire or picnic table setup. The eclectic nature of the sites becomes even more varied when you consider that some have electric hookups and some are walk-in sites for tent campers. There is something for everyone here, and return campers certainly have their favorite sites in mind when they book. But don't stress about getting the best site if you are a first timer—save your stress for just getting any site at all because the Platte River Campground is just that popular. Its location within Sleeping Bear Dunes National Lakeshore is excellent, and its proximity to an epic tubing or kayak run on the Platte River is very convenient.

-------- **Budget-Camping Gear: Stormy Kromer Caps** --------

Stormy Kromer has been making great caps in the Upper Peninsula of Michigan since 1903. At first glance, you might think they are a bit expensive, but considering they are handmade in the United States and built to last a lifetime, we think they are an absolute bargain. The iconic Stormy Kromer earband can be pulled down to keep your ears warm on those chilly fall nights at your favorite Michigan campground. These caps have a unique styling that is all their own. Embrace the lace and go get yourself a Stormy Kromer. Just make sure you measure your noggin first and consult their size chart so you get a perfect fit!

ALSO GREAT

Bay Furnace Campground/Hiawatha National Forest

▷ Munising, Michigan

▷ recreation.gov

▷ RV and Tent Sites

▷ $

If you feel like traveling further up and further in, then head to the Hiawatha National Forest in Michigan's Upper Peninsula. Bay Furnace Campground is simple and rustic, but that is a huge part of its appeal, as is its location on the shores of Lake Superior. The sites here do not have hookups but are spacious enough for RVs and private enough for tent campers. Pictured Rocks National Lakeshore is about forty-five minutes away, so this campground makes a great base camp for the lakeshore and for all that Hiawatha National Forest has to offer, including great hiking and nearby waterfalls.

Wilderness State Park

▷ Carp Lake, Michigan

▷ www2.dnr.state.mi.us/parksandtrails

▷ RV and Tent Sites, Cabins, Bunkhouses

▷ $

Wilderness State Park is located on the extreme northern tip of Michigan's Lower Peninsula, about 10 miles west of Mackinaw City. Michiganders from this part of the state absolutely love camping here, and it is easy to understand why. This is an incredible place to get away from it all and reconnect with nature. The West Lakeshore Campground is located right on the water inside the park, and it has more than 150 sites with electric hookups. The quality of these sites varies widely—some are magnificent, and some are just nice grassy parking spots in the woods. Across the street from this campground is a second campground called Pines, which also has a nice range of sites, but it is not as close to the water.

Ausable River Camping/Huron-Manistee National Forests

▷ Oscoda, Michigan

▷ recreation.gov

▷ Tent Sites

▷ $

Camping along the Ausable River in Huron-Manistee National Forests is one of the most special camping experiences in the Midwest. This is not one physical campground, but instead it is a series of more than one hundred campsites along the river. Some of them are only accessible by boat. Many of the campsites sit on bluffs that can be quite high above the river, and the river can be hard to access from your site in some situations. Locals do better picking their spots here and developing their knowledge of the individual sites over many years of camping. So, when you camp here for the first time, consider it a fact-finding mission and an epic adventure—because it certainly will be!

Getting to Know Michigan's State Park Campgrounds

▷ RV and tent sites in Michigan's state parks can be booked up to six months in advance.

▷ Other state park accommodations can be booked up to one year in advance.

▷ Michigan state parks have a new alert system that will send you an email when a chosen site becomes available. This is a great way to track cancellations.

▷ Michigan.gov has an incredibly useful page about pet-friendly recreation within the state's parks. It lists every pet-friendly accommodation and every pet-friendly shoreline within the state.

▷ Several Michigan state parks are offering safari tent rentals through a partnership with Tentrr.

▷ Many small businesses rent RVs and can have them dropped off within Michigan's state parks. Michigan.gov lists all state-approved vendors.

▷ Winter camping is available in many of Michigan's state parks. Check Michigan.gov for details.

▷ Michigan also offers 140 state forest campgrounds with rustic camping for those who want a more remote experience. These campgrounds are all located on rivers or lakes.

RECOMMENDED CAMPGROUNDS

★ BEST IN STATE   ○ ALSO GREAT

Itasca State Park
Park Rapids, Minnesota

Clubhouse Lake Campground/ Chippewa National Forest
Marcell, Minnesota

Tettegouche State Park
Silver Bay, Minnesota

Gull Lake Recreation Area
Brainerd, Minnesota

Split Rock Lighthouse State Park
Two Harbors, Minnesota

Lebanon Hills Regional Park
Eagan, Minnesota

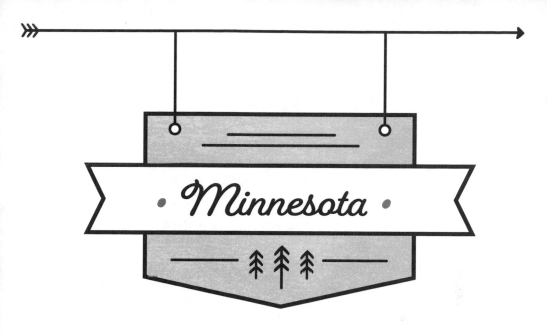

You could spend your entire life camping in Minnesota and never run out of wonderful and budget-friendly places to camp. Many of the best spots here are situated directly on stunning lakes or, in some cases, right on the breathtaking shores of Lake Superior. Minnesota's state park system has a robust list of camping options that span the state, and it is one of the few state park systems in the country to still be building new campgrounds—so kudos to Minnesota for expanding its already-excellent system. There is so much great National Forest Service camping here as well. Many of those spots have only a handful of sites and are rustic and secluded in the very best of ways.

BEST IN STATE

Split Rock Lighthouse State Park

▷ Two Harbors, Minnesota

▷ dnr.state.mn.us

▷ **RV and Tent Sites**

▷ **$**

There are so many breathtaking campgrounds on America's Great Lakes, and the Shipwreck Creek Campground at Split Rock Lighthouse State Park is certainly one of them. This campground opened in 2022, and it is an absolute delight. The sites are large, spacious, and lovingly carved into the landscape. Many of them are also surrounded by wildflowers and a diverse mix of trees that provide shade and natural beauty. There are forty-six electric sites here with pads that measure around seventy feet long, so this is a great place for larger rigs. The freshly paved roads are also great for biking and strolling around the campground. People love to walk around here and check out each individual site, because they are all unique and they are all beautifully designed. Plan on spending your time hiking and exploring Pebble Beach and taking in stunning views of Lake Superior. Tours of the lighthouse are available through the Minnesota Historical Society for a moderate fee.

------------------- **Budget-Camping Hacks:** -------------------

Make an Affordable Camping Meal with Spam!

Spam was created in Austin, Minnesota, by Hormel Foods and is certainly one of Minnesota's greatest contributions to American popular culture. Spam was developed as an inexpensive and durable meat alternative during the Great Depression, and its popularity exploded during World War II because it could be stored for long periods of time and shipped around the world. It is still popular today among campers and budget-conscious home cooks. We recommend slicing it thin and cooking it up well done for amazing Spam, egg, and cheese breakfast sandwiches on English muffins—or dicing it up for Spam fried rice with whatever ingredients you want to toss in. Both of these options are cheap, easy to make, and can feed a hungry army at the campground.

Tettegouche State Park

▷   Silver Bay, Minnesota

▷   dnr.state.mn.us

▷   RV and Tent Sites, Cabins

▷ $

Tettegouche State Park is just fifteen minutes farther north up the coast of Lake Superior from Split Rock Lighthouse State Park. It amazes us that two majestic state parks with great campgrounds are so close to each other. Located about an hour north of Duluth, Tettegouche has a stunning shoreline on Lake Superior, beautiful hikes to waterfalls, and most importantly, a terrific campground. But please note, the campground is 1.5 miles away from the water. The sites here are large and private and some of them have electric, but they do lack the whimsical charm of the sites at Split Rock. They do, however, offer more privacy and shade, so they might be preferable for tent campers or those who don't like to see their neighbors. Make sure you bring your hiking boots to this park because it has some amazing trails. You can hike along the cliffs above Lake Superior and take in wonderful vistas, or hike to three waterfalls within the park. There is also rock climbing and mountain biking along with excellent nature programs that are kid friendly.

Itasca State Park

▷   Park Rapids, Minnesota

▷   dnr.state.mn.us

▷   Douglas Lodge Rooms, Cabins, RV and Tent Sites, and Lodge Rooms

▷ $

The Mighty Mississippi River starts here! Itasca State Park was established in 1891 and is Minnesota's oldest state park. It is also gigantic. It encompasses 32,000 acres and has more than one hundred lakes. Park-run lodging options here are top-notch. The Douglas Lodge has been hosting lovers of the great outdoors for more than one hundred years, and a variety of other classic Civilian Conservation Corps–built cabins are also available for rent. There are two campgrounds here, Bear Paw and Pine Ridge, and both offer excellent sites that are large and wooded—when combined they offer 223 campsites and 160 of them have electric hookups. Bear Paw campsites are a little bit more out in open than Pine Ridge, which has very private sites. The park is packed with recreational opportunities, and it has its own camp store and bait-and-tackle shop called Itasca Sports. It also rents out bikes, canoes, kayaks, paddleboards, and much more. Make sure to check out the visitor center after you check in—the staff will get you situated and help you figure out how to best spend your time in this magnificent state park.

ALSO GREAT

Lebanon Hills Regional Park

▷   **Eagan, Minnesota**

▷   **co.dakota.mn.us**

▷   **RV and Tent Sites**

▷   **$**

This campground is a quiet and shady oasis located right smack in the suburbs of the Twin Cities. Downtown Minneapolis is only thirty-five minutes away, and the Mall of America is less than twenty minutes away. Lebanon Hills Regional Park Campground is the perfect base camp for those destinations, but it is also a destination in its own right. This spotless park is filled with trails and lakes for hiking, biking, and boating and the swimming at Schulze Lake Beach is also good, so don't forget your bathing suit. The full hook-up sites here are an absolute bargain.

Gull Lake Recreation Area

▷   **Brainerd, Minnesota**

▷   **recreation.gov**

- ▷ **RV and Tent Sites**
- ▷ **$**

This U.S. Army Corps of Engineers campground is a very special place. It is immaculately clean and lovingly maintained, and each of the shaded and private campsites is an absolute delight. The sites here all have electric hook-ups, and they look like they were carved into the landscape by an artist, not an engineer. The waters of Gull Lake are crystal clear, and they are near-wild heaven for fishing, swimming, and kayaking—at least during Minnesota's all-too-short summer season.

Clubhouse Lake Campground/Chippewa National Forest

- ▷ **Marcell, Minnesota**
- ▷ **recreation.gov**
- ▷ **RV and Tent Sites**
- ▷ **$**

This National Forest Service campground is nestled right alongside Clubhouse Lake, and the best sites are right on the water. Rustic camping without hookups doesn't get much better than this. A thick stand of fragrant 200-year-old white and red pine trees blankets the campground and provides shade and privacy at just about every campsite. There is a swimming beach and fishing pier here and not much else. This place is all about enjoying the simple pleasures of lake life and nature.

Let's Go Ice Fishing in Minnesota!

Ice fishing and camping? Count us in! Icehouses are similar to camping trailers, but they are made to be towed onto frozen lakes. Anglers sit inside the comfortable little "house" and fish through a hole in the floor. Icehouses come in many sizes and at many price points. You can find small icehouses that have canvas walls and are similar to tents. There are also large icehouses that sleep nearly a dozen people and have all the amenities of an RV.

One of the more famous icehouse builders is Ice Castle Fish Houses. Many of the big icehouses have slide outs, kitchens, and bathrooms. Icehouses are built to be warmer and better insulated than typical camper trailers.

The season for ice fishing starts in the beginning of December in Minnesota and many other far northern states. That's when people can usually walk out on the ice. By the end of December, people can often drive a pickup truck across the ice. This all varies by how far north the lake is. Ice fishing usually ends sometime in March.

Safety is important, so the season depends on the thickness of ice. Ice is safe to walk on when there are four inches of clear ice. To drive a truck on the ice, it's better to wait until the ice is twelve to fifteen inches thick. It's important to note that ice will not be consistent all the way across a lake, so use an auger to check the depth of the ice before driving on it.

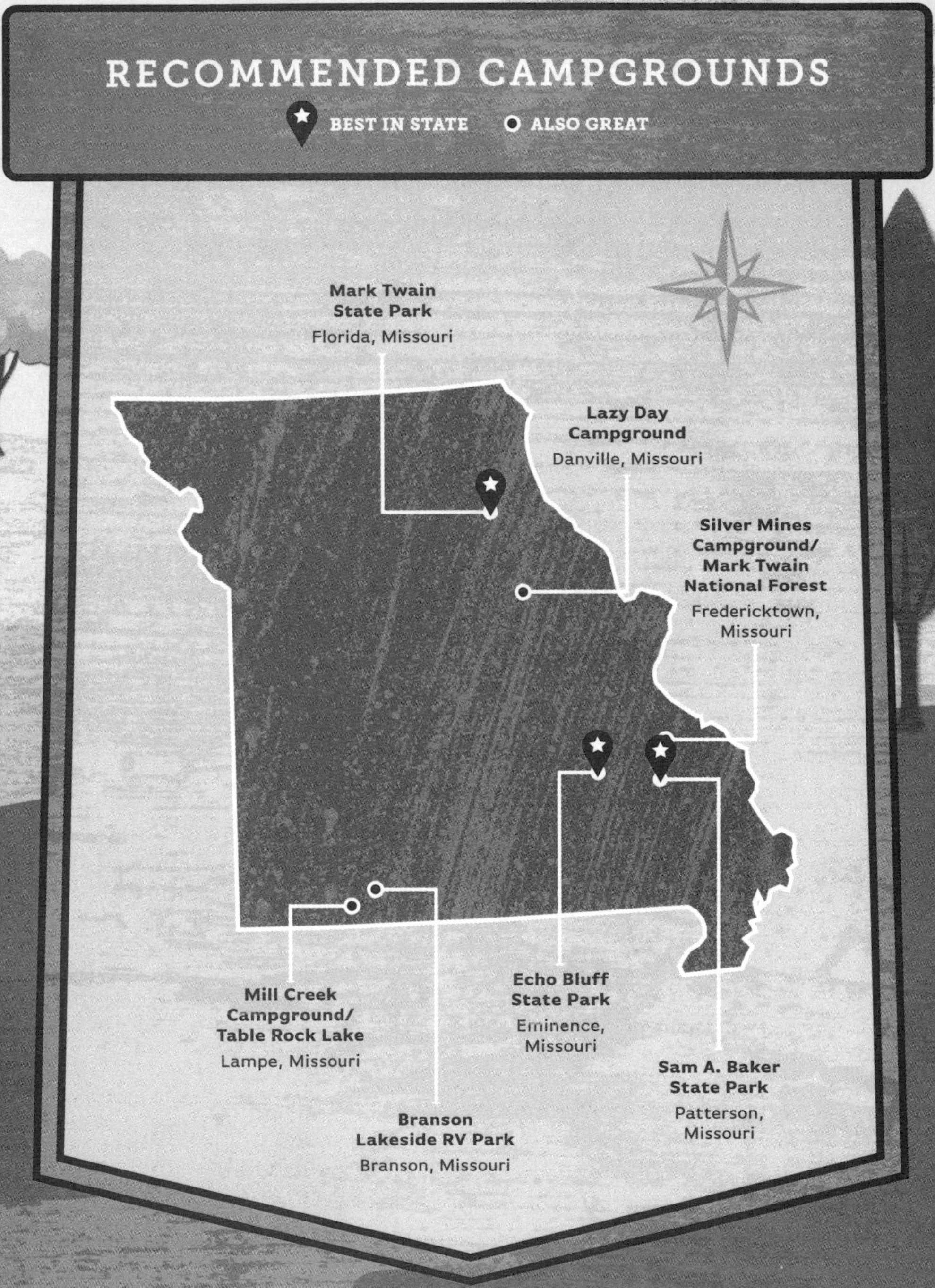

RECOMMENDED CAMPGROUNDS

★ BEST IN STATE   ○ ALSO GREAT

**Mark Twain
State Park**
Florida, Missouri

**Lazy Day
Campground**
Danville, Missouri

**Silver Mines
Campground/
Mark Twain
National Forest**
Fredericktown,
Missouri

**Mill Creek
Campground/
Table Rock Lake**
Lampe, Missouri

**Echo Bluff
State Park**
Eminence,
Missouri

**Sam A. Baker
State Park**
Patterson,
Missouri

**Branson
Lakeside RV Park**
Branson, Missouri

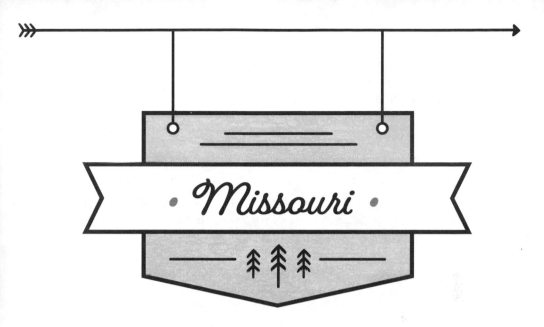

Missouri is yet another midwestern state with terrific options for budget camping. Many of the state parks border on the magnificent, and Missouri has more than its fair share of great U.S. Army Corps of Engineers and national forest campgrounds. Upscale RV resorts are starting to pop up in the state, but there are still plenty of bargain-priced mom-and-pop campgrounds that offer tons of activities and amenities for families. So why isn't Missouri on more people's bucket lists for epic outdoor adventures? It's hard to say. When it comes to camping, the state has so much to offer—including surprisingly good hiking, epic fishing, and boating. We would like to see more people visit places like Missouri, Michigan, Wisconsin, and Minnesota because the camping there is grand, and the best sites are out there waiting for all of us.

BEST IN STATE

Mark Twain State Park

▷ Florida, Missouri

▷ **mostateparks.com**

▷ **RV and Tent Sites, Cabins**

▷ **$**

This is a really cool campground and state park for anyone, but it is especially fun for book lovers and fans of the great American writer Mark Twain. The Mark Twain Birthplace State Historic Site is located in Mark Twain State Park, and it showcases the two-room cabin that Samuel Clemens was born in. First editions of the author's books are also on display and so is a handwritten manuscript of *The Adventures of Tom Sawyer*. Reading one of Twain's books while you are camping here would be a very special experience indeed. There are three campgrounds within the park, and all of them are good. Badger has electric sites and is good for RVs, Coyote has primitive sites and sites with electric, and Puma has electric sites and extra-large family sites that cost a bit more but are absolutely terrific. These family sites have two of everything and can accommodate two families camping together. The hiking on the bluffs around the lake is excellent, so bring your hiking shoes and plenty of water. It gets hot here in the summertime.

------------------ **Budget-Camping Hack:** ------------------
Stock Up on Shirts, Hoodies, and Hats at Bass Pro Shops
Bass Pro Shops was born in a liquor store in 1972 in Springfield, Missouri. That's when founder Johnny Morris began selling fishing gear out of his dad's store. Today, Johnny Morris is a billionaire and owns more than 200 hundred stores across North America. We love stocking up on camping and fishing shirts and hoodies at Bass Pro Shops because they are affordable and the quality is good. We also like their branded baseball camps that come in a wide variety of styles and colors.

Echo Bluff State Park

▷   Eminence, Missouri

▷   echobluffstatepark.com

▷   RV and Tent Sites, Cabins, Lodge Rooms

▷ $

The Timbuktu Campground at Echo Bluff State Park looks more like a modern RV park than a state park campground, and we don't mean that in a bad way. The sites lack shade and privacy, but they have full hookups, and they are paved, level, and reasonably sized. While the sixty RV sites are out in the open sun, the twelve walk-in tent sites are wonderfully private and well shaded. Some of them are even handicap accessible. Tent camping doesn't get much better than this. The lodge rooms and cabins at Echo Bluff are also pretty awesome. They are comfortable, modern, and incredibly well-equipped. All the accommodations here are world class by state park standards, but the park itself is the star of the show. The Sinking Creek is surrounded by otherworldly bluffs and a lush green forest that is filled with great hiking and mountain biking. The smallmouth bass fishing is legendary in this part of the country, so bring your fishing gear and get ready for a day on the water. The lodge rents bikes if you don't have your own, and the Creekside Grill has indoor and outdoor dining. It is a great place to break bread after a long day of adventuring in the park.

Sam A. Baker State Park

▷   Patterson, Missouri

▷   mostateparks.com

▷   RV and Tent Sites, Cabins

▷ $

Sam A. Baker State Park may not be the most famous state park in Missouri, but many campers from the Show-Me State call it their favorite. The Saint Francis River and Big Creek attract those who love fishing, swimming, and kayaking, and those who just love to dip their toes in the crystal clear water. There are two campgrounds in Sam A. Smith, creatively named Campground 1 and Campground 2. Both have a mix of primitive sites and sites with electric. Both also have "family" campsites that have room for two families and two of everything at an extra-large site. The cabins here also win rave reviews from guests. They may look rustic and charming on the outside, but don't be fooled because they are well-equipped with kitchens, heating, air conditioning, and full bathrooms. Make sure you don't miss the Mudlick Mountain Store in the park—it is filled with charming gifts, ice cream, jams, jellies, fresh produce, and more.

---------------- Three More Amazing State Parks ----------------
in Missouri with Campgrounds

1. **Johnson's Shut-Ins State Park in Middle Brook, Missouri:** What the heck is a shut-in? It's kind of like a natural water park in a river created by rock that is resistant to erosion. The shut-ins at this state park are filled with all kinds of neat little swimming holes and spots for rock jumping and exploring.

2. **Bennett Spring State Park in Lebanon, Missouri:** Known for its excellent hiking and trout fishing, this state park in the southwest corner of Missouri has an idyllic campground and also offers cabins and motel rooms. It is just one hour away from Springfield and three hours away from St. Louis, so it is far from an undiscovered gem.

3. **Lake of the Ozarks State Park in Kaiser, Missouri:** The RV and tent sites are great at Missouri's most visited state park, but the real star of the show is the aptly named "Outpost" area in the heart of the park. Here you will find eight picture-perfect and Instagram-worthy cabins surrounded by an oak-hickory forest.

ALSO GREAT

Mill Creek Campground/Table Rock Lake

▷ Lampe, Missouri

▷ recreation.gov

▷ RV and Tent Sites

▷ $

Missouri is absolutely jam-packed with great U.S. Army Corps of Engineers campgrounds, and Mill Creek, which is less than forty-five minutes away from Branson, is definitely one of the best. Some of the sites are out on a peninsula and have spectacular water views that wrap around the campsites. These may just be some of the best campsites in the entire state. Don't fret if you can't reserve one of these—all sixty-seven sites here are very good and all of them come with water and electric hookups.

Branson Lakeside RV Park

▷ Branson, Missouri

▷ bransonlakesidervpark.com

▷ RV Sites

▷ $$$

The campsites are close together at this super clean RV park, but everything else is wonderful. If you want to be close to everything that Branson has to offer, definitely check this place out. There is a trolley that will take you downtown or to the shopping at Branson Landing, which has more than one hundred retail shops. A gigantic Bass Pro Shops is half a mile away. There is also an on-site marina here and a fishing dock. Full hook-up sites are reasonably priced, and we think they are definitely worth the splurge.

Silver Mines Campground/Mark Twain National Forest

▷ Fredericktown, Missouri

▷ recreation.gov

▷ RV and Tent Sites

▷ $

This campground and the entire area around it are absolutely beautiful. A river runs past the campground, and there are hiking trails and swimming holes nearby. There are several camping areas here with seventy total sites, and eleven of them have electric hookups. This is National Forest Service camping at its best—simple, natural, and unplugged. Make sure you bring a net for catching tadpoles and tubes for floating on the river. Kayakers fill this place up on spring weekends, so it may actually be easier to reserve in the summertime.

Lazy Day Campground

▹ **Danville, Missouri**

▹ **lazydaycampground.com**

▹ **RV and Tent Sites**

▹ **$$**

Missouri has lots of good mom-and-pop campgrounds with excellent amenities, activities, and customer service—and Lazy Day Campground in Danville is one of the best of them. The pool here is delightful on a hot summer's day, and the catch-and-release fishing pond is popular with those who love to wet a line while camping. If the weather is good, they run a movie night every Saturday during peak season—make sure you grab some ice cream at the camp store before showtime.

RECOMMENDED CAMPGROUNDS

★ BEST IN STATE   ○ ALSO GREAT

Bessey Recreation Complex and Campground/ Nebraska National Forest at Halsey
Halsey, Nebraska

Ponca State Park
Ponca, Nebraska

Two Rivers State Recreation Area
Waterloo, Nebraska

Cottonwood Campground/Lewis and Clark Lake
Waterloo, Nebraska

Platte River State Park
Louisville, Nebraska

Eugene T. Mahoney State Park
Ashland, Nebraska

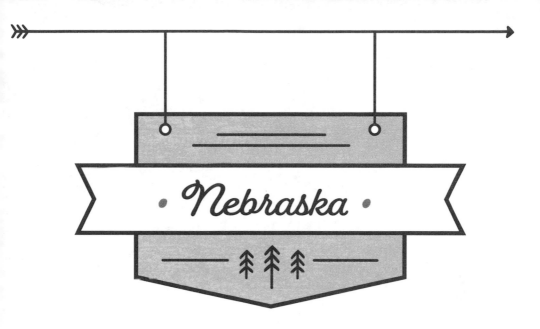

Nebraska

Some of you may be surprised to read this, but we want to make a claim here: several of Nebraska's state parks are among the best in the country. Hands down. The state has invested tremendous resources into these parks, and it shows in every single way. They have world-class facilities for all kinds of outdoorsy activities, and they have lodging that could easily be featured in a glossy travel magazines. Their campgrounds are also excellent. So, if you want to camp in Nebraska and save money, start by looking at the state park campgrounds that are reviewed in this chapter. There are also very good camping options at U.S. Army Corps of Engineers campgrounds in the state, and there is some surprisingly good National Forest Service camping—but those options may be best for those living in-state and looking for quiet getaways. If you are traveling through Nebraska and want to see the best camping the state has to offer, then head to a Nebraska state park for an epic and unforgettable camping experience that rivals other state park masterpieces like Custer State Park in South Dakota and Gulf Shores State Park in Alabama. When it comes to budget-friendly camping, the Cornhusker State delivers for campers of all ages.

BEST IN STATE

Platte River State Park

▷ Louisville, Nebraska

▷ outdoornebraska.gov/location/platte-river/

▷ RV and Tent Sites, Cabins, Glamping Cabins

▷ $

Platte River Campground is awesome in just about every way. Whether you are getting your feet wet at its spray park or at the Stone Creek Waterfall, this is a great place to spend a summer weekend. Crawdad Creek is another great place to get wet and search for crawdads and minnows—but you will also get muddy, which is just fine for the kids who love to spend time there. The campground here is on the smaller side but offers the holy trinity of water, sewer, and electric hookups at a bargain-basement price. Shade is almost non-existent at the campground, but the sites are fairly spacious. The glamping cabins at Platte River State Park are gorgeous and amazing—private campground owners should take note. The bright and airy space is designed so that you can sleep inside or outside by simply rolling the bed out onto the private deck. Fully equipped "modern" cabins are also available, as are rustic camper cabins. Platte River gets our Worth the Splurge badge for its glamping cabins only—the campsites and rustic cabins here are definitely super affordable.

Eugene T. Mahoney State Park

▷ Ashland, Nebraska

▷ outdoornebraska.gov/location/eugene-t-mahoney/

▷ RV and Tent Sites, Cabins, Lodge Rooms

▷ $

Mahoney State Park may be one of the best and most modern state parks in the country when it comes to amenities, activities, events, camping, and lodging. This park, which is located between Omaha and Lincoln, is a special place that is deeply loved by Nebraskans. Campers from all over the country should put this place on their "where should we camp next" lists, and get there as soon as they can—especially if they love outdoor adventure. Mahoney has a ropes course, a wave pool, an ice-skating rink, climbing walls, golf, mini golf, and a gigantic indoor playground with slides and a ball pit for rainy days. There are almost sixty cabins here, and there are options with two, four, and six bedrooms, making this a great place for multi-family trips. The Peter Kiewit Lodge also has forty lodge rooms, and some of them have sleeping lofts for the kids. As if all of that is not enough, Mahoney has two modern campgrounds that are great for tents and RVs. Both campgrounds have sites with hookups, and specific sites are listed as "tentable" if they have a level grassy area for pitching a tent.

Ponca State Park

▷ Ponca, Nebraska

▷ outdoornebraska.gov/location/ponca

▷ RV and Tent Sites, Cabins, Tentrr Safari Tents

▷ $

When it comes to modern lodging and camping options and robust offerings for activities and events, Ponca State Park, which overlooks the Missouri River, is another Nebraska state park that could serve as a model for the rest of the country. The lodging options are particularly impressive. Ponca has more than thirty cabins, and all but four rustic cabins are open year-round. Its two- and four-bedroom mini-lodges are downright exquisite and come with wood or electric fireplaces, gas grills, full kitchens—and much more. The park even has two so-called "green cabins" that are made of straw bales. Those who want a more rustic and outdoorsy experience can of course bring their own tents, or they can rent a canvas safari tent from Tentrr that will be set up and ready to go upon arrival. Ponca also has three small campgrounds that are very cozy and quite popular with guests. The campgrounds offer a mix of sites without hookups and sites with electric. Plan on hiking, fishing, swimming, and golfing during your stay at Ponca—and don't forget to stop in at the visitor center during your trip. It's one of the best state park visitor centers in the country.

ALSO GREAT

Two Rivers State Recreation Area

▷ Waterloo, Nebraska

▷ outdoornebraska.gov/location/two-rivers/

▷ RV and Tent Sites, Cabooses

▷ $

Two Rivers State Recreation Area has ten Pacific Union cabooses that have been converted into quirky and charming family-friendly accommodations that won't break the bank. That alone makes Two Rivers an awesome place to spend a weekend, but there is much more. There is great swimming and fishing here, and there are almost 150 modern campsites spread across several campgrounds. The sites here are spacious and most are shady. We like the waterfront sites at Lakeside Campground the best.

Cottonwood Campground/Lewis and Clark Lake

▷ Waterloo, Nebraska

▷ recreation.gov

▷ RV and Tent Sites

▷ $

Located alongside the western side of Lake Yankton, this U.S. Army Corps of Engineers park offers seventy-seven spacious and level campsites with electric hookups. There is great kayaking here, and there is a good swimming beach near the campground. The campground has a modern playground for the kids and a disc golf course—but beyond that, it is kind of far away from everything, which is certainly part of its appeal. So, if you go, just make sure you bring your own fun and a couple of good books.

Bessey Recreation Complex and Campground/ Nebraska National Forest at Halsey

▷ Halsey, Nebraska

▷ recreation.gov

▷ RV and Tent Sites

▷ $

All-terrain vehicle (ATV) lovers who camp love this place dearly because there are excellent trails nearby, and you can ride your ATV from your campsite to the trailheads. However, this does create noise that can disturb those who are not there to ATV. There is also a train that goes by several times a day. But if you are there to ATV, you probably won't even notice. The campsites are spacious and some of them have electric. Opportunities for hiking, biking, and bird-watching are abundant in this national forest setting.

Getting to Know Nebraska's State Park Campgrounds

▷ Campsites in Nebraska's state parks can be reserved up to 180 days in advance.

▷ Cabins and lodge rooms can be reserved up to 365 days in advance.

▷ Nebraska has a state call center for reservations that is open Monday through Friday from 9:00 a.m. to 6:00 p.m. local time.

▷ Nebraska has almost seventy-five state parks with camping options.

▷ Only bring firewood that was purchased or cut from within a 50-mile radius of your campground.

▷ Please do not bring firewood home after bringing it into a Nebraska state park campground—burn all of it before leaving.

▷ Alcohol is allowed at campsites except during quiet hours from 10:00 p.m. to 6:00 a.m.

▷ Several Nebraska state parks, such as Platte River, offer excellent modern lodging and glamping opportunities that are among the best public lodging options in the country.

Budget-Camping Gear at Cabela's

Cabela's was founded in 1961 in Chappell, Nebraska, when Dick and Mary Cabela started selling fishing flies from their kitchen table. The company is now owned by Bass Pro Shops, but its history and lineage will always be associated with Nebraska. Today, it is still a great place to find moderately priced camping gear. Here are a few of our favorites:

▷ **Cabela's Polar Cap Coolers** are certainly not cheap in the grand scheme of things—but they are quite a bit cheaper than a Yeti and many cooler aficionados think they are even better.

▷ **Cabela's Polar Cap Tumblers** are less than half the price of their Yeti counterparts, and they come with an integrated bottle opener on the bottom.

▷ **Cabela's line of Intensity Binoculars** are a great value for those who want a rugged and durable pair of binocs that won't break the bank.

▷ **Cabela's Mountain Trapper Sleeping Bags** cost more than the sleeping bags that you will find in a big-box store, but they are incredibly well made and will last a lifetime. We've had ours for seven years and they look brand new.

RECOMMENDED CAMPGROUNDS

★ BEST IN STATE   ○ ALSO GREAT

Fort Stevenson State Park
Garrison, North Dakota

CCC Campground/ Little Missouri National Grassland
Grassy Butte, North Dakota

Downstream Campground/ Sakakawea Lake
Hazen, North Dakota

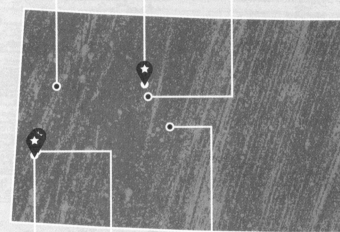

Theodore Roosevelt National Park
Medora, North Dakota

Cross Ranch State Park
Center, North Dakota

Medora Campground
Medora, North Dakota

Very few American campers get to North Dakota, and it is an absolute shame that they don't. This state is far away for most of us, but it is absolutely worth getting to, and not just because of the Fargo-Moorehead Visitors Center's hilarious "Best for Last Club" (it's worth looking up). North Dakota is worth visiting at any time because of the wonderful and underrated Theodore Roosevelt National Park and because of its excellent state parks. Those state parks are mostly visited by residents of the state, but many of them have excellent options for campers who are passing through. To round things out, North Dakota also offers great U.S. Army Corps of Engineers camping and excellent National Forest Service camping. Pretty much all camping in North Dakota is budget camping—so a trip here definitely won't break the bank.

BEST IN STATE

Theodore Roosevelt National Park

▷ Medora, North Dakota

▷ nps.gov

▷   RV and Tent Sites

▷ $

Theodore Roosevelt National Park is an underrated gem. Roosevelt's time spent here as a young man in the 1880s shaped his life and the future of our nation. World-class wildlife viewing and hiking opportunities can be found in this park without the crowds that are often associated with Yellowstone, Badlands, and Glacier. There are two NPS campgrounds inside the park (Cottonwood Campground and Juniper Campground), and both of them are very good— but like most NPS campgrounds, they do not have hookups. Cottonwood Campground is partially situated along the banks of the Little Missouri River, and it is the only campground in the more popular south unit of the park. Half of the sites here are reservable, and half are first-come, first-served—but all of them are simple, quiet, and beautiful. Book as early as possible because Cottonwood does fill up despite the generally uncrowded nature of the park— and bring your own soap to the bathhouse because they often run out. If you are lucky, you will see bison wandering through the campground and maybe even onto your campsite. Keep your distance and get ready to be in awe of these mighty and magnificent creatures. Wild horses also roam through this park, so keep an eye out for them as well. Juniper is the only campground in the north unit of the park and all the sites are first-come, first-served, so it is a much trickier option for tourists visiting from out of state. The campground is grassy and shady, and it is also nestled next to the Little Missouri River.

Medora Campground

▷   Medora, North Dakota

▷   medora.com/medoracampground

▷   RV and Tent Sites, Cabins, Conestoga Wagons

▷ $$$

If you don't want to dry camp inside Theodore Roosevelt National Park, book a full hook-up site right outside the park at Medora Campground. This private campground offers an excellent location and basic amenities just a short walk away from the town of Medora—and a very short drive away from the south unit of the national park. The RV sites are certainly not huge, but most people don't plan on spending much time at the campground anyway. This is a base camp destination intended to provide a clean, comfortable, and convenient place to come home to after a long day of exploring the national park—and it does a bang-up job of delivering those things to its guests. There are cabins and Conestoga wagons for rent here that also get the job done nicely—just don't expect a glamping experience if you book them. The tent-camping sites are much more beautiful inside the park at Cottonwood Campground and Juniper Campground, so we would only consider Medora Campground for tenting if we couldn't get a site in the park. Facilities here include a laundry room, a campground, and a playground for kids. There is no pool, but there is a nice city pool right next door, which is open to the public for a small fee.

Fort Stevenson State Park

▷ **Garrison, North Dakota**
▷ **parkrec.nd.gov/fort-stevenson-state-park**
▷ **RV and Tent Sites, Cabins**
▷ **$**

North Dakota has a surprisingly robust and modern state park system with lots of great options for tent and RV owners and lots of comfortable cabins and yurts. Fort Stevenson State Park is just one of many North Dakota state parks that is loved by campers from within the state and seldom visited by campers from the rest of the country. The sites here are large, and about half of them have full hookups. Some sites are shady while others offer full sun. Many of the sites are private and have trees between them. This park does a great job when it comes to renting out fun equipment and recreational gear at budget prices. Want to rent an aqua-pad, a kicksled, or a stand-up paddleboard? Fort Stevenson has got you covered for all of these and a whole lot more. Visitors also love the hiking and biking trails, and there is an on-site marina where you can rent boats.

---------   **Budget-Camping Gear: Toas-Tite Pie Irons**   ---------

When you are camping out in the Badlands of North Dakota, it just feels right to cook a simple and delicious meal over the campfire. If you don't have the time or patience for a Dutch oven, why not grab yourself a couple of Toas-Tite pie irons and make some delicious hot sammies that the whole family will love? These American-made retro pie irons have been around since 1949 and are almost as iconic as old TR himself. Toas-Tite pie irons can make a hot toasted sandwich in about three minutes—and they are definitely budget priced. We recommend getting the XL Toas-Tite with the longer handle so you and your kids can keep a safe distance from the campfire. And make sure you use plenty of cooking spray so the bread doesn't stick.

ALSO GREAT

CCC Campground/Little Missouri National Grassland

▷ Grassy Butte, North Dakota

▷ recreation.gov

▷ RV and Tent Sites

▷ $

If you are feeling adventurous and you're equipped for camping without hookups, the CCC Campground in Little Missouri National Grassland is another great option for a base camp near the north unit of Theodore Roosevelt National Park. A well-maintained gravel road leads into the campground, which has thirty-two sites, five of which are reservable. This is primitive camping with pit toilets, but the sites are large and level, and the area is filled with great hiking. The Little Missouri River runs right by the campground, and Medora is one hour away.

Cross Ranch State Park

▷ Center, North Dakota

▷ parkrec.nd.gov/cross-ranch-state-park

▷ Cabins, Yurts, Tipis, RV and Tent Sites

▷ $

Cross Ranch State Park is located along a wild and peaceful stretch of the Missouri River and offers outdoor recreation of just about every type—but it is particularly excellent for hiking, mountain biking, and cross-country skiing. RV and tent sites are spacious, private, and primitive, and some of the lodging options, like the cabins and yurts, offer full kitchens and bathrooms. The York Cabin and Pretty Point Yurt are particularly impressive, as both offer comfortable digs and stunning views of the Missouri River. There are three distinct campgrounds within Cross Ranch, and Sanger is probably the prettiest, but big rigs need not apply—it is designed for tent campers and smaller RVs.

Downstream Campground/Sakakawea Lake

▷ Hazen, North Dakota

▷ recreation.gov

▷ RV and Tent Sites

▷ $

North Dakota has several U.S. Army Corps of Engineers campgrounds that are absolute gems, but the Downstream Campground on the Missouri River is probably the best among them. The setting is peaceful and lovely, and the sites are large and shaded, and most have electric hookups. This Army Corps of Engineers campground also makes a point to be very kid and family friendly, especially on the weekends when they show movies or have organized games at the amphitheater. Kudos to them, because most Corps of Engineers campgrounds do not have organized events or activities like this. There are also three playgrounds within the campground and excellent fishing nearby.

Six Great Things to do in Medora, North Dakota

If you find yourself in Medora, then there is a very good chance that you are there to spend most of your time in Theodore Roosevelt National Park. But definitely plan on spending some time (and money) in the gateway town of Medora. Here are six great options.

1. The **North Dakota Cowboy Hall of Fame** is educational and entertaining, and the price of admission is dirt cheap. Kids seventeen and under are free on Wednesdays and Sundays. The Chad Berger Bucking Bulls exhibit is a favorite for kids and adults.

2. Thanks to generous donors, kids seventeen and under can golf for free at the **Bully Pulpit Golf Course** Sunday to Thursday all day and Friday and Saturday after 3:00 p.m. Regular admission for adults is quite a bit more expensive than at a typical public course.

3. The **Medora Musical** is not the only show in town, but it comes pretty close. This outdoor country and western variety show is moderately priced, but it really packs a punch. Most visitors think it will be kitschy—and maybe it is—but this is high-quality entertainment that pleases the masses.

4. Taking a trail ride on the beautiful horses with the **Medora Riding Stables** is not exactly cheap, but we think it is worth the splurge! The guides here are friendly and the views of the Badlands are unforgettable.

5. The town of Medora is challenging for dining out. There are not that many options, and some of them are expensive tourist traps. But we think the **Badlands Pizza Parlor** is the real deal when it comes to offering quality pizza at a budget price. We like the "Badlands Bob" and the "Pesto Chicken" pizzas the best.

6. The **Medora Fudge and Ice Cream Depot** is a great place to get a sweet treat after a long day of exploring Theodore Roosevelt National Park—just make sure you get there before 8:00 p.m. when they close. The licorice ice cream is an out-of-the-box pick but is a real fan favorite.

RECOMMENDED CAMPGROUNDS

 BEST IN STATE ○ **ALSO GREAT**

Mill Creek Campground/ Berlin Lake
Berlin Center, Ohio

East Harbor State Park
Marblehead, Ohio

Findley State Park
Wellington, Ohio

Yogi Bear's Jellystone Park Camp-Resort: Whispering Hills
Big Prairie, Ohio

Hocking Hills State Park
Logan, Ohio

Iron Ridge Campground at Lake Vesuvius/ Wayne National Forest
Pedro, Ohio

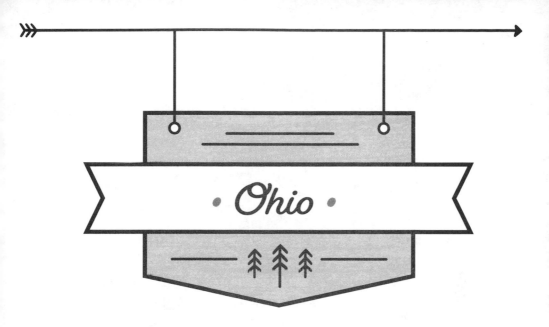

· Ohio ·

When it comes to state park campgrounds, Ohio does not mess around—there is a long list of very good ones and they are clean, well cared for, and carefully managed. Many of them also offer great cabin and yurt options for those without tents or RVs. The Buckeye State also has some great budget camping entries, compliments of the National Forest Service and the U.S. Army Corps of Engineers. Resort camping has not taken hold in the state as much as it has in the Northeast and the South, so many private campgrounds are still reasonably priced and well worth considering. Ohio's state parks also have some truly wonderful lodges (and some that could use some help), so please check out the sidebar in this chapter to learn about four of our favorites. These lodges are terrific for a romantic weekend away without the kids, and the prices are very good.

BEST IN STATE

Findley State Park

▷ Wellington, Ohio

▷ ohiodnr.gov/go-and-do/plan-a-visit/find-a-property/findley-state-park

▷ RV and Tent Sites, Cabins, Shelterhouses

▷ $

Findley State Park is located in northeast Ohio, and it is a favorite place for outdoor enthusiasts across the region. The hike is particularly popular with mountain bikers and bike lovers of every kind, because it has direct access to the popular cross-state Buckeye Trail. There is even a self-serve bike repair station inside the park. There are really no bad sites at the campground here—most are spacious and shady. There are more than 250 sites in the park, and a few have full hookups, almost one hundred have electric, and about 150 have no hookups. There are two very nice camping areas here—one has a mix of the aforementioned sites, and the other only has sites without hookups. There are also three cabins with electricity for rent. The nature center is very popular, and there is an old-school playground that still sees lots of action. Findley Lake has a designated swimming area, but it is on the opposite side of the lake from the campground.

Budget-Camping Hack:
Seniors, Get Your Buckeye Pass!

Ohio residents aged sixty and up can save some serious money when they camp in a state park with a Golden Buckeye Card. Campground reservations are 50 percent off on Sunday through Thursday nights and 10 percent off on Friday and Saturday nights. A 10 percent discount is available for cabins and other overnight accommodations on any day of the week.

East Harbor State Park

▷ Marblehead, Ohio

▷ ohiodnr.gov/go-and-do/plan-a-visit/find-a-property/east-harbor -state-park

▷ RV and Tent Sites, Yurts, Cabins

▷ $

This may just be the most popular state park campground in Ohio. With more than 500 campsites, it is definitely the largest. There are more than 50 sites here with full hookups and more than 350 with electric, while the rest have no hookups. The location of this campground along the shores of Lake Erie is excellent, and there is a very nice swimming beach just a short bike ride away. If you don't bring your own bikes, you can rent them at the camp store. Lake Erie is famous for its walleye fishing, and there are good spots nearby. You can also take a ferry over to Kelleys Island State Park, which also has a great campground. Ohioans often debate which campground is better. We think they are both great—but taking an RV on the ferry isn't exactly cheap, so East Harbor is the better option for budget camping.

Hocking Hills State Park

▷ Logan, Ohio

▷ parks.ohiodnr.gov/hockinghills

▷ RV and Tent Sites, Cabin Rentals

▷ $

Hocking Hills State Park is one of the most beautiful state parks in the country. The park is a hiker's delight and features cliffs, gorges, and waterfalls that will surprise and delight nature lovers of all ages. The campground is not quite as spectacular as the park itself, but its location within walking distance of Old Man's Cave and a variety of excellent hiking trails can't be beat. The campground has a wide variety of site offerings, and some even offer full hookups. Many of the sites are not level, so come prepared with blocks to straighten out your rig. If you are in a tent, resourcefulness may be required to get comfortable. This campground is incredibly popular and is full almost all summer long. It can be noisy on weekends, but most folks settle down at a reasonable hour. RV owners with self-contained rigs will have an advantage here, because the public restrooms can get messy at peak season. If you aren't picky about every little detail, you will love it here. Plan on bringing comfortable hiking shoes so you can spend hours exploring this magnificent park.

Yogi Bear's Jellystone Park Camp-Resort: Whispering Hills

▷ Big Prairie, Ohio

▷ whisperinghillsjellystone.com

▷ RV and Tent Sites, Cabins, Multifamily Cabins

▷ $$$

This charming Jellystone is located among peaceful rolling hills, and just about every inch of it is clean and charming. Camping here will cost more than at an Ohio State Park, but the campground has so much to offer in terms of amenities and activities that we think the price is actually very reasonable. Once your kids are here, you will not need to leave to seek out (and pay for!) other family entertainment. The pool and sports courts are very good, and there is a super fun corn maze behind the campground. There is also a nice hike that rings around the campground if you want to get some steps in during your visit and burn off some calories from the ice cream at the snack stand. This park is a great value when you consider how much it offers for the price. If you go, tell Yogi, Cindy, and Boo Boo that we said hello!

ALSO GREAT

Iron Ridge Campground at Lake Vesuvius/ Wayne National Forest

▷ Pedro, Ohio

▷ recreation.gov

▷ RV and Tent Sites

▷ $

Iron Ridge Campground is simple and peaceful and surrounded by the natural beauty of Wayne National Forest. This is one of two National Forest Service campgrounds in the Vesuvius Recreation Area, and it is a very good one. Most of the campsites here are large and deeply wooded and offer privacy, so this is a great place for back-to-basics camping—think grilling, hanging out with friends and family, and long nights around the campfire. There are great options for swimming and fishing in Lake Vesuvius, which is situated just below the campground.

Mill Creek Campground/Berlin Lake

▷　Berlin Center, Ohio

▷　recreation.gov

▷　RV and Tent Sites

▷　$

With almost 300 campsites, Mill Creek Campground is one of the largest U.S. Army Corps of Engineers campgrounds in the country. All of the sites here are spacious; some have shade and some do not. You can select "shaded" or "unshaded" as an option when you reserve your site at recreation.gov, which is a super handy feature. The waterfront sites are always the most in demand at an Army Corps of Engineers campground—and that's no different here, where campers love to fish directly from their sites.

Take a Break from Camping at Ohio's Best State Park Lodges

We are big believers in leaving the RV or tent at home from time to time and spending a weekend in a gorgeous state or national park lodge. Ohio has an incredible list of state park lodges that will give you a warm and cozy place to stay in some stunning natural settings. Is it camping? Or is it glamping? You can call it whatever you want—we are calling it lots and lots of fun at a budget-friendly price. Here are four of Ohio's best options for a state park lodge getaway.

▷ **The Lodge at Geneva-on-the-Lake** has spectacular views of Lake Erie and is located in Ohio's underrated wine country. Try one of its packages that combines wine tasting with lodge accommodations to save even more money.

▷ **The Mohican Lodge & Conference Center** is nestled alongside Pleasant Hill Lake and offers terrific outdoor and indoor recreation. This would be a great one to try in the winter because of the indoor pool and comfortable on-site dining at Bromfield's.

▷ **The Maumee Bay Lodge & Conference Center** offers up a stunning location directly on Lake Erie and has its own golf course and marina. Kids enjoy the Splash Garden here, but we think you should consider leaving them at home so you can enjoy the saunas, hot tubs, and whirlpools in peace.

▷ **The Salt Fork Lodge & Conference Center** has excellent rooms and cozy cabins near Salt Fork Lake. The outdoor pool is huge and looks like something you would see at a much more expensive resort. There is great hiking and fishing just steps away, and the on-site restaurant, Timbers, is solid if not spectacular.

RECOMMENDED CAMPGROUNDS

 BEST IN STATE ○ ALSO GREAT

Sheridan Lake South Shore Campground/ Black Hills National Forest
Rapid City, South Dakota

Left Tailrace Campground/Big Bend Dam
Fort Thompson, South Dakota

Palisades State Park
Garretson, South Dakota

Horse Thief Lake Campground/ Black Hills National Forest
Mount Rushmore, South Dakota

Custer State Park
Custer, South Dakota

Newton Hills State Park
Canton, South Dakota

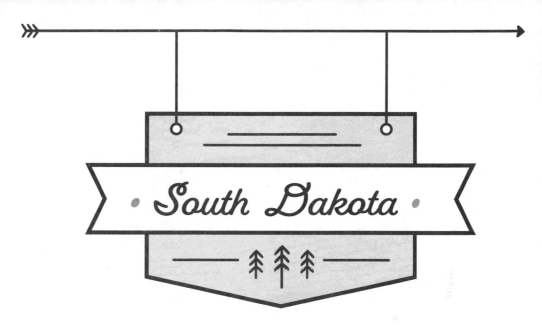

South Dakota

When it comes to camping, South Dakota has an embarrassment of riches. The western part of the state is a magical wonderland for tent campers, RV owners, cabin campers—and even those who like outdoorsy lodging. The eastern section of the state gets much less love from the national camping community, but citizens of the state know there are some real gems there too. The abundance of great camping in the state is because it has campgrounds from just about every possible company or agency. There are KOAs and Good Sam Parks along with NPS campgrounds, national forest campgrounds, U.S. Army Corps of Engineers campgrounds, and a magnificent list of state park campgrounds. It even has a budget-friendly Jellystone Park just outside of Sioux Falls. When it comes to budget camping, what more can you ask for of a state?

BEST IN STATE

Custer State Park

▷ Custer, South Dakota

▷ gfp.sd.gov/parks/detail/custer-state-park/

▷ RV and Tent Sites, Cabins, Lodge Rooms

▷ $

It is not crazy to make the case for Custer State Park as the single best state park in the country. This park is magnificent in every way and just as grand as many of our more famous national parks. When it comes to camping (and lodging), Custer quite simply takes things to another level. There are nine separate campgrounds, and all of them are worth considering. Blue Bell is probably the most famous and perhaps the most beautiful—it has great sites for tent campers as well as sites with electric hookups for RVs. Center Lake Campground is also pretty and is recommended for tent campers and those with small RVs—and the swimming beach is nice in the summertime. Game Lodge Campground is close to Highway 16A, which cuts through the park. It is not as perfectly situated as Blue Bell and Center Lake, but it is a great option if you can't get sites elsewhere. Grace Coolidge Campground is good for tent campers and offers good fishing, so bring your gear if you go. Legion Lake Campground is small and pretty and is another very popular campground in Custer—but sites go quickly, so grab one on opening day if you can. Stockade North and South are also good, and North can accommodate just about any size RV. Large RVs struggle to navigate some of the other campgrounds in Custer, so this one is popular with big rig owners. Sylvan Lake Campground is very close to the water, and some think it is the most beautiful campground in the park, but it is harder to get to and there are size limitations for both tents and RVs—so know before you go. Lastly, French Creek Horse Camp is specifically designed for those camping with horses. People often wonder which campground to choose at Custer, but sometimes it just comes down to taking whatever spot you can get. And that should be quite all right, because all of them are good and all of them are inside one of the best state parks in America.

---------- **Interesting Facts about Custer State Park** ----------

✧ Custer was designated as a state park in 1919. Before that it was a game preserve. The park contains over 71,000 acres, and it is South Dakota's oldest and largest state park. It is named after Lt. Colonel George Armstrong Custer.

✧ Over 1,200 bison call the park's 71,000 acres home, and they are usually easy to spot. Many visitors claim that they see more bison in Custer State Park than they do in Yellowstone National Park, even though there are three to four times more of them in America's oldest national park.

✧ Custer is one of the greatest state parks in our country, and it is also surrounded by a handful of amazing NPS sites that are all easily reachable for day trips. With Custer as your base camp, you can easily visit Mount Rushmore National Memorial, Wind Cave National Park, Jewel Cave National Monument, Badlands National Park, and Minuteman Missile National Historic Site.

✧ Custer State Park has five excellent lodges (State Game Lodge, Creekside Lodge, Sylvan Lake Lodge, Blue Bell Lodge, and Legion Lake Lodge) that are each quite different—but all charming. Each one also has its own on-site restaurant with good food and drink. The dining here is more upscale than at most other state parks in the country, so wear pants and Patagonia fleece and leave your cargo shorts at home.

✧ Custer State Park has its own theater! The Black Hills Playhouse offers a variety of performances each summer. The quality of the shows is excellent, and the prices are very good. Discounted tickets are offered for seniors, military, students, and youth.

Newton Hills State Park

▷ Canton, South Dakota

▷ gfp.sd.gov/parks/detail/newton-hills-state-park

▷ RV and Tent Sites, Cabins, Group Lodge

▷ $

The campsites at Newton Hills State Park, which is located thirty minutes from Sioux Falls, are large and mostly situated in a parklike setting with a mix of shade and sun. In a general sense, the campground is much more popular with RV owners than tent campers. There are some semi-private sites here for tent campers, but they are a bit harder to find. If you are a tent camper and want to try this park, consider renting one of its excellent cabins with bathrooms, full kitchens, heat, and air conditioning. They are very comfortable and well worth the splurge. So is the group lodge, especially if you want to vacation with another family. There is even a campsite next to the lodge that is only reservable for lodge guests, so you can bring a third family with an RV along as well. The park is very good for hiking and biking, and the trails are well shaded by oak and ash trees. Lakota Lake is a short drive or bike ride from the campground, and you can rent paddleboards and kayaks there for a budget-friendly price. The water here is clear and inviting and provides a great place to beat the heat in the summertime.

Budget-Camping Hack: Become a State Park Campground Host

Most state parks offer a free campsite for the season to those willing to volunteer as campground hosts. These hosts typically work several days a week (it's twenty-four hours per week in South Dakota), and they have several days off to enjoy camping at the park and exploring the area. Camp hosts often get the best sites and often have water, electric, and sewer hookups for their RVs. If you want to spend a summer in South Dakota (or just about any other state) without spending a single dollar on campground fees, then these are great programs to investigate.

ALSO GREAT

Palisades State Park

▷ Garretson, South Dakota

▷ gfp.sd.gov/parks/detail/palisades-state-park

▷ RV and Tent Sites, Cabins, Group Lodge

▷ $

Palisades State Park is just a few miles from the Minnesota border, and it is an underrated gem in the South Dakota State Park system. A lovely creek runs through the park with stunning quartzite foundations along either side of it in some sections. This state park has lots of opportunities for outdoor recreation, even including family-friendly rock climbing. There are seventy-one newer campsites here, some with electric and some without. The campground is charming and quiet.

Left Tailrace Campground/Big Bend Dam

▷ Fort Thompson, South Dakota

▷ recreation.gov

▷ RV and Tent Sites

▷ $

The sites here are large and level, and many of them overlook the water. This campground is pretty far off the beaten path, so come here to relax and unwind at your site in a quiet, peaceful setting. Make sure to bring bug spray in the summer and bring your kayaks if you have them. This is a really fun place to explore on a personal watercraft, but the water can get very choppy when the wind is up. This U.S. Army Corps of Engineers park has around one hundred sites. All of them are good, and most have electric hookups.

Sheridan Lake South Shore Campground/ Black Hills National Forest

▷ Rapid City, South Dakota

▷ recreation.gov

▷ RV and Tent Sites

▷ $

White-tailed deer often roam through this national forest in the evening, and they love this campground every bit as much as the campers do. This is rustic Black Hills camping at its best—the sites are large and shaded by towering ponderosa pines. The sites in Rocky Loop and Woodsy Loop with water views are our favorites at Sheridan Lake, so catch one if you can. The lake here is an absolute joy. Plan on swimming, fishing, or kayaking, or just going for a stroll around its clear and peaceful waters.

Horse Thief Lake Campground/Black Hills National Forest

▷ Mount Rushmore, South Dakota

▷ fs.usda.gov

▷ RV and Tent Sites

▷ $

Horse Thief Lake Campground has four major things going for it besides its amazing name. First, it's only 2 miles from Mount Rushmore and is the closest campground to the historic landmark. Second, it's beautiful and peaceful, though close to the road. Third, the lake is small but delightful, so bring kayaks or stand-up paddleboards if you have them. Lastly, the affordable price point is attractive to those on a budget. Be forewarned, Horsethief only has thirty-six sites and is far more accommodating to smaller RVs. Book early, campers.

RECOMMENDED CAMPGROUNDS

★ BEST IN STATE   O ALSO GREAT

**Two Lakes Campground/
Chequamegon-Nicolet
National Forest**
Drummond, Wisconsin

**Boulder Lake
Campground/
Chequamegon-Nicolet
National Forest**
White Lake, Wisconsin

**Peninsula
State Park**
Fish Creek,
Wisconsin

**Stoney Creek
RV Resort**
Osseo,
Wisconsin

**Blackhawk
Park**
De Soto,
Wisconsin

**Mirror Lake
State Park**
Baraboo,
Wisconsin

**Devil's Lake
State Park**
Baraboo,
Wisconsin

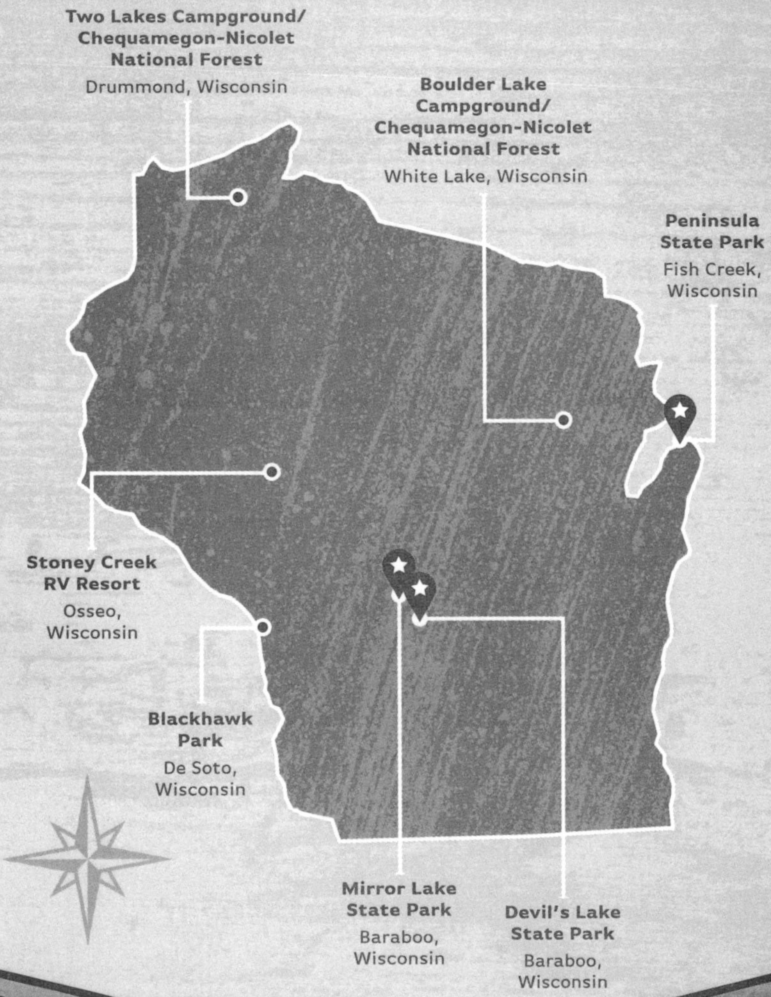

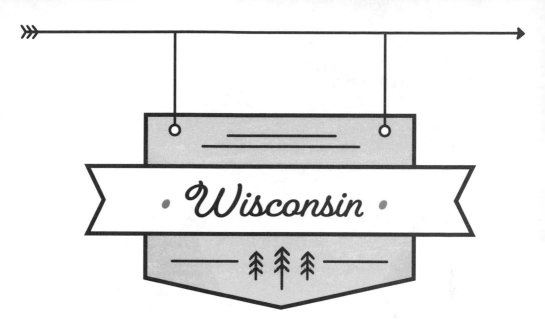

Wisconsin

The good people of Wisconsin are among the friendliest people on planet Earth—and the campers among them are even happier and nicer than the rest of them. Are they so happy because they have an amazing and underrated state park system that is absolutely packed with great campgrounds? Or is it because the state also offers national forest camping that is dirt cheap and much easier to reserve than national forests in the great American West? Or is it because many of the in-state RV resorts are actually reasonably priced for most families? We think it is because of all the above. We are so glad we spent time in Wisconsin on our way out West, because now we know that the state is a great camping destination and not just a stopover state for those buzzing back and forth between the coasts. We think you should plan an entire summer camping vacation in Wisconsin— and then come back again in the fall. As for the winter—let's leave that alone for right now. Rugged and outdoorsy Wisconsites may camp in their great state year-round, but you won't catch us there in the winter months. Rumor is it gets mighty cold in those great northern woods.

BEST IN STATE

Peninsula State Park

▷ Fish Creek, Wisconsin

▷ dnr.wisconsin.gov/topic/parks/peninsula

▷ RV and Tent Sites

▷ $

Peninsula State Park is an absolutely magnificent place to go camping and is certainly one of the most popular places to camp in the state. Camping here should be a bucket-list item for every American with a tent or RV, but not enough out-of-staters get here, which is a shame. Hopefully we can inspire you to go. But take fair warning—this place is hard to book in summer because many in-state campers return over and over again. Tennison Bay Campground alone has almost 200 sites and about half them have electric hookups. The trees are lovely here and provide lots of shade and fairly good privacy between the sites. Nicolet Bay Campground has a north and a south section. The north section has no hookups and is very nice for tent camping. There are many double sites in this section, so friends and family can camp together. The south section has the same look and feel of the north sections, but more than fifty sites have electrical hookups. Welcker's Point Campground is on the northeastern side of the park and offers about eighty campsites without hookups. This is a pretty campground, but the facilities need improving. Weborg Point Campground is very small, but all of the sites have electric. Recreational opportunities within this park are close to endless, especially for hikers and bikers. There is even an eighteen-hole golf course for those who can fit their clubs inside their tents or RVs.

Mirror Lake State Park

▷ Baraboo, Wisconsin

▷ dnr.wi.gov/topic/parks/name/mirrorlake

▷   Cabin and Cottage Rentals, RV and Tent Sites

▷ $

Mirror Lake State Park would be incredibly popular even if it was not such a great base camp for the highly touristed Wisconsin Dells, which is just across the interstate. This beautiful state park has three different campgrounds that offer over 150 combined sites. The Bluewater Bay campground is close to the visitor center and has over sixty non-electric sites. The sites here are large and surrounded by thick trees, so they offer a lot of privacy and are terrific for tent campers. The Sandstone Ridge Campground is close to a medium-sized beach and fishing pier and offers sixty-eight sites—some with electric and some without. Sandstone looks just like Bluewater, but it is better for RV owners because of the hookups. The sites are not exactly huge here, though, so smaller RVs will rule the day. The Cliffwood Campground is smaller than the other two and most of the sites have electric. A bunch of the sites here are double sites, which are described in more detail in the "Getting to Know Wisconsin's State Park Campgrounds" sidebar in this chapter. Overall, this is a gorgeous state park for fishing, hiking, boating, and swimming. It's no wonder Wisconsites love their state parks so much!

Devil's Lake State Park

▷   Baraboo, Wisconsin

▷   dnr.wi.gov/topic/parks/name/devilslake

▷   RV and Tent Sites

▷ $

Devil's Lake is only creepy on cool, foggy mornings during the offseason. In the summer, it is a magical place for swimming, hiking, picnicking, and camping. Five-hundred-foot quartzite bluffs provide stunning views of the 360-acre lake, and there are over two dozen miles of stellar hiking trails, making this a virtual wonderland for those who love the great outdoors. Wisconsin's most visited state park has three campgrounds with more than

420 combined sites, and each one has different strengths with few draw-backs. The Quartzite Campground, which is largely open and parklike, is best for larger RVs, and many of the sites have electric hookups. Quartzite is also closest to the lakeshore. The Northern Lights Campground has a mixture of shady, wooded sites and sites out in the open and also offers electric hookups. It is a half mile from the lakeshore. The Ice Age Campground is the most popular with tent campers and those with pop-up campers and other small RVs. It is about one mile from the lakeshore. Unfortunately, there are no cabin options at Devil's Lake. Rock climbing is allowed here, but the park warns that you do so at your own risk. Boating, canoeing, and kayaking are great options here, and the park offers rentals and two no-fee boat landings. Mirror Lake State Park is only twenty minutes away and well worth a visit if you are camping at Devil's Lake—and vice versa.

ALSO GREAT

Stoney Creek RV Resort

▷ **Osseo, Wisconsin**

▷ **Stonycreekrvresort.com**

▷ **RV and Tent Sites, Cabins, Cottages**

▷ **$$$**

This is one of the few RV resorts that we have included in this book because very few meet our pricing criteria as laid out in the introduction. But Stoney Creek RV Resort does. Considering how awesome this place is, the price is truly a bargain—especially for families. Everything here is nice and looks brand new, including the jumping pillow, the mini golf course, and the swimming pool with splash area. The resort even has a skate park for skateboarders and laser tag for kids of all ages. The campsites are also immaculate and super big rig friendly.

Blackhawk Park

▷   De Soto, Wisconsin

▷   recreation.gov

▷   RV and Tent Sites

▷ $

The swimming in the Mississippi River is surprisingly good here in the summertime when the water is shallow and warm. But be forewarned: in the springtime, the campground does sometimes close partially or completely due to flooding. The 150 sites here are immaculate and spacious, and almost half of them have electric hookups. This park is also a bit more family friendly than some of the other U.S. Army Corps of Engineers parks reviewed in this book. Besides swimming, kids can fish, kayak, play horseshoes or volleyball, and burn off some energy at one of two different playgrounds. In a general sense, this is quiet, peaceful, and relaxing old-school camping that is terrific for those who love the great outdoors and living life at a slower pace.

Boulder Lake Campground/Chequamegon-Nicolet National Forest

▷   White Lake, Wisconsin

▷   recreation.gov

▷   RV and Tent Sites

▷ $

This is a terrific campground in Nicolet National Forest for those who like to keep it simple in a rustic and natural environment. The swimming is good here in the summertime (and surprisingly warm considering how far north it is), and some of the sites have direct access to the water. Bring bug spray in the summer or visit in the shoulder seasons to avoid mosquitoes.

Two Lakes Campground/Chequamegon-Nicolet National Forest

▷   Drummond, Wisconsin

▷   recreation.gov

▷   RV and Tent Sites

▷ $

The sites at Two Lakes Campground in Chequamegon National Forest are gigantic and private—two qualities that please just about every camper on planet Earth. This is a great place to kick back and relax with family and friends and enjoy time together around the picnic table or campfire. There are two swimming beaches for those camping here and the fishing is very good, so make sure you bring your fishing gear.

----   **Budget-Camping Hack: Get a Good Sam Membership**   ----

A Good Sam membership can be a terrific way to save money if you plan on camping at Good Sam campgrounds for more than a few nights per year. Good Sam members get 10 percent off their camping stays (with some blackouts and limitations) at more than 2,000 campgrounds. The Stoney Creek RV Resort reviewed in this chapter is a Good Sam campground, and if you stayed there for three to four nights, you would make the money back that you spent on your membership. We recommend checking its list of member campgrounds before you purchase the membership to see if you will really use it.

Getting to Know Wisconsin's State Park Campgrounds

▷ There are more than 6,000 state park operated campsites in Wisconsin. That's a lot of campsites!

▷ Reservations for Wisconsin state park campgrounds can be made up to eleven months in advance.

▷ State park campgrounds have a very convenient "automatic" check-in policy. When you arrive at the campground at your appointed check-in time, you can head directly to your campsite.

▷ Many of Wisconsin's state park campgrounds have old-school yellow phones that campers can use to ask questions about their reservations or get help if needed.

▷ Wisconsin state parks only allow you to bring firewood that originated from within 10 miles of the park's boundaries. Please consider applying this same rule on all of your camping trips.

▷ The Wisconsin state park system has ten beautiful cabins that can only be reserved by people with disabilities and their guests. Eight of these accessible cabins are fully appointed with kitchens, bathrooms, air conditioning, and heat. Two of the accessible cabins are rustic but do have electric.

▷ Remote and primitive camping options are available at seventeen different locations in Wisconsin. These locations are not at campgrounds and cannot be reserved, but a permit may be needed to camp there.

▷ Many Wisconsin state park campgrounds have "double sites" (also sometimes called buddy sites) for families and friends who want to camp together and need more than one site. Six people are allowed per site, so twelve campers can share one space without obstructions between them.

THE WEST

RECOMMENDED CAMPGROUNDS

★ BEST IN STATE   ○ ALSO GREAT

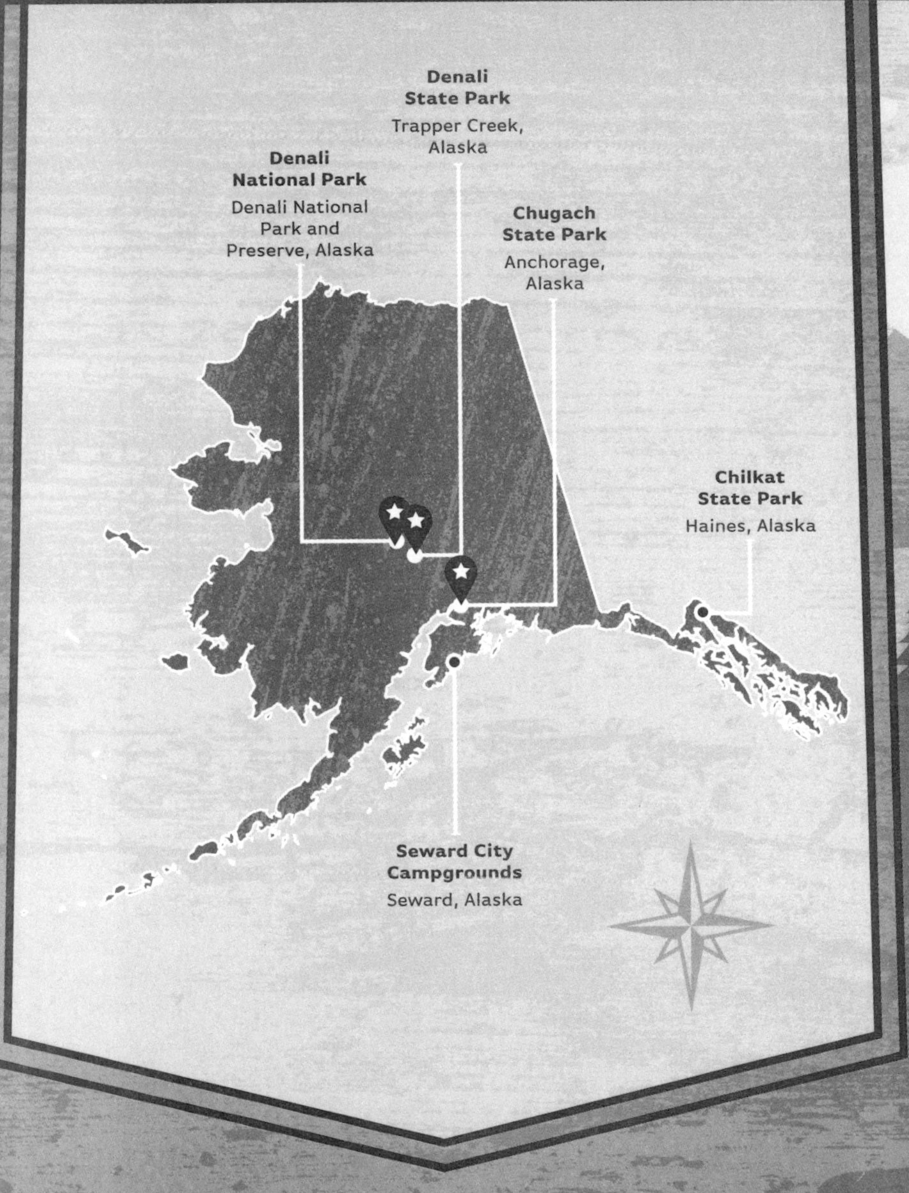

Denali State Park

Trapper Creek, Alaska

Denali National Park

Denali National Park and Preserve, Alaska

Chugach State Park

Anchorage, Alaska

Chilkat State Park

Haines, Alaska

Seward City Campgrounds

Seward, Alaska

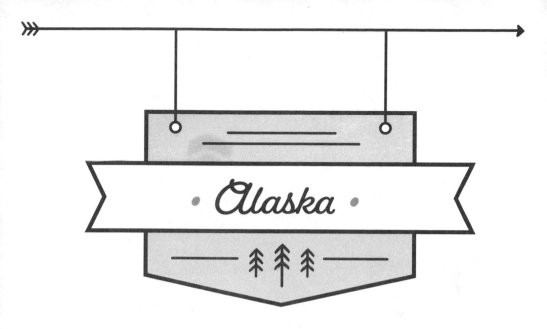

Alaska

Alaska is vast and wild and not for the faint of heart. This is a place where veteran campers and RVers go after they have honed their skills in friendlier climates in the lower forty-eight. If you want to tackle Alaska as a rookie camper, we would suggest that you cut your teeth elsewhere first—or at least do lots of research before showing up here. The state is nicknamed "The Last Frontier" for very good reasons. Thankfully, once you do show up in Alaska, you will find that pretty much all the camping here is budget camping. And thank God that's the case, because it can cost a small fortune getting here. But be forewarned: much of the camping is cheap because it is wild and remote, and hookups and amenities are close to non-existent here. Having a strong boondocking setup is essential if you are RVing in Alaska. If you are a tent camper, you must be prepared for cold nights, even in the summertime. All this preparation is, of course, very much worth it. Alaska is America's last true wilderness, and its beauty is very much unrivaled.

BEST IN STATE

Chugach State Park

- ▷ Anchorage, Alaska
- ▷ dnr.alaska.gov
- ▷ RV and Tent Sites, Cabins
- ▷ $

Chugach State Park encompasses almost half a million acres, and it is one of the largest state parks in America. The west side of the park is near Anchorage, Alaska, so making a pit stop here makes sense for many travelers. There are several campgrounds within this massive state park. Bird Creek Campground and Bird Creek Overflow offer more than sixty sites for visitors. The sites at the campground are spacious and wooded, but they offer no hookups, and the campground only offers pit toilets. The overflow area is basically a parking lot, but still a safe place to rest your head in a beautiful area. The Eagle River Campground is very close to the Eagle River, but you can't see it from most of the sites—happily, you can hear it as you fall asleep each night. Eklutna Lake Campground is larger than the others with fifty large, wooded, and private sites. Kayaking and fishing are excellent here, and so are the hiking trails along the lake. More adventurous souls also ride ATVs in the park, and the Eklutna Trail is open for them Sunday to Wednesday. There are a small handful of cabins to rent at each of these campgrounds in Chugach State Park. This is a state park that feels wild and remote, but civilization is not too far away at all, so it is great place to get your feet wet when it comes to camping in Alaska.

Denali State Park

- ▷ Trapper Creek, Alaska
- ▷ dnr.alaska.gov/parks
- ▷ RV and Tent Sites, Cabins
- ▷ $

Everything about Alaska is gigantic—and Denali State Park is no exception. This state treasure is almost half the size of Rhode Island, yet it flies under the radar of most visitors to the state who blow by it to get to Denali National Park. Byers Lake Campground has seventy-five sites that are situated near the water at the foot of the Kesugi Ridge, but the real star of the show here is the K'esugi Ken RV and Tent Campground. The RV sites at K'esugi Ken have electric hookups and accommodate the biggest of big rigs. The tent sites are large and private, and some of them border a peaceful stream. The cabins are adorable but sparse and have wood stoves for heat. A few of the campsites have stunning views of Denali, but everywhere you look here is beautiful. This is a near-perfect campground in one of the most beautiful places on earth. If you do make it to Denali State Park and you feel like a big adventure, consider hiking (at least part of) the K-esugi Ridge Trail. On a clear day the views of Denali are astonishing.

Affordable Coffee, Culture, and Food in Anchorage, Alaska

✦ Start your day early at the **Dark Horse Coffee Company** on the corner of Seventh and F in downtown Anchorage for the best cup of coffee in town. Want a healthy breakfast? Try the avocado toast. Feel like something sweet? Try the cinnamon roll. Neither will disappoint.

✦ Admission to the **Anchorage Museum** is reasonable for adults, half price for kids ages six to twelve, and free for those five years old and under. The three permanent exhibits on Alaskan history and culture are all excellent, and your visit to the museum should begin there.

✦ For a delicious and affordable lunch, head to the **Alaska Crepery**, which is a short walk from the Anchorage Museum. The Alaskan Reindeer Crepe gets all of the attention, but we prefer the Cubano. We think you will too.

Denali National Park

▷ Denali National Park and Preserve, Alaska

▷ nps.gov

▷ RV and Tent Sites

▷ $

For most campers a bucket-list trip to Alaska isn't complete without a stop in Denali National Park. Denali is true wilderness, and it attracts those who want to come face-to-face with majestic natural beauty on an epic scale. There are six campgrounds inside the park, but most visitors will choose Riley Creek or Savage River. Riley Creek is the biggest campground in the park, offering the most services and the most convenient location. The campground is right inside the park's entrance, and it offers almost 150 sites for tents and RVs up to forty feet. Sites are semi-private and situated near fragrant spruce trees along Riley Creek. This campground is a good choice for most people, because it is close to the visitor center (which is a hub for hiking trails) and the Riley Creek Mercantile, which offers basic camping supplies, groceries, and fresh coffee. Savage River Campground is located at mile marker 14 on Denali Park Road and offers spacious, private, and beautiful RV and tent sites with fewer amenities (and fewer people around!) than Riley Creek Campground. But on clear days you can take a short walk from your site and see Denali in all its magnificent splendor. There is also an easy hiking trail that takes you down to the Savage River where you might see caribou feeding along its banks and playing in the water.

ALSO GREAT

Chilkat State Park

▷ Haines, Alaska

▷ dnr.alaska.gov/parks

- ▷ RV and Tent Sites
- ▷ $

This is a stunning state park situated around Chilkot Inlet near Haines, Alaska, that has snow-capped mountain peaks as its backdrop. The campground has thirty-five spacious and deeply wooded sites that can accommodate rigs up to 35 feet. If you are up for an adventure, make sure you do the Seduction Point Trail—it's one of the best hikes in the Northern Alaskan Panhandle.

Seward City Campgrounds
- ▷ Seward, Alaska
- ▷ cityofseward.us/departments/parks-recreation/campgrounds
- ▷ RV and Tent Sites
- ▷ $$

Seward Alaska is a welcoming seaside village just 2 miles from Anchorage filled with good bars and restaurants and surrounded by opportunities for epic outdoor adventures. This postcard-worthy town is located directly on Resurrection Bay and also serves as the gateway to Kenai Fjords National Park—home to nearly forty glaciers and the world-famous Harding Icefield. Seward manages a series of ten campgrounds that sprawl across the waterfront and provide a wide variety of sites for tent campers and RV owners. The sites are not much to speak of, but the location is spectacular. Mountains surround you, and the bay is a short walk from your site no matter which campground you choose.

RECOMMENDED CAMPGROUNDS

 BEST IN STATE ○ **ALSO GREAT**

Mather Campground and Trailer Village RV Park/ Grand Canyon National Park
Grand Canyon Village, Arizona

Aspen Campground/ Apache-Sitgreaves National Forest
Payson, Arizona

Lake Havasu State Park
Lake Havasu City, Arizona

Lost Dutchmen State Park
Apache Junction, Arizona

Catalina State Park
Tuscon, Arizona

Reef Townsite Campground/ Coronado National Forest
Hereford, Arizona

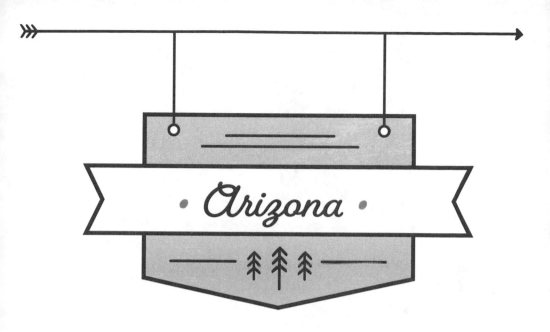

Arizona

rizona is a majestic place for camping and road tripping, and it is filled with epic surprises from one corner of the state to the other. The Grand Canyon is obviously the main attraction, but the state has so much more to offer when it comes to amazing camping accommodations. Some of Arizona's state parks have the look and feel of some of our nation's greatest national parks, just on a somewhat smaller and much less crowded scale. The state is also filled with dozens of excellent National Forest Service campgrounds that are popular with locals but fly somewhat under the radar with campers from out of state. If you are planning your first trip to Arizona, we certainly think that you should hit the Grand Canyon, but we also think you should tack on a stop to one of the state or national forest campgrounds reviewed in this section. They are breathtaking places that are waiting to welcome you with open arms.

BEST IN STATE

Lost Dutchman State Park

▷ Apache Junction, Arizona

▷ azstateparks.com/lost-dutchman

▷ RV and Tent Sites, Cabins

▷ $

Lost Dutchman State Park is a terrific option for camping and outdoor recreation for those who live in the greater Phoenix area. This magnificent park is named after a lost gold mine and sits near the bottom of Superstition Mountain, which lurks in the background in a dramatic fashion. So just make sure you tell some spooky ghost stories about the ghosts of long-lost miners if you come here, okay? The campsites have some privacy that is provided by ground shrubbery, but most still have sweeping views of the mountains and the Sonoran Desert all around them. The campground has 135 sites and about half of them have water and electric, while the offer half offer no hookups. Cabins are also available, and though they are not exactly cute, they have spectacular views on all sides. There are trails that lead directly from the state park into the Superstition Mountain Wilderness—just be careful if you go for a hike. Anything can happen here, especially if you are superstitious.

- - - - - - - - - - Budget-Camping Hack: Save Money and - - - - - - - - - -
Get Outside with an America the Beautiful Pass

If you plan on visiting more than one national park in any given year, consider getting an America the Beautiful Pass. The pass covers entry fees (not camping fees) to lands under the jurisdiction of the National Park Service, U.S. Fish and Wildlife Service, U.S. Forest Service, Bureau of Land Management, Bureau of Reclamation, and U.S. Army Corps of Engineers. Having the pass can save you a small fortune and inspire you to get outside even more. Getting this pass is a must-have for most outdoorsy families.

Lake Havasu State Park

▷   Lake Havasu City, Arizona

▷   azstateparks.com/lake-havasu

▷   RV and Tent Sites, Cabins

▷ $

The campground at Lake Havasu State Park is located in the Mojave Desert and is situated right on the water with California mountain views right on the other side of the lake. It gets mighty hot here in the summer. The clear waters of the lake do provide some relief, but they get mighty warm too! The campground (and the park in general) fills up with campers and boaters on the weekends, but they both stay fairly quiet during the week. All of the sites have 50-amp hookups, and most of them are spacious and sunny. Shade is at a premium here, so plan on having lots of direct sunlight at your site. The two-bedroom waterfront cabins at Lake Havasu are excellent and have terrific views, but they do not have privacy between them, so plan on saying hello to your neighbors while you are here. Please remember to bring linens if you rent a cabin—they are not included.

Mather Campground and Trailer Village RV Park/Grand Canyon National Park

▷   Grand Canyon Village, Arizona

▷   nps.gov

▷   RV and Tent Sites

▷ $

The Grand Canyon is one of the most magnificent places on planet Earth— and thankfully it has very good campground options for tent campers and RV owners. With more than 320 sites, Mather is the largest campground inside Grand Canyon National Park. Fifty-five of the sites at Mather are tent only, and the rest of them can accommodate both tents and RVs. Those sites do have size limitations for RVs, and those size limits are different based on whether you have a towable rig or a motorhome, so double-check the details before you book. Mather is a beautiful campground, but it can feel like a camping village in the summer when it fills up. We recommend embracing the crowd and always remembering that you are a part of it. The Grand Canyon Trailer Village RV Park scores points for its excellent location near the South Rim and for truth in advertising when it comes to its own name. This is a place to eat, sleep, and take breaks from the heat during your visit to one of the most breathtaking places on earth. Wi-Fi is not available, but cell phone service may be, depending on your carrier. This campground is not necessarily beautiful like Mather, but you get full hookups less than a mile from the South Rim of the Grand Canyon. Few people complain about the simplicity of the campground or the small size of the sites because they get to run their AC during the heat of the summer—and for most RV owners visiting the Grand Canyon, that's more than enough to make them happy.

ALSO GREAT

Catalina State Park

- ▷ Tucson, Arizona
- ▷ azstateparks.com/catalina
- ▷ RV and Tent Sites
- ▷ $

The Arizona State Park system is pretty amazing, and many people think Catalina State Park is the crown jewel, especially RV owners and tent campers. The campground has 120 water/electric sites, and big rigs are welcome. The sites at this state park are large, paved, and lovely. Shade and privacy vary from site to site, but everyone has plenty of elbow room and many sites have stunning views of the Santa Catalina Mountains.

---------------- **Coffee, Culture, Food, and Fun** ----------------

at Affordable Prices in Tucson, Arizona

✦ Start your morning at **Tucson Coffee Roasters** for an affordable and unpretentious cup of joe and a casual breakfast that won't break the bank. The staff here is friendly and there is comfortable seating if you feel like staying for a while.

✦ **The Tucson Museum of Art** has an excellent permanent collection and shines in the areas of Western American art and Latin American art. Admission is affordable and kids twelve years old and under can always enter for free. Thanks to an anonymous donor, admission is free on the first Thursday of every month from 5:00 p.m. to 8:00 p.m.

✦ If you have little kids, skip the Tucson Museum of Art and head to **Children's Museum Tucson** instead. But be forewarned—you may have even more fun than they do. Kids love the painting wall and the banana cars, and so will you.

✦ **The El Charro Café** is more than one hundred years old and was named one of the twenty-one "most legendary" restaurants in the USA by *Gourmet* magazine. This place isn't taco-truck cheap, but it is surprisingly affordable for a family meal, considering that its enchiladas and chimichangas are so famous.

Reef Townsite Campground/Coronado National Forest

▷ Hereford, Arizona

▷ fs.usda.gov

▷ Tent Sites, Van/Car Camping

▷ $

Reef Townsite sits at 7,200 feet on the site of a former mining town, and it has spectacular views and offers visitors a cool mountain escape from the summer heat below. There are only sixteen sites here, and they are not reservable, but the group campsite can be reserved. Be forewarned: the road does make for a somewhat adventurous drive. RVs twelve feet and under are technically allowed in the campground, but we don't recommend towing anything up there. Bring your tent or van and a pair of good hiking boots and enjoy one of the best National Forest Service campgrounds in a state that is jam-packed with them.

Aspen Campground/Apache-Sitgreaves National Forest

▷ **Payson, Arizona**

▷ **recreation.gov**

▷ **RV and Tent Sites**

▷ **$**

Campers from the Phoenix Metroplex love to escape to places like Aspen Campground in the summer because its higher elevation provides relief from the heat back in the city. The parking pads are not always huge here, but most of the 136 non-hook-up sites are spacious when considered in their entirety. There is a shaded asphalt trail that connects the campground to Woods Canyon Lake—a terrific little spot for swimming, fishing, and kayaking.

RECOMMENDED CAMPGROUNDS

 BEST IN STATE   ○ ALSO GREAT

Redwood National and State Parks

Various Locations in Northern California

Heritage Oak Winery (Harvest Hosts)

Acampo, California

Yosemite National Park

Yosemite National Park, California

Sonoma Coast State Park

Bodega Bay, California

Pfeiffer Big Sur State Park

Big Sur, California

Point Mugu State Park

Malibu, California

Crystal Cove State Park

Laguna Beach, California

· California ·

When it comes to camping, California shouldn't be considered a state, it should be considered a country—and picking the best campgrounds in this country is a fraught and foolhardy task. We will proceed to do so anyway—but please know we would rather research and write an entire book on California camping than have to make such difficult choices here. California has magnificent budget camping in its state parks and national parks—but many of those sites can also be notoriously difficult to book. So, what's a camper to do? Wake up on the day that sites are released and get ready to start refreshing your browser, of course. If you don't get the site of your dreams at Yosemite or in a state park along the California coast, check back regularly for cancellations. State and national park campgrounds are not the only show in town when it comes to budget camping in California, but they do rise above the competition. In this chapter, we will focus strictly on them—because when it comes to budget camping in California, they simply can't be beat.

BEST IN STATE

Pfeiffer Big Sur State Park

▷   Big Sur, California

▷   parks.ca.gov

▷   RV and Tent Sites

▷ $

Those who drive up the California coast for the first time often don't fall in love with the state until they reach Big Sur. This wild and rugged stretch of the California coastline is one of the most beautiful places in the world—and Pfeiffer Big Sur State Park is the place to camp on this side of paradise. This state park is not directly on the ocean, nor does it have direct ocean access, but Pfeiffer Beach is just about a mile away. What the park does have is incredible hiking trails, some of which have sweeping ocean views. It also has a gorgeous campground with 189 huge and mostly private sites that are situated on and around the Big Sur River. Sites are famously difficult to book here, so make sure you get on it right when the reservation window opens six months in advance. Camping at Pfeiffer Big Sur is well worth the extra effort.

Crystal Cove State Park

▷   Laguna Beach, California

▷   parks.ca.gov

▷   RV and Tent Sites

▷ $

The highlight of Crystal Cove State Park is its 3 miles of stunning Pacific coastline right smack in the heart of busy and bustling Orange County, California. This place is a straight-up coastal oasis right in the middle of one of the most densely populated parts of the state. The park is often packed with hikers, bikers, surfers, sunbathers, swimmers, and those simply strolling along on the beach in one of the park's seven coves, exploring the tide pools.

The Moro Campground is situated above the beach with sweeping views of the ocean from some of the campsites—and the sunsets, as you might expect, are colorful and often epic. Most of the sites are large and offer some scrubby bushes that create privacy between the sites, though there isn't much shade. Tent campers love the clean restrooms and hot showers, and everyone loves that the park is clean and well maintained by its famously friendly staff. Keep your eyes peeled for pods of dolphins swimming by and don't forget your hiking shoes—there are real trails in the park if you want a break from the beach.

Yosemite National Park

 ▷ **Yosemite National Park, California**
 ▷ **nps.gov**
 ▷ **RV and Tent Sites**
 ▷ **$**

Getting a campsite inside Yosemite National Park is the holy grail of American camping. Yosemite (which is only about four hours away from San Francisco) gets more visitors than Yellowstone—but Yellowstone is three times the size. The sites here are that difficult to book...but someone has to get them, so why not you? Most people try to book Upper or Lower Pines first. Upper Pines has 238 sites that can handle trailers up to twenty-five feet long and motorhomes up to thirty-five feet long, and it is a tent camper's paradise. Lower Pines is nestled along the Merced River and is located near many of the park's most iconic destinations. For the most part, the campground is shady and deeply wooded, but some sites have incredible views of Half Dome in the not-so-far distance. If you can't get reservations in Upper or Lower Pines, Wawona Campground is worth considering as a backup. It's a forty-five-minute drive from Yosemite's most iconic locations, but so are most of the private campgrounds outside of the park. Wawona is rustic and peaceful, and it has great site options for tent campers and those in small- to medium-sized RVs.

ALSO GREAT

Redwood National and State Parks

▷ Various Locations in Northern California

▷ nps.gov

▷ RV and Tent Sites

▷ $

Camping in the Redwoods in northern California is a magical and almost spiritual exercise for many tent campers and RV owners. There are not many campground options within this unique state and national park collaboration, so please try to book your sites as early as possible. The Jedediah Smith Campground is our favorite option. Hiking the Hiouchi Trail and then returning to the campground for a dip in the Smith River is an incredible way to spend a summer day. Also make sure to check out Gold Bluffs Beach Campground, Mill Creek Campground, and Elk Prairie Campground. They put you into the heart and soul of the action.

------------------ **Budget-Camping Hack:** ------------------
Rent Your RV When It Is Not Being Used

Are you considering purchasing your first RV but worried about the cost? Or are you a current RV owner who could use some extra scratch so you can afford a few more trips? Why not consider renting your RV when you are not using it? Peer-to-peer rental platforms like RV Share and Outdoorsy make it easy to rent your rig and turn your family memory machine into a small business instead of letting it sit in your driveway when you're not camping. Worried about damage being done to your rig? Both companies offer extensive insurance to give you extra peace of mind.

Sonoma Coast State Park

▷ Bodega Bay, California

▷ parks.ca.gov

▷ RV and Tent Sites

▷ $

The 16-mile stretch of California coastline that belongs to Sonoma Coast State Park is among the most beautiful stretches of beach in the United States, but it is wild and fierce. The surf is strong, the water is cold, and rip tides are almost constantly present. So, take caution—even if you are just strolling along the beach. There are three campgrounds here, and Bodega Dunes is the largest and most popular. If you are an Alfred Hitchcock fan, make sure to visit the town of Bodega Bay—just keep your eye open for apocalyptic herds of birds that may or may not be waiting to attack.

Point Mugu State Park

▷ Malibu, California

▷ parks.ca.gov

▷ RV and Tent Sites

▷ $

Some will complain and say that Thornhill Broom's campsites are nothing more than parking spots on the side of the road. But oh, what a glorious road it is! You can step out of your RV and walk on to the sandy beaches of Point Mugu State Park. Tent campers can pitch their tents directly on the sand. When you are settled around the campfire under a bed of California stars, your parking spot will become one of the most magical places to camp in all of America.

Heritage Oak Winery (Harvest Hosts)

▷ Acampo, California

▷ harvesthosts.com

▷ Self-enclosed RVs Only

▷ $

There are more than 350 Harvest Hosts locations in California, and many of them are beautiful wineries that craft superb wines. So, if you want to explore California's wineries by RV—where should you even start? We think you should put Heritage Oak Winery near Lodi at the top of your list. This delightful vineyard (and its RV parking spots) is situated next to a peaceful river. Pricing for tasting flights and bottles is very reasonable considering the quality, making this a budget-friendly stop for California wine lovers.

Escape from LA: Planning a Trip to Joshua Tree National Park

Like Death Valley, Joshua Tree National Park is just a few hours from Las Vegas and Los Angeles, and it's a very popular outdoor destination during the spring when temperatures are mild and the wildflowers are in bloom. The fall is another lovely time to visit, and the crowds are often lighter than in the spring months. Summers are scorching hot, some campgrounds are closed, and most ranger programs are on pause. Winters bring wildly fluctuating temperatures and a chance of snow, but there are campgrounds open—so if you are up for an adventure, then Joshua Tree will be waiting. Here are our three favorite campgrounds in Joshua Tree. Start your planning here.

▷ **Jumbo Rocks Campground** looks and feels like another planet. The rock formations look like they belong on the moon, not in California. These dusty-looking formations change dramatically from one end of the campground to another, so the sites here are all quite different.

▷ **Indian Cove Campground** is in a much more secluded section of the park than Jumbo Rocks, and you may find yourself driving quite a bit more if you camp here, but the campground is beautiful and the sites are typically large and private.

▷ Joshua Tree rookies rarely look to pitch their tents or park their RVs at **Ryan Campground** first, but it is an absolute favorite among those who have experience camping in the park. The campground is small (there are only thirty-one sites) and it has a mystical, spiritual quality to it.

RECOMMENDED CAMPGROUNDS

★ BEST IN STATE   ○ ALSO GREAT

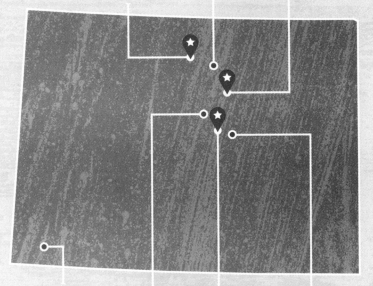

Wild Cider (Harvest Hosts)

Longmont, Colorado

Rocky Mountain National Park

Rocky Mountain National Park, Colorado

Cherry Creek State Park

Aurora, Colorado

Morefield Campground/Mesa Verde National Park

Mesa Verde National Park, Colorado

Mueller State Park

Divide, Colorado

Cheyenne Mountain State Park

Colorado Springs, Colorado

Spruce Grove Campground

Lake George, Colorado

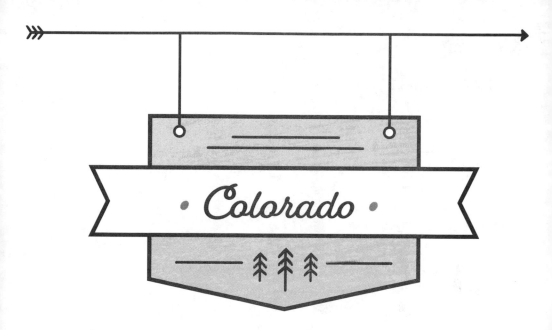

Colorado

You could take an epic camping trip to Colorado and never step foot in a national park—the state parks here are that good. Though the natural landscape is much different, the camping landscape reminds us very much of Utah with overcrowded national parks and amazing state parks. But in both cases, are those state parks less crowded than the national parks? In a general sense they are, with only a few exceptions. If you want to explore Colorado (or neighboring Utah), then consider skipping the national parks and heading to the state parks. Colorado also has excellent national forest camping, with more than 300 sites available. Many of the campgrounds are small and only offer a handful of sites, but many of them also offer spaces for thirty or forty campers. The sheer size and scope of the camping options in Colorado is astonishing. Rocky Mountain National Park is amazing and is in no way overrated, but consider all of your Colorado camping options when you are planning a trip here. You won't regret spreading your camping net very widely when you visit Colorado.

BEST IN STATE

Cherry Creek State Park

▷ Aurora, Colorado

▷ cpw.state.co.us/placestogo/parks/CherryCreek

▷ RV and Tent Sites

▷ $

The natural beauty and serenity of Cherry Creek State Park is astonishing, considering it is only 12 miles from downtown Denver. This is probably the best large state park in the country that is so close to a major American city. It's no wonder that Denverites adore recreating and camping here so very much. Many of the park's highlights are centered around Cherry Creek Reservoir—and the campground, which is very popular with RV owners, is located along its northwest corner. There are over 130 sites and most of them have full hookups. Many of them are also big rig friendly, so the fifth wheel and motorhome crowd definitely like to show up. The campground is not the prettiest part of the park by any stretch of the imagination, but it puts you close to all the action. Biking, boating, fishing, and swimming are all popular here—and splendid views of the Rocky Mountains provide an astonishing backdrop for most activities.

Mueller State Park

▷ Divide, Colorado

▷ cpw.state.co.us/placestogo/parks/Mueller

▷ RV and Tent Sites, Cabins

▷ $

When it comes to natural beauty and opportunities for outdoor adventure, Mueller State Park, which is located less than an hour west of Colorado Springs, is one of the best state parks in America. What makes this park so beautiful? Is it the Aspen groves and stacks and stacks of pine and spruce?

Or the views of Pikes Peak? Is it the hiking trails along wooded ridges? Or is it the abundance of wildlife that frolics around the park? It is, quite simply, all of the above. The camping here is also world class. There are seven different camping areas here with different names. Many folks think of them as separate campgrounds, but the state park numbers them all together and they are technically all just sections of one overarching campground. There are about one hundred sites here with electric that are popular with tent campers and RVers, and there are about twenty-five beautiful walk-in sites for tent campers only.

Rocky Mountain National Park

▷ Rocky Mountain National Park, Colorado

▷ nps.gov

▷ RV and Tent Sites

▷ $

Rocky Mountain National Park was the fourth most-visited national park in 2022 with more than four million visitors—and to say that people love to camp here would be a colossal understatement. Unfortunately, this national park only has five campgrounds, and booking a campsite at any of them can be challenging. Our three favorites are Moraine Park Campground, Glacier Basin Campground, and Timber Creek Campground. Moraine Park Campground (which sits at an elevation of 8,160 feet) has stunning views of snow-capped mountains that defy description. With almost 250 sites, this is the largest campground inside the park, but sadly it is still incredibly difficult to book in the summer. Those who can score a coveted site have a very good chance of spotting elk, mule deer, and wild turkeys wandering through the campground—so have your camera ready. Glacier Basin Campground is a terrific second choice if you can't get a site at Moraine. The campsites here are shaded and semi-private thanks to rows upon rows of lodgepole and ponderosa pines. Timber Creek Campground is the only NPS campground on the west side of the park, and it is worth recommending for that reason alone. The location is quiet and beautiful, as is the entire west side of Rocky Mountain National Park. Plan on getting over there if time allows.

ALSO GREAT

Morefield Campground/Mesa Verde National Park

▷ Mesa Verde National Park, Colorado

▷ nps.gov

▷ RV and Tent Sites

▷ $

Mesa Verde National Park in southwest Colorado is endlessly fascinating. The park protects and preserves the ancestral homes of the Pueblo people, and it is a UNESCO World Heritage Site and an International Dark Sky Park—which is a pretty awesome one–two punch for a national park. Thankfully there is an amazing NPS campground just 4 miles from the park's entrance. Morefield Campground has more than 250 sites, and it is the rare national park campground that pretty much never fills up. There are fifteen full hook-up sites here, but getting one of those is another matter entirely.

--------- **Affordable Family Fun in Denver, Colorado** ---------

✦ **The Denver Museum of Nature & Science** has excellent permanent exhibits on wildlife, Egyptian mummies, outer space, and much more. Admission is reasonably priced, and if you have a bunch of kids, do the math and consider getting an annual family membership. Even if you are only coming for one day, it could save you a nice chunk of money.

✦ Hitch a ride on the historic **Denver Trolley** from Memorial Day to Labor Day. Ticket prices for this thirty-minute ride are dirt cheap, and you will learn fun facts about the history of the area. The trolley operates on the weekends—check its website for current information about times and booking.

✦ **The Denver Botanic Gardens** has an astonishing permanent collection of gardens known as Gardens of the West. These eighteen gardens display the best and most beautiful of Colorado's native plants. There is so much more on offer, and ticket prices are affordable.

Cheyenne Mountain State Park

▷ Colorado Springs, Colorado

▷ cpw.state.co.us/placestogo/parks/CheyenneMountain

▷ RV and Tent Sites, Cabins

▷ $

This delightful park opened its doors (as a state park) in 2006, making it a very young campground. Some of the campsites here are incredibly spacious, especially those that have two levels carved into a ridgeline. The upper level of these sites is for your car or RV, and there is a step down to an area with a tent pad and picnic table. These sites have incredible views, and they are really the size of two sites wrapped into one. Most of the campsites here are out in the open on the ridge with little shade, and the wind can whip through, but it's worth it for the spectacular views of the valley down below.

Spruce Grove Campground

▷ Lake George, Colorado

▷ recreation.gov

▷ RV and Tent Sites

▷ $

Spruce Grove Campground in Pike National Forest is a little gem with thirty campsites surrounded by cool rock outcroppings and sporadic stacks of spruce trees. This is a terrific place for tent camping, but the sites can accommodate RVs up to thirty-five feet. Tarryall Creek is right next to the campground and is a great place for tubing, fly fishing, and dipping your feet in its cool, clear waters.

Wild Cider (Harvest Hosts)

▷ Longmont, Colorado

▷ harvesthosts.com

▷ Self-enclosed RVs Only

▷ $

There are almost 200 Harvest Hosts locations in Colorado, and Wild Cider in Longmont is one of our absolute favorites. Enjoy a wide variety of cider flavors such as agave peach and pineapple at this delightful orchard with Rocky Mountain views as the backdrop. Live music and food are also offered on select nights. Call in advance for more info. The best part is that you can enjoy a couple of drinks and walk back to your RV for a peaceful night of sleep after you are done.

RECOMMENDED CAMPGROUNDS

 BEST IN STATE   ○ **ALSO GREAT**

**Mālaekahana State
Recreation Area**
Oahu, Hawaii

**Haleakalā
National Park**
Maui, Hawaii

**Spencer
Beach Park**
Hawaii, Hawaii

**Hawaiʻi Volcanoes
National Park**
Hawaii, Hawaii

• Hawaii •

Hawaii is a tough state for camping in many ways. RV culture does not really exist here for obvious reasons, so van camping and tent camping rule the day. Many of the campgrounds are only open for extended weekends and are closed mid-week. Many of those same campgrounds are locked up early every night, so you can't drive out for dinner. Hawaii's state websites also have an almost complete lack of information about the campgrounds, and booking them online is often a bit tricky. Some of the state-managed campgrounds (on various islands) also struggle with crime and homelessness. Most people camping in Hawaii are locals who know the insides and outsides of the parks from personal experience. To be quite frank, most campers from the mainland who visit Hawaii do not camp there when they go—it's a hotel or resort trip for most of them. However, if you are feeling adventurous and you are on a tight budget, then camping in Hawaii can be an absolutely epic experience with oceanfront sites that look like something from out of a dream. There are some amazing opportunities for national park camping here that are also worth exploring, but sites are limited and some of them are quite difficult to get to.

BEST IN STATE

Hawai'i Volcanoes National Park

▷   Hawaii, Hawaii

▷   nps.gov

▷   Lodge Rooms, Cabins, Tent Sites

▷ $

Hawai'i Volcanoes National Park is astonishing and otherworldly in so many ways. Its landscape stretches from sea level to almost 14,000 feet, and it is home to two volcanoes (Kīlauea and Mauna Loa) that are very active—which means that the shape and size of this national park are constantly changing. There is some pretty epic driving within Hawai'i Volcanoes on both Crater Rim Drive and Chain of Craters Drive. Both roads have breathtaking vistas and overlooks, so plan on taking your time and making lots of stops during the drives. Crater Rim Drive will take you almost directly to Chain of Craters, so consider them both together as one epic drive. The two campgrounds at Volcanoes National Park (Namakanipaio and Kulanaokuaiki) are very small and do not accommodate RVs, which are rarely seen in Hawaii, but you can rent a tent from the concessionaire (who will set it up and break it down for you) or bring your own and do it the old-fashioned way. The Volcano House also offers thirty-three comfortable rooms that are a great option for those who are not camping but want to stay inside the park. Like many national park lodges, the rooms are lovely but not luxurious. The lodge sits at the edge of the Kīlauea Caldera, providing guests with views of the volcano from the dining room and many of the guest rooms.

Haleakalā National Park

▷   Maui, Hawaii

▷   nps.gov

▷   Tent Sites and Campervan Sites

▷ $

Haleakalā National Park is a stunning national park for those with adventurous spirits. The park has two districts that have distinct features, and thankfully, each of them has a campground. The Kipahulu District is accessed by driving 12 miles on the beautiful, but occasionally dangerous, Hana Highway. Once you arrive (hopefully in one piece), you will be treated to once-in-a-lifetime ocean views, waterfalls, and incredible options for swimming and hiking. You can hear waves crashing onto ocean cliffs just a short walk away from your basic site at the Kipahulu Campground. There is no water available here, so bring your own or plan on getting it nearby at the visitor center. The Summit District of Haleakalā is like no other place on earth. At an elevation of over 10,000 feet, this place gets cold and can be challenging for those not physically prepared for those heights. The Hosmer Grove Campground is tiny and intimate, and it puts you pretty close to the summit— and there is drinking water. But even campers at Hosmer Grove need reservations to see the sunrise at the top. You can get them at recreation.gov.

-------------- **Budget-Camping Gear: The Kala Satin** --------------
Mahogany Ukulele (Classic or Hawaiian Edition)

Adding a ukulele to your camping kit is a no-brainer if you have a musician in your family. The gentle sounds of a ukulele strumming around the campfire could calm a baby or a savage beast. Kala makes beautiful ukuleles that are also budget priced. Its "Classic" model is an absolute steal, and its "Hawaiian Island Edition" with the Hawaiian Islands laser-etched on the front only costs a few bucks more.

ALSO GREAT

Mālaekahana State Recreation Area

▷ Oahu, Hawaii

▷ camping.ehawaii.gov/camping

▷ Tent Sites

▷ $

This somewhat remote recreation area in northern Hawaii is far away from the crowds in more popular spots on the beautiful and surf crazy island of Oahu, but you are not exactly in the middle of nowhere because there is a grocery store and hardware store nearby for supplies. The white sand beaches here are beautiful, and more adventurous travelers can wade across the water to Goat Island and usually have the entire place to themselves—but wading across is not recommended for kids. The tent sites here are right by the beach,

and they are spacious and beautiful. The park is locked in the early evening hours, so don't plan on leaving the campground in the late afternoon for any stretch of time—you will be locked out when you get back.

Spencer Beach Park

▷ Hawaii, Hawaii

▷ hawaiicounty.ehawaii.gov

▷ Tent Sites

▷ $

The beach here is stunning, and it is very family-friendly in a couple of different ways. The waves tend to be gentle here and good for younger swimmers, and the park is considered to be very safe compared to some others on the Hawaiian Islands. There is a grassy field for tents here that is right by the sand, so you won't have any privacy if you camp here, but you will fall asleep to the sound of gentle waves and wake up in paradise.

RECOMMENDED CAMPGROUNDS

★ BEST IN STATE   O ALSO GREAT

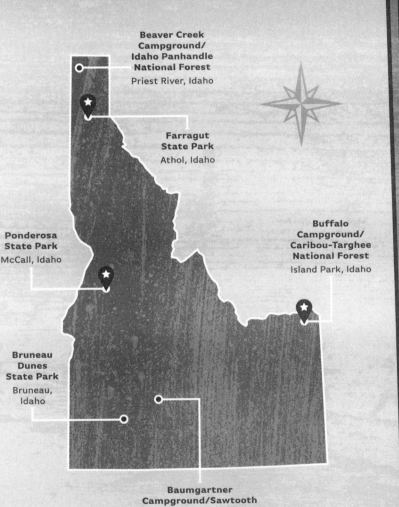

Beaver Creek Campground/ Idaho Panhandle National Forest
Priest River, Idaho

Farragut State Park
Athol, Idaho

Buffalo Campground/ Caribou-Targhee National Forest
Island Park, Idaho

Ponderosa State Park
McCall, Idaho

Bruneau Dunes State Park
Bruneau, Idaho

Baumgartner Campground/Sawtooth National Forest
Mountain Home, Idaho

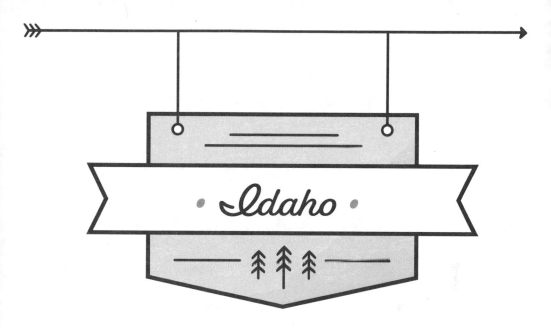

Idaho is definitely the most underrated state for camping in the American West, and we know why: the Gem State is the only state in the West that does not have a national park. Idaho is surrounded by states with some of the most iconic national parks in the world, and those places (think Yellowstone, Olympic, Glacier, and Crater Lake) clearly draw more attention—and more visitors. But Idaho doesn't lack a great national park because it is not epic and beautiful—because it is. It lacks a national park because competing interests within the state have never been able to agree with one another about whether their state should have a national park or not. Instead, Idaho has a vast wilderness called Sawtooth Mountain National Forest, which allows for a greater degree of private use than a national park. When it comes to camping, Sawtooth National Forest is an underrated and underappreciated wonderland. You could spend an entire lifetime camping here—and some people do just that. Idaho also has a great state park, but when it comes to camping, the National Forest Service steals the show in this astonishingly beautiful western state.

BEST IN STATE

Buffalo Campground/Caribou-Targhee National Forest

▷ Island Park, Idaho

▷ recreation.gov

▷ RV and Tent Sites

▷ $

Located about thirty-five minutes southwest of the West Gate of Yellowstone, this hidden gem serves as a perfect base camp for exploring America's first national park. Buffalo Campground has six loops with 127 sites, and every site is beautiful, private, shady, and just a little bit different than the site right next to it. There are some double-family sites, so grab one of those if you are camping with friends. Loop C has electric hookups, but the rest of the loops do not. The campground is quiet and peaceful, and kids love to ride their bikes around the loops. The beautiful Buffalo River runs through the park, and the fishing and tubing are very good. Enjoy the smell of lodgepole pines as you cast your line or float through the campground. Smokey Bear makes appearances at the amphitheater for evening interpretive programs during holiday weekends and select weekends throughout the summer. This may just be one of the best National Forest Service campgrounds in America—and its location within striking distance of Yellowstone is pretty hard to beat.

 ### Ponderosa State Park

▷ McCall, Idaho

▷ parksandrecreation.idaho.gov/parks/ponderosa

▷ RV and Tent Sites, Cabins

▷ $

This popular campground borders Lake Payette and is sold out on most weekends in the summer. The more than 120 RV sites and tent sites are large and private, and the majority of them have electric hookups, while forty of them have full hookups. The entire campground is terrific and shaded by beautiful trees, but the Aspen Loop is probably the best. The campsites in this loop are private and all of them are just a short walk away from the Peninsula Trail, which has views of Payette Lake. In the mornings and evenings, deer love to wander through the campground, so keep your eyes peeled. The Lakeview Deluxe Cabins, which may be the star of the show here, are just as good as the campground. They have nine of them with names like Moose, Bear, Eagle, and Elf—and they are all lovely and perfectly situated. Osprey Point has panoramic views of water with mountains in the backdrop, so make sure you get there before you go. Charming downtown McCall is nearby. Head into town for good eats and artsy and outdoorsy shopping.

Budget-Camping Gear:

Idaho's Very Own Rolla Roaster

The Rolla Roaster was invented in 1980 by Idaho's own Bob Holzer when he dreamed up a way to make roasting hot dogs and marshmallows easier and more fun. The Rolla Roaster is an extendable camping fork that telescopes from twelve inches to forty-two inches long. Our favorite feature is the rotating knob on the handle that allows you to easily cook all sides of your marshmallows or hot dogs evenly—and with one hand. We don't leave for a camping trip without our Rolla Roasters, and neither should you.

Farragut State Park

▹ Athol, Idaho

▹ parksandrecreation.idaho.gov/parks/farragut

▹ RV and Tent Sites, Cabins

▹ $

Located at the southern tip of Lake Pend Oreille, Farragut State Park has a fascinating history worth learning. This 4,000-acre park was once the site of the Farragut Naval Training Station during World War II. Views of the lake were stunning for naval officers back then, and they are stunning for campers and day-trippers now. There are several campgrounds here and each one has its devotees, but all of them are great for different reasons. Waldron is the largest and the best suited for bigger rigs, Gilmore is shadier and feels a bit more remote, and Whitetail is more deeply wooded, has no hookups, and is better suited for tent campers. All campers will struggle with cell service, no matter which campground you choose. There are vast recreational opportunities at this park, including bird-watching, boating, fishing, and hiking. The campground is packed during summer weekends, so plan accordingly. If you get bored of this park's beauty and tranquility, take a day trip to Silverwood Theme Park, the Pacific Northwest's largest theme park, which is less than fifteen minutes from Farragut.

ALSO GREAT

Bruneau Dunes State Park

▷ Bruneau, Idaho

▷ parksandrecreation.idaho.gov/parks/bruneau-dunes

▷ RV and Tent Sites, Cabins

▷ $

Did you know that Idaho has some amazing sand dunes? Most people don't. You can explore the dunes by foot or, if you are feeling adventurous, rent a sandboard from the visitor center. Either way, it gets mighty hot in high summer here, so come before or after July and August if you don't want your feet to melt. There are more than one hundred campsites here split between two different campgrounds called Broken Wheel and Eagle Cove. Some of the sites have electric hookups.

Baumgartner Campground/Sawtooth National Forest

▷ Mountain Home, Idaho

▷ recreation.gov

▷ RV and Tent Sites

▷ $

Baumgartner Campground, which is nestled alongside the South Fork Boise River, is just as pretty as many of the campgrounds in Yellowstone National Park. The massive ponderosa pines smell like butterscotch and shoot upward toward the sky in dramatic fashion. The campsites here are shady and private, and the river is filled with rainbow trout. There is also a hot pool on-site that is terrific for relaxing after a long day of outdoor adventure.

Beaver Creek Campground/Idaho Panhandle National Forest

▷ Priest River, Idaho

▷ recreation.gov

▷ RV and Tent Sites

▷ $

Beaver Creek Campground feels like it is located in a magical forest that time forgot. The campsites are shaded by hemlock and cedar trees, and most of them are private and spacious and can even accommodate larger RVs— which is far from a given at National Forest Service campground. The waters of Priest Lake are crystal clear and beckon campers in for a cool dip in the summer months, and there are views off the Selkirk Mountains in the distance. This is a great place to get lost in nature for a while—far from the cares and worries of everyday life.

Eight Interesting Facts about Sawtooth National Forest in Idaho

1. Sawtooth National Forest is located in south-central Idaho and was first established in 1905.
2. Four percent of Sawtooth National Forest is actually located in northern Utah.
3. There are over two million acres of land in Sawtooth National Forest.
4. There are more than sixty-five campgrounds in Sawtooth National Forest.
5. Dispersed camping (non-campground camping) is allowed throughout Sawtooth National Forest. Check the National Forest Service's website for more information.
6. Idaho is the only western American state without a national park.
7. The Sawtooth National Recreation Area in Sawtooth National Forest has more than 700 miles of hiking trails.
8. The Hemingway-Boulders Wilderness is a protected area in Sawtooth National Recreation Area named after author Ernest Hemingway, who lived in nearby Ketchum for a time.

RECOMMENDED CAMPGROUNDS

 BEST IN STATE   ○ ALSO GREAT

Big Creek Campground/ Flathead National Forest

Columbia Falls, Montana

Glacier National Park

Glacier National Park, Montana

Polson/ Flathead Lake KOA Holiday

Polson, Montana

Bannack State Park

Dillon, Montana

Soda Butte Campground/ Gallatin National Forest

Cooke City, Montana

Lewis & Clark Caverns State Park

Whitehall, Montana

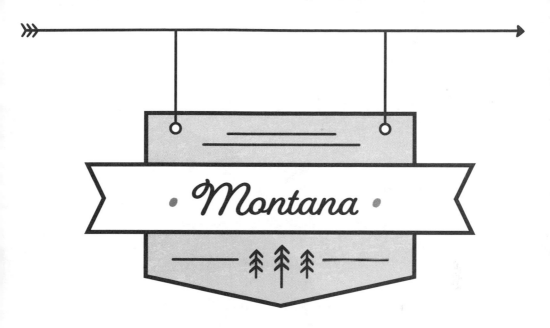

Most Americans have heard of Glacier National Park, and the vast majority of campers can probably tell you what state it is in. But how many of you can name a single state park in Montana? Montana's excellent state parks are dramatically overshadowed by the colossal national park in its northwest corner. Montana's state parks are surprisingly unassuming, especially when you consider that everything else in the state seems to operate on such a grand scale. Many of the best state parks in Montana are far off the beaten track—and though many of them have great campgrounds, they are often very small, with only twenty or thirty sites. Even so, some of these state parks are definitely bucket-list worthy. Whether you want to take a tour of a limestone cavern or camp right next to a ghost town, Montana has you covered. There are also an incredible number of national forest campgrounds in Montana that are dirt cheap, but they are often at least somewhat difficult to get to. Budget camping in Montana favors the adventurous.

BEST IN STATE

Bannack State Park

▷ Dillon, Montana

▷ fwp.mt.gov/stateparks/bannack-state-park

▷ RV and Tent Sites, Tipi

▷ $

If you are a history buff or a lover of the Old West, then put Bannack State Park (located in southwest Montana) at the very top of your bucket list. A major gold rush ignited here in 1862, and by 1863 there were more than 3,000 people living in Bannack. Now it is one of the best-preserved gold rush towns in the American West. Many visitors also claim that it is haunted. The state park even hosts ghost walks in the fall, where macabre scenes from the town's past are acted out by costumed performers. If you become frightened and need to leave, just remember that tickets are nonrefundable. The campground here is small with only twenty-eight dry-camping sites, but it is cute as a button and serves as a terrific base camp for exploring this ghostly town. There is also a rental tipi and a walk-in group site with four tent pads. We have not been able to confirm if the campground is haunted, so please take the necessary precautions if you do decide to go.

Glacier National Park

▷ Glacier National Park, Montana

▷ nps.gov, koa.com

▷ RV and Tent Sites, Cabin Rentals

▷ $

Glacier National Park is known as the "Crown of the Continent" for good reason. Its beauty is majestic and resplendent and awe-inspiring. It may very well be the best national park for hiking in the country. It is also one of the best national parks for camping in the country. There are seven reservable campgrounds in the park, and St. Mary Campground is our favorite on the east side, while Apgar Campground is our favorite campground on the west side. These are our favorites because they serve as excellent base camps for exploring those sides of the park. More seasoned Glacier campers will probably choose more remote locations to pitch their tents, but for first timers, these are very hard to beat. St. Mary Campground has easy access to the Going to the Sun Road that runs through the park, great wildlife viewing opportunities, and otherworldly mountain views. Plus, it is close to the St. Mary visitor center and shuttle service. Apgar Campground is just steps away from Apgar Village and the busiest section of the Lake McDonald shoreline. If you want to camp inside the western side of the park near food, shopping, and kayak and SUP rentals, this is the perfect spot. Glacier's free shuttle service stops at this campground, making it ideal for those who don't want to search for parking at popular trailheads in the early morning hours.

Lewis & Clark Caverns State Park

▷ Whitehall, Montana

▷ fwp.mt.gov/stateparks/lewis-and-clark-caverns/

▷ RV and Tent Sites, Cabins

▷ $

Much like Bannack State Park, which is less than two hours away, Lewis & Clark Caverns State Park draws day-trippers from around the region because of its rich history and built-in attractions. Many first-time visitors come just for the limestone cavern tours—and those tours are excellent and varied in their offerings—but this park has so much more to offer, especially when it comes to outdoor recreation. Montana's first state park also has hiking, biking, kayaking, bird-watching, fishing, and of course great camping. This open and airy campground has mountain views and offers forty sites, about half of which have electric hookups. There are also three cabins here that are absolutely adorable, and the price to book them is beyond reasonable. Lewis & Clark Caverns State Park is in a somewhat remote location, and few visitors from out of state think about visiting it when they come to Montana, but they should. This is a terrific state park, and it is clearly the crown jewel in Montana's state park system.

------------------- **Budget-Camping Hack:** -------------------
Join the KOA Rewards Camping Loyalty Program

Kampgrounds of America (KOA) was founded in 1962 in Billings, Montana, and it is one of the most iconic names in camping today. There are more than 500 KOA campgrounds in North America, and their prices can range widely from budget friendly to quite expensive, depending on location and amenities offered. If you plan on doing more than a few nights of camping in any given year, then getting a KOA Rewards membership is a no-brainer. You get 10 percent off daily registration rates and points for cash off future stays. You also get a free night of camping during KOA's annual Rewards Weekend. The West Glacier KOA is one of the most beautiful privately owned campgrounds in the country—and it is also quite expensive. A KOA Rewards membership would definitely save you some money if you planned on camping there during a trip to the Crown of the Continent.

ALSO GREAT

Soda Butte Campground/Gallatin National Forest

▷ Cooke City, Montana
▷ fs.usda.gov
▷ Hard-Sided RVs Only
▷ $

There are bears in these parts—let's just get that out of the way first. Please take all precautions and educate yourself about bear safety in this neck of the woods before camping here. This campground may be in Montana, but it is a really good option for getting into Lamar Valley from Yellowstone's northeast entrance, and Lamar Valley is one of the best places for viewing wildlife in

the entire American West. The sites here are gigantic, and the entire area is beautiful, but there is no reservation system. This is first-come, first-served camping—so please have a backup plan if you want to camp here.

Big Creek Campground/Flathead National Forest

- ▷ Columbia Falls, Montana
- ▷ recreation.gov
- ▷ RV and Tent Sites
- ▷ $

This campground is located 2 miles south of the northwest entrance to Glacier National Park and could easily be used as a base camp for heading into Glacier if you can't get a site inside the park. It is also a wonderful place to visit in its own right. The dirt road into the campground is quite bumpy, so be super careful if you are trying to get an RV here. In that sense, it may be better for tent campers with rugged vehicles. There are only twenty-two sites, the river is nearby, and the campground is shady and beautiful.

Polson/Flathead Lake KOA Holiday

- ▷ Polson, Montana
- ▷ koa.com
- ▷ RV and Tent Sites, Cabins
- ▷ $$$

Because Montana is KOA's home state, we wanted to give a nod to one of its best campgrounds here, which also fits our criteria for budget camping. This campground has great views of Flathead Lake and the Mission Mountain Range and is known for its cleanliness and great customer service. This entire area is terrific, and Flathead Lake, the largest freshwater lake in the West, is stunning. While the campground does not have direct access to the lake, it is easy to get to. This KOA makes for a nice stop on your way up to (or home from) Glacier National Park.

Eight Fun Facts about The Beartooth Highway—America's Most Spectacular Drive

1. Legendary CBS Correspondent Charles Kuralt famously called this "America's Most Scenic Drive."
2. Beartooth Highway is 68 miles long and begins near the town of Red Lodge on the east side and ends near Yellowstone's northeast entrance.
3. Though it is only 68 miles long, you should plan on taking three hours to complete the drive—or longer if you are planning on stopping to take in the sights along the way.
4. Beartooth Highway is generally open from the beginning of Memorial Day Weekend to mid-September or mid-October. It all depends on the weather.
5. Clearing the highway of snow is a monumental task. The Montana Department of Transportation posts regular videos of the progress being made once the clearing of the snow begins. This has to be the strongest flex made by any state DoT in the country.
6. Beartooth Highway's highest point is Beartooth Pass, at 10,947 feet above sea level.
7. Construction on the highway began in 1932 and ended in 1936. Initially the route was used to bring supplies to mining towns and military posts in the area.
8. The state of Montana and the National Park Service each control separate portions of the road.

RECOMMENDED CAMPGROUNDS

★ BEST IN STATE   ○ ALSO GREAT

Cave Lake State Park
Ely, Nevada

Cathedral Gorge State Park
Panaca, Nevada

Nevada Beach Campground/ Lake Tahoe Basin
Zephyr Cove, Nevada

Valley of Fire State Park
Moapa Valley, Nevada

Lake Mead National Recreation Area
Boulder City, Nevada

Nevada

When it comes to camping, Nevada really does have it all. It has National Park Service camping in places like Great Basin National Park and Lake Mead National Recreation Area. It also has a very good state park system with a handful of truly epic campgrounds, along with a few of the best National Forest Service campgrounds in the country. The bright lights of Las Vegas shine over some truly excellent RV resorts that put you right smack in the middle of the action—but those are certainly not budget-camping options by any stretch of the imagination. Some of them are certainly worth the splurge if you simply must stop in Las Vegas on your epic road trip out West. Always consider the heat when you are traveling through Nevada in the summer. Waking up early and hitting your favorite outdoor activities in the early morning hours is a good plan in the Silver State.

BEST IN STATE

Nevada Beach Campground/Lake Tahoe Basin

▷ Zephyr Cove, Nevada

▷ recreation.gov

▷ RV and Tent Sites

▷ $

Let us not mince words here—Nevada Beach Campground is, quite simply, one of the most beautiful campgrounds in the American West. The pine tree forest here provides shade and much beauty, but it is not very thick, so in between each tree you will see the sparkling blue waters of Lake Tahoe—which can be directly accessed from the campground. On a sunny day, golden shafts of light spill across the roads and campsites, giving the entire place a heavenly look that is hard to describe. The campsites here (which do not have hookups) are all quite large, and each one is very different. Some have shade and some have more direct sunlight. Take a gander at the site pictures on recreation.gov to pick one that is right for you. But be forewarned: this little slice of heaven is very popular, and the campground is fairly small, so you probably should grab whatever you can get. The amenities here are very basic, but who needs a playground when there is so much natural beauty to explore? Snap some family photos on the sandy beach just steps away from the campground—the contrast of the sand and blue water with mountains in the backdrop is quite astonishing.

Cave Lake State Park

▷ Ely, Nevada

▷ parks.nv.gov

▷ RV and Tent Sites

▷ $

Cave Lake State Park is a bit of an under-the-radar desert oasis that is quite a bit less crowded than other more popular Nevada state parks. The clear waters of the lake are stocked with rainbow trout, and it is a terrific place to fish in an uncrowded setting. Depending on when you come, you could bring a kayak here and have the entire lake to yourself. There are two small campgrounds at Cave Lake: Elk Flat Campground and the Lake View Campground, which both have excellent sites without hookups. These sites are surrounded by fragrant juniper trees and tend to have plenty of space and privacy, but they can be difficult to navigate in larger rigs. Tent campers will love the level spots and the clean restrooms with showers and hot water. There is some very rigorous hiking here, and it can get very, very hot, so stay hydrated if you decide to tackle one of the hikes in the hills around the campground.

------------------**Family-Friendly Las Vegas:**------------------
Four Budget-Friendly Activities You Don't Want to Miss

1. Admission for the **Discovery Children's Museum** is reasonably priced, and permanent exhibits like Toddler Town and Young at Art are very good. Older kids love The Summit. It's a 70-foot tower filled with physical and mental challenges. There is a view of downtown Las Vegas at the top.

2. Take a family selfie at the famous **"Welcome to Fabulous Las Vegas, Nevada" welcome sign.** This 25-foot-tall sign is iconic in every way, and, fun fact, it has been completely solar powered since 2014!

3. **The Pinball Hall of Fame** offers up some of the most affordable and fun family-friendly entertainment in Las Vegas. The pinball machines here all work, and they are not just on display! You can play all of them for twenty-five or fifty cents. The best part about the Pinball Hall of Fame is that it donates most of the money that gets plunked into its machines to the Salvation Army. How cool is that?

4. General admission to the **Neon Museum Las Vegas** is very reasonable, and kids six and under are always free. This place is wild, wacky, kitschy, colorful, and will please the whole family. Purchase your tickets in advance because this museum often sells out.

Valley of Fire State Park

▷ **Moapa Valley, Nevada**

▷ **parks.nv.gov**

▷ **RV and Tent Sites**

▷ **$**

There are a small handful of state parks in this country that seem every bit as grand as many of our national parks, and Valley of Fire State Park is one of them. Visitors love taking pictures of the pink, red, and white colors of the rock formations contrasted against a bright blue Nevada sky. The red Aztec sandstone outcrops are visually stunning, and hikes through shaded slot canyons beckon adventurous campers and day-trippers of all ages. Though many of the hikes are pretty easy, many day-trippers enter the park just to enjoy a picnic and a short stroll and then leave when it closes at sunset. But for those camping within the state park, the real show starts after the sun goes down. The night skies are spectacular here, and the stargazing is incredible on clear nights. Valley of Fire has two campgrounds that are perfectly posi-tioned to enjoy the best that this park has to offer. The RV and tent sites at Atlatl Rock Campground are absolutely epic. Many back right up to the bright red rock formations and form the perfect backdrops for Instagram photos that will wow your friends. About twenty of these sites have water and electric hookups so you don't have to rough it in the heat of the summer. Arch Rock Campground is also beautiful, but there are no hookups there. Neither of these campgrounds accept reservations, so getting a site is first-come, first-served. We don't like this policy here (or at any other public campground), because we think it discourages tourists from out of state from camping in this park. Who wants to drive for hours and pull into paradise only to find they can't get a campsite for the night? We know tent campers who will book the first night at a reservable campground, then move to a first-come, first-served site the next day—but this is a much more challenging strategy for RV owners.

ALSO GREET

Lake Mead National Recreation Area

▷ Boulder City, Nevada

▷ nps.gov

▷ RV and Tent Sites, Hotel Rooms

▷ $

This is the nation's oldest and largest National Recreation Area, and it is magnificent in every way. Lake Mead and Lake Mojave both have an other-worldly beauty and offer plenty of opportunities for epic swimming, fishing, and boating. Hiking through the rock formations here is also a grand way to spend a day, so don't forget your hiking boots and plenty of water. There is an entire camping ecosystem located inside this park's boundaries, which includes fifteen campgrounds and RV parks with more than 900 combined sites—some of which are actually in Arizona. There are also three resorts here with motel room–like accommodations for those wanting a break from their tents or RVs.

Budget-Camping Hack: How to Find Black Friday Camping Deals
Have you ever wanted to splurge on a fancy RV resort (like the ones on the strip in Vegas?) but didn't want to pay the steep price for a reservation? We recommend you hunt down some great Black Friday camping deals. Here is how to do it: pick the resorts that you want to visit, follow them across all their social media channels, and sign up for their newsletters. A surprising number of RV resorts (and private campgrounds of every kind) offer discounts on Black Friday every year. Some offer a free night if two are booked, or special discounted camping during the week or shoulder seasons. Why pay full price if you don't have to?

Cathedral Gorge State Park

▷ Panaca, Nevada

▷ parks.nv.gov

▷ RV and Tent Sites

▷ $

Camping at Cathedral Gorge State Park is like camping on another planet. The campground here is small, but this state park is mighty. It is located in a narrow valley where erosion has created a stunning landscape of cathedral-like spires that change color when the sun rises and sets. The hiking is amazing, and some trails feature slot canyons with dramatic walls. There are only twenty-two sites, but they are spacious and private. Some even offer picnic tables under shelters that provide much-needed shade.

RECOMMENDED CAMPGROUNDS

★ **BEST IN STATE**   ○ **ALSO GREAT**

Jacks Creek Campground/ Santa Fe National Forest
Tererro, New Mexico

Hyde Memorial State Park
Santa Fe, New Mexico

Columbine Campground/ Carson National Forest
Red River, New Mexico

Manzano Mountains State Park
Mountainair, New Mexico

City of Rocks State Park
Faywood, New Mexico

Oliver Lee Memorial State Park
Alamogordo, New Mexico

· New Mexico ·

The beauty of New Mexico takes many travelers by surprise. We know several people who have headed into the Land of Enchantment for a week but then quickly changed their plans and stayed for a month—or longer. It is also one of the best places for budget camping in the country. When it comes to camping, the state park system is one of the cheapest in the country, and National Forest Service campgrounds are also abundant. One of the reasons why some RV owners spend months here at a time is because it is so affordable—and of course, because it is so very, very beautiful.

BEST IN STATE

City of Rocks State Park

- ▷ **Faywood, New Mexico**
- ▷ **emnrd.nm.gov**
- ▷ **RV and Tent Sites**
- ▷ **$**

Most people have a national parks bucket list—but do most people have a state parks bucket list? Probably not. But they should—and City of Rocks State Park should be on it. It is located about 30 miles north of Deming in southwestern New Mexico, but it feels like it is on another planet. The quality of the individual sites here varies. Some of them are quite simply some of the best campsites we have ever seen in the United States—especially the tent sites that are surrounded by or built around the otherworldly rock pinnacles that make this place so special. These sites can have shade from the rocks and trees, and even two levels, one for parking and one for pitching your tent. Other sites are badly sloped and look like pull-through sites at a mediocre RV park. Doing your homework before booking a site here will pay off in spades—or you can just come prepared for an unlevel site and make the best of it. City of Rocks State Park only takes up a single square mile of desert, but it is packed with great hiking, mountain biking, bird-watching, stargazing, and more. There is even a desert botanical garden here. If you are camping in a tent or tiny trailer without a bathroom, you will also love the park's modern restroom and hot showers.

Stargazing at Cosmic Campground International Dark Sky Sanctuary

Cosmic Campground in Gila National Forest must be the coolest campground in the country for stargazing, and that's partly because the campground exists purely for that activity. There are only seventeen certified IDA International Dark Sky Sanctuaries in the world, and Cosmic Campground is one of them. Campsites are first-come, first-served here, and campfires are not allowed. Visitors are also asked to arrive before dark so their vehicle lights do not disturb the experience of other stargazers. You should also avoid using flashlights, lanterns, or any other source of artificial light when others are stargazing nearby. Please come prepared if you camp here. There are few services at the Cosmic Campground beyond pit toilets, and the nearest place for gas or food is 8 miles away in Alma.

Hyde Memorial State Park

▷ Santa Fe, New Mexico

▷ emnrd.nm.gov

▷ RV and Tent Sites, Yurts

▷ $

Hyde Memorial State Park is the oldest state park in the Land of Enchantment, and it scores huge points because of its natural beauty and proximity to Santa Fe, New Mexico's, stunning state capital. The park is only fifteen to twenty minutes away from downtown, and it provides a wonderful base camp for tourists who want to day trip into the city while simultaneously providing a great escape for campers who live in the capital city. The skies here are incredibly dark at night, and there is excellent stargazing, which is astonishing considering its proximity to the city. There are fifty-seven campsites and seven of them have electric. Group camping facilities are also available. Campers also love the three new yurts—they are straight up adorable, have mountain views, and are surrounded by fragrant trees.

Oliver Lee Memorial State Park

▷ Alamogordo, New Mexico

▷ emnrd.nm.gov

▷ RV and Tent Sites

▷ $

The rugged landscape and ravishing views of the Sacramento Mountains on one side and a sweeping desert landscape on the other will make you fall in love with Oliver Lee Memorial State Park the second you back into your spacious and private site. New Mexico natives love this park and often use it as a base camp when visiting White Sands National Park, which is about thirty minutes away. Though plenty of folks also like to just kick back here and enjoy all that Oliver Lee has to offer. Enjoy a leisurely stroll on the Riparian Nature Trail or challenge yourself with a strenuous hike up the Dog Canyon Trail for stunning views on all sides. Sunrise and sunset are typically beautiful here, so plan on bringing an extra SD card! Jackrabbits run through the park, and a wide variety of birds, such as owls, hummingbirds, and mockingbirds, also pass through depending on the season. The exhibits at the visitor center are also worth checking out, and the rangers and camp hosts are friendly and helpful.

ALSO GREAT

Jacks Creek Campground/Santa Fe National Forest

▷ Tererro, New Mexico

▷ fs.usda.gov

▷ RV and Tent Sites

▷ $

National Forest Service campgrounds are plentiful in New Mexico, and Jacks Creek is one of the best in the state. It is also fairly close to Santa Fe and is popular with campers from the state capital region. It is first-come, first-served, so travelers who do not have a nearby home to return to might think twice about coming. This is high-mountain camping at its best, with lakes and rivers nearby and majestic fir and aspen trees everywhere you look. The thirty-nine sites here do not have hookups, and potable water is not available, so come prepared for some truly delightful rustic camping!

Manzano Mountains State Park

▷ Mountainair, New Mexico

▷ emnrd.nm.gov

▷ RV and Tent Sites

▷ $

This cozy state park sits at an elevation of 7,250 feet and provides a great escape for campers from the Albuquerque area, which is about an hour and fifteen minutes away. This is a family-friendly park with easy trails and lots of room for kids to play right at your own spacious and shady campsite. The pine trees here are delightful, and they make a lovely sound when the wind whistles through them. There are only about thirty campsites here, and only a handful of them have electric. The diminutive size of this campground is not a negative—it is a defining feature of its charm.

Budget-Camping Hack: New Mexico's Annual Camping Permit

If you plan on doing a lot of camping in New Mexico's state parks, getting their annual camping permit is an absolute no-brainer. If you are taking a long road trip here, do the math and figure out if it makes good financial sense. The annual camping permit allows for unlimited free camping on campsites without hookups. If sites do have hookups, your pass covers most of the price, but you will have to pay a few bucks each night for the utilities. We wish every state had an annual camping pass. Kudos to New Mexico's state park system for being so budget friendly!

Columbine Campground/Carson National Forest

▷ Red River, New Mexico

▷ recreation.gov

▷ RV and Tent Sites

▷ $

Columbine Campground is yet another National Forest Service gem in the Land of Enchantment. The gentle music created by the creek that runs through the campground can be heard from just about every campsite, and there are mountain views here and there when the trees open up to the sky. You can make reservations ahead of time, which makes this National Forest campground an appealing option for those who are traveling from far away.

RECOMMENDED CAMPGROUNDS

★ BEST IN STATE   ○ ALSO GREAT

Silver Falls State Park
Marion County, Oregon

Fort Stevens State Park
Hammond, Oregon

Oxbow Regional Park Campground
Gresham, Oregon

Blue Heron French Cheese Co. (Harvest Hosts)
Tillamook, Oregon

Cape Blanco State Park
Port Orford, Oregon

Black Canyon Campground/ Willamette National Forest
Oakridge, Oregon

Aspen Point Campground/ Fremont-Winema National Forest
Klamath Falls, Oregon

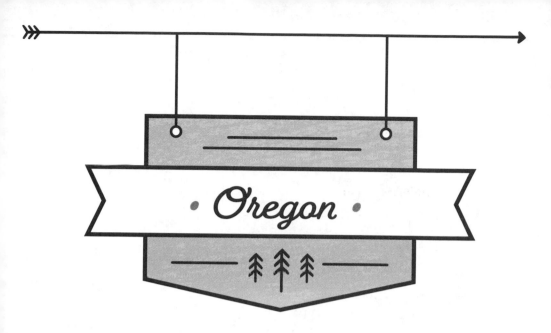

• Oregon •

Does Oregon have the best state park system in the country? It would be an interesting argument to have around the campfire— preferably in an Oregon state park campground. A few of its state parks—like the ones reviewed in this chapter—feel more like national treasures than regional parks for locals, because that's exactly what they are. But when it comes to budget camping in Oregon, state park campgrounds are not the only show in town. Some of the most beautiful National Forest Service campgrounds in the country are in Oregon, and nabbing good sites in them may be easier than you think, especially if your schedule is flexible. There is also great national park camping in Crater Lake National Park. If you decide to visit that amazing national park and you can't get a site, we suggest checking the many national forest campgrounds nearby. Visitors from out of state may be tempted to only explore coastal Oregon, but we do suggest that you also visit the state's interior. There is magical camping to be found there—and it is often dirt cheap.

BEST IN STATE

Fort Stevens State Park

▷ Hammond, Oregon

▷ stateparks.oregon.gov

▷ RV and Tent Sites, Cabins, Yurts

▷ $

The *Peter Iredale* shipwreck on the wide, sandy beach at Fort Stevens
State Park may be the most photographed spot in this magical state park
near the northern tip of coastal Oregon, but the entire park is picturesque and an absolute dream for photographers. It's pretty much a dream
come true for campers too. The year-round campground has almost 500
shady campsites; more than 300 of them have water and electric, and
174 sites have full hookups. At the time of this writing, another loop was
being added specifically for tent campers. It is encouraging to see that
the Oregon state park system is still making improvements and updating the infrastructure to this already-excellent campground. Despite its
massive size, it still feels cozy and relaxed here, probably because of the
number of individual loops. Each one of them feels like a tiny camping
village. Just make sure you can find your way back to your campsite after
a long and relaxing stroll on the beach—the loops do look somewhat the
same. The campground also has eleven cabins and fifteen yurts that are
charming and nicely tucked among Sitka spruce, shore pine, and western
hemlock trees.

Silver Falls State Park

▷ Marion County, Oregon

▷ stateparks.oregon.gov

▷ RV and Tent Sites, Cabins

▷ $

The Trail of Ten Falls in Silver Falls State Park is one of the most magnificent hikes in any state park in the entire country. This 7.2-mile-long hike takes you to ten waterfalls, and most of them are spectacular—especially the ones you can walk behind. This is bucket-list hiking for many people, and it's easy to see why. Thankfully, this completely epic state park has a great campground you can return to after a long day of hiking. The campground isn't gigantic (at least not when compared to Fort Stevens), but it does offer forty-eight electric sites and forty-three tent sites without hookups. It also has fourteen rustic cabins, half of which are pet friendly. At the time of this writing, the Oregon state park system was developing the North Gateway of the park and building a second campground there and a new visitor center. The state must know that it has a national treasure on its hands, and it is incredibly heartening to see Oregon investing in another campground within the park. We wish other states would take notice.

Cape Blanco State Park

▷ Port Orford, Oregon

▷ stateparks.oregon.gov

▷ RV and Tent Sites, Cabins

▷ $

It may be hard to believe, but there are many Oregonians who love Cape Blanco State Park just as much, or more, than they love Silver Falls State Park. At the end of the day, waterfalls are nice, but if you love the beach more, you won't get an argument from us. The location of this state park is magnificent. It sits on a bluff above the Pacific Ocean that also happens to be Oregon's furthest western point. All fifty-two of the campsites here are large and very private with majestic trees on either side of them, and all of them have electric. Most of the sites are also big rig friendly, so this place is popular with the motorhome set. But if you are tent camping, don't worry—you won't have a gigantic Class A looming over your site here.

In fact, you won't be able to see your neighbors while you are relaxing at your site. You will barely be able to even hear them. But you will be able to hear the sound of the mighty Pacific from your campsite, so plan on letting it lull you to sleep each night. When you wake up each morning, make sure you head down to the sand with a cup of coffee in your hand for a morning stroll. The beach here is wide, walkable, windswept, and magnificent. There are not many activities or amenities here, because there does not need to be. The beach is the star of the show, as is the Cape Blanco Lighthouse, so make sure to pay it a visit when you go. Cabin rentals are also available.

ALSO GREAT

Aspen Point Campground/ Fremont-Winema National Forest

- ▷ Klamath Falls, Oregon
- ▷ recreation.gov
- ▷ RV and Tent Sites
- ▷ $

Aspen Point is a terrific national forest campground located on the shores of Lake of the Woods, less than forty-five minutes away from Klamath Falls, Oregon. The forty campsites here feel like they are located in a magical forest far away from the stresses of everyday life. It would be worth it to simply come here to kick back, relax at your site, read a book, and enjoy a crackling campfire. If you are feeling energetic, you can also hike, bike, fish, and swim. This place is a wooded wonderland, but the Lake of the Woods Resort is also nearby and has good food, a charming general store, and boat rentals at its marina.

Black Canyon Campground/Willamette National Forest

▷ Oakridge, Oregon

▷ recreation.gov

▷ RV and Tent Sites

▷ $

Black Canyon offers gigantic private sites along the Willamette River and is widely considered to be one of the best campgrounds in the majestic North Cascades section of the Beaver State. There are sites here, but only nineteen are reservable. A handful of them are situated right alongside the river, and they are the best sites in the campground. Lookout Point Lake is nearby and is a great place to wet a line or drop a kayak in the water.

Oxbow Regional Park Campground

▷ Gresham, Oregon

▷ oregonmetro.gov

▷ RV and Tent Sites

▷ $

Oxbow Regional Park Campground wins high points in our book because it is beautiful, affordable, and less than forty-five minutes from downtown Portland. There are eighty-six campsites here, and twelve of them are specifically for RV owners. The campground is situated in an old-growth forest that is calm and peaceful during the week and bursting with life and laughter on the weekends. The Sandy River is close to the campground, and its sandy beaches provide a great place for swimming and fishing.

Blue Heron French Cheese Co. (Harvest Hosts)

▷ Tillamook, Oregon

▷ harvesthosts.com

▷ Self-enclosed RVs Only

▷ $

This terrific Harvest Hosts location is found at a gorgeous spot along the Oregon coast. Don't be fooled by the name of this place—it does make and sell legendary cheese, but it also sells local wines, gourmet foods, and micro-brews. The highlight for many visitors may be its locally famous delicatessen. Its soups are to die for, and often hit the spot on a rainy, windswept Oregon day.

Budget-Camping Gear: Three Rainy-Day Games for Kids with Camping Themes

Rainy days can happen at the campground, especially in the lush and beautiful Pacific Northwest, so it is best to be prepared and have some rainy-day games permanently stored in your RV or tent-camping kit. These three games have been crowd-pleasers in our family for years—and they are compact, affordable, and super fun to play for kids (and adults) of all ages.

1. **Spot It!** was probably our sons' favorite card game when they were young. We still keep a regular edition of the game in our house and the camping edition in our RV. The camping edition is the same game, but the graphics (which have to be matched together during play) include images of campfires, cabins, lanterns, marshmallows, and more. This card game is compact, easy to play, and fast paced.

2. **Uno's Wilderness Edition** is also the same game as classic Uno, but the playing cards each have a wilderness or great outdoors theme. Just like with Spot It!, we keep the regular edition at home and bring the wilderness version camping and leave it in our RV.

3. There are a surprising number of games that have a National Park Foundation edition, and **National Parks Jenga** is one of the best of them. You have to pull out blocks without crashing the tower in this game—so it can get a little bit rowdy and noisy. The blocks also have national park facts and trivia on them, so this game is fun and educational.

RECOMMENDED CAMPGROUNDS

★ BEST IN STATE   ○ ALSO GREAT

Antelope Island State Park
Syracuse, Utah

Ashley National Forest
Vernal, Utah

Dead Horse Point State Park
Moab, Utah

Sand Hollow State Park
Hurricane, Utah

Duck Creek Campground/Dixie National Forest
Cedar City, Utah

Goblin Valley State Park
Green River, Utah

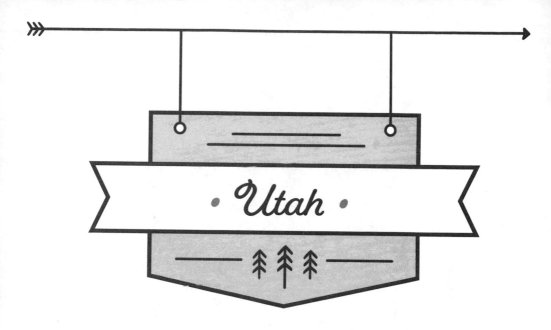

Utah

When it comes to overcrowding in our national parks, Utah has been ground zero. While this chapter does give the Utah national parks a nod, we are very pleased to report that there are many other wonderful options for budget camping in the Beehive State. The state park campground system is awe-inspiring. You could easily do an epic trip to Utah and never visit a single national park, and not just because of the great options for state park camping. There is also national forest camping in Utah that is relatively uncrowded for those who love a rustic, back-to-nature camping experience. There are times when we think that Utah may be the greatest state for budget camping in the country. There is just so much public land in this colorful and otherworldly state. And there are so many public campgrounds—hundred and hundreds of them.

BEST IN STATE

Antelope Island State Park

▷ Syracuse, Utah

▷ stateparks.utah.gov

▷ RV and Tent Sites

▷ $

Antelope Island is less than two hours away from Salt Lake City, and it serves as a great escape into the natural world for the denizens of that city. This place is packed with wildlife. While you are camping here, you might see free-ranging bison and stunning pronghorn, among many other species. This state park is also one of the best spots in the country—so bring your binoculars if you come. There are two campgrounds here, and both of them are stunning. Bridger Bay is larger and more popular and offers water and electricity in its upper loop. It also has bathrooms and showers. White Rock Bay Campground does not have hookups, but it does offer group camping sites and two equestrian sites if you camp with your loyal steed. There are only pit toilets here, which is partly why Bridger Bay is the more popular option. The hiking and mountain biking are amazing at Antelope Island—so come ready for an adventure.

Dead Horse Point State Park

▷ Moab, Utah

▷ stateparks.utah.gov

▷ RV and Tent Sites, Yurts

▷ $

The Kayenta and Wingate Campgrounds at Dead Horse Point State Park are among the most desirable places to camp in Utah. This state park is drop-dead gorgeous and a destination in its own right, but it is also located about fifteen minutes from Canyonlands National Park and forty minutes from Arches National Park, so it can serve as base camp for both of them if you can't get sites at either location. There are two campgrounds inside Dead Horse State Park. Kayenta Campground has twenty-one campsites and each of them comes with a sun shelter, tent pads, and electrical hookups for RVs. Spectacular hiking starts right from the campground. The East Rim Trail leads to the popular and oft-photographed Dead Horse Point Overlook. The West Rim Trail is more rugged but also boasts breathtaking views. Wingate Campground was built in 2018 and offers thirty-one campsites. Twenty of those sites have electrical hookups for RVs. These sites can also accommodate big rigs. Each site has a sun shelter with a picnic table underneath that makes eating outside much more comfortable in the summer heat. The roads here are paved and easy to navigate, both for RV owners in big rigs and kids on bikes. Spacious and well-equipped yurt rentals are also available at Wingate; just make sure to bring your own bedding.

Budget-Camping Gear: Blackstone's 22-inch Tabletop Griddle

Blackstone griddles have taken the camping world by storm over the past ten years. The company is headquartered in Logan, Utah, and a love of the great outdoors runs deep in the company's DNA. One of our all-time favorite pieces of camping gear is the Blackstone 22-inch tabletop griddle. We can cook breakfast, lunch, and dinner on it, and there is plenty of cooking space so we can feed our hungry army—and feed them fast. The price is also really good—especially if you pick up one of the Adventure Ready models at your local Walmart. Our 22-inch griddle is five years old, and it still works like it is brand new—so they are also built to last.

Ashley National Forest

▷ Vernal, Utah

▷ fs.usda.gov

▷ RV and Tent Sites

▷ $

The overcrowding in places like Arches and Zion has made national news in the past five years—and there is no doubt that campsites can be hard to find and so can parking spots at popular trailheads. So, what is to be done to solve the problem? How about inspiring visitors to head to other stunning spots in Utah like Ashley National Forest in the northeastern part of the state? Knowledgeable travelers know that this is one of the most beautiful and underrated spots in the state. There are more than fifty National Forest Service campgrounds to choose from here with more than 1,000 combined campsites. So where should you camp first? For once we will let you decide. You just need to know that there are sites open right now waiting for you. If you listen, you can hear them calling your name.

ALSO GREAT

Sand Hollow State Park

- ▷ Hurricane, Utah
- ▷ stateparks.utah.gov
- ▷ RV and Tent Sites
- ▷ $$

Sand Hollow State Park in southwest Utah is a baby in state park years at just over twenty years old, but in the decades since it opened, it has become a real under-the-radar favorite for many Utah campers. This park is all about bright blue water contrasting against pink and red sand dunes. It's a great place to kayak and a great place for off-highway vehicle lovers. There are three campgrounds that all have a variety of hookup options.

Goblin Valley State Park

- ▷ Green River, Utah
- ▷ stateparks.utah.gov
- ▷ RV and Tent Sites, Yurts
- ▷ $

Goblin Valley State Park gets its awesome name from the thousands of hoodoos (mushroom-shaped rock formations) that fill the park and are known locally as "goblins." The National Park Service's "Night Sky Team" has determined that Goblin Valley State Park also has one of the darkest night skies in the world. There are only twenty-five campsites in the park, and none have hookups, but each one is otherworldly at night surrounded by hoodoos and situated under a thick blanket of bright stars.

Duck Creek Campground/Dixie National Forest

▷ Cedar City, Utah

▷ recreation.gov

▷ RV and Tent Sites

▷ $

Much like Ashley National Forest, Dixie National Forest is one of Utah's best-kept secrets. There are more than twenty campgrounds here, and Duck Creek is among the best of them. This campground, like so many national forest campgrounds, has a rustic charm that is created by towering trees (in this case ponderosa pines and aspens) and campsites that feel like they were carved into the woods by magic elves. Some of the sites here have shade and privacy, while some have sunlight. The fishing in Duck Creek and Duck Creek Pond is very good. Because of the high elevation, summer days can be in the '70s while it is in the 100s in Cedar City at the bottom of the mountain. Duck Creek is something of an oasis—at least in the summertime.

Utah's Mighty Five:
Our Top Campground Picks

1. **Arches National Park:** Devil's Garden is the only campground in Arches National Park, and the views of slick rock outcroppings make this place look and feel like another planet. Even the rock formations right inside the campground are fascinating and worth exploring.

2. **Bryce Canyon National Park:** North Campground is not as magnificent as Devil's Garden in Arches or Needles in Canyonlands, but it still earns our top pick because of its location near the visitor center. Sunset campground has more privacy and shade, but its sites are tighter and more difficult for RVs to navigate.

3. **Canyonlands National Park:** The Needles Campground in Canyonlands has large and level sites that offer a surprising amount of shade on summer days. The location on the east side of the park is quiet and peaceful. Islands in the Sky Campground is also amazing, but Needles has twice as many campsites, so it earns our top pick.

4. **Capitol Reef National Park:** Fruita Campground is the only developed campground in Capitol Reef. Thankfully, it is an absolute gem. Campers can pick fruit (like apples, apricots, cherries, and more) during the daytime, and the stargazing at night is beyond spectacular.

5. **Zion National Park:** South Campground earns our top pick for Zion National Park because you can walk to the shuttle and visitor center. This is worth its weight in gold, considering Zion is one of America's most overcrowded national parks.

RECOMMENDED CAMPGROUNDS

📍 **BEST IN STATE**   ⭕ **ALSO GREAT**

Deception Pass State Park
Oak Harbor, Washington

Eightmile Campground/ Okanogan-Wenatchee National Forest
Leavenworth, Washington

Salt Creek Recreation Area
Port Angeles, Washington

Cape Disappointment State Park
Ilwaco, Washington

Seaquest State Park
Castle Rock, Washington

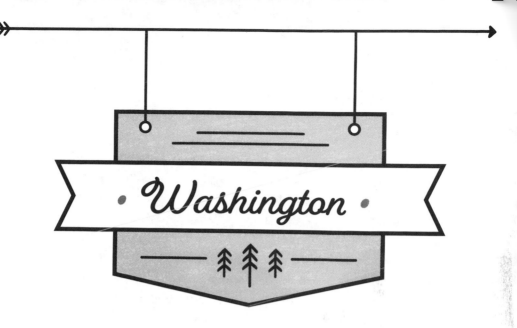

Washington

Washington State is a majestic state for budget camping in every single way. Olympic National Park is packed with great camping options inside the park and in nearby national forest campgrounds. You could spend several months exploring the entire Olympic Peninsula and not come close to seeing all its magical places—and that's just one part of this beautiful state. There are also excellent state park campgrounds along Washington's rugged and windswept coastline and in its wild and mountainous interior. There is also a lifetime of camping to be had in and around Washington's Cascade Range—and another great national park to explore there. We also recommend putting Mount Saint Helens and Mount Rainier somewhere very close to the top of your bucket list—both locations are epic and breathtaking and affordable to visit if you are camping on a budget.

BEST IN STATE

Deception Pass State Park

▷ Oak Harbor, Washington

- ▷ parks.wa.gov
- ▷ **RV and Tent Sites**
- ▷ **$**

Deception Pass State Park is located on Fidalgo and Whidbey Islands about 80 miles north of Seattle. Its proximity to that great city helps make it Washington's most visited state park—and so do its cliffs, beaches, tide pools, and sunsets. This park, which recently turned one hundred years old, is packed with coastal hiking trails, and there are numerous places to launch a boat or kayak along its shores. There are three camping locations within Deception Pass. Cherry Lake is the largest and most popular. There are about 230 sites there and about one-third of them have hookups. Quarry Pond is a medium-sized campground and Bowman Bay is very small and intimate. There are some awesome concessions in this park worth checking out. Blue Otter Kayaks is located at Cranberry Lake and does a nice job with a variety of rentals, and Campstuff Coffee operates out of a vintage camp trailer right by the camp loop entrance to Cranberry Lake. Fidalgo and Whidbey Islands are connected by the iconic and immensely photographable Deception Pass bridge, so bring your camera when you go.

---- Budget-Camping Gear: Bodum Outdoor French Press ----

Coffee is important, especially when you are camping in cool or wet weather in the Pacific Northwest. We love the Bodum outdoor French press for camping trips because it is made of shatterproof plastic. That's good news for RV owners and tent campers who haul their gear from campground to campground. It also makes a delicious cup of java at an extremely budget-friendly price. It's available at target.com for less than the price of two pounds of Starbucks coffee.

Cape Disappointment State Park

▷ Ilwaco, Washington

▷ parks.wa.gov

▷ RV and Tent Sites, Cabins, Yurts, Vacation Houses

▷ $

For another epic coastal camping option, look no further than Cape Disappointment State Park on the Long Beach Peninsula. Here you will find secluded sandy beaches, dramatic cliffs near the edge of the sea, and lighthouses that are as pretty as a picture. Bring your hiking boots and a rain jacket because there are many trails to explore that wander through old-growth forest or lead to views of the park's lighthouses. There are more than 200 sites here, and fifty of them have full hookups. The best sites here are closest to the windswept beach. These sites do have some shade and protection from the rugged stretch of sand and sea just beyond the trees, but plan on windy conditions and don't leave the RV awning out when unattended. You may want to leave your tent or RV at home anyway and rent one of Cape Disappointment's fourteen family-friendly yurts. They are cozy, comfortable, and heated—and just steps away from the beach.

Salt Creek Recreation Area

▷ Port Angeles, Washington

▷ clallamcountywa.gov

▷ RV and Tent Sites

▷ $

The campground at Salt Creek Recreation Area is situated on a bluff above the Strait of Juan de Fuca, and most of the sites (half of which have hookups) have views of the sparkling water. Our friendly neighbors in Canada are located directly across the strait. The location of this campground is stunning and dramatic in every way. The tide pools located just steps below the campsites will keep your kids occupied for hours, as will the basketball and volleyball courts. Outdoor activities abound for thrill seekers and nature lovers. Whether you love hiking, biking, kayaking, bird-watching, or even surfing, there is something for you on property or nearby. Downtown Port Angeles is also close and filled with hip food, coffee, and shopping. Check the sidebar in this chapter for a few of our favorite picks in that super cool gateway town. If summertime on the Olympic Peninsula isn't near-wild heaven, it's pretty damn close.

ALSO GREAT

Seaquest State Park
▷ Castle Rock, Washington
▷ parks.wa.gov
▷ RV and Tent Sites, Yurts
▷ $

Seaquest State Park is an excellent base camp for visiting Mount Saint Helens, which is one of the most epic destinations in the Pacific Northwest. There is actually a pedestrian tunnel that connects this deeply wooded state park with the Silver Lake Mount Saint Helens visitor center, which is a must-stop before heading up to the top. The park has close to one hundred campsites, and about thirty of them have either partial or full hookups. There are also five yurts with bunk beds that would make a really fun option for an adventurous family on a budget.

Eightmile Campground/Okanogan-Wenatchee National Forest
▷ Leavenworth, Washington
▷ recreation.gov
▷ RV and Tent Sites
▷ $

Washington State is jam-packed with top-notch national forest campgrounds and choosing any single one of them as the best is dangerous work, but if Eightmile Campground on Icicle Creek (near downtown Leavenworth) is not the best one, then it is certainly close. The campsites are private and are lovingly carved into the lush pine, fir, and maple trees around them, and the creek is directly accessible from the campground. In the springtime, that creek rushes by like a river, and the area is filled with adventurous kayakers. There is no cell service here, so why not turn your phone off and slip into the mystic? The natural beauty of your surroundings at Eightmile will transform you if you let it.

Six Great Campgrounds Inside Olympic National Park

1. **Kalaloch Campground** is right on the beach. Only a handful of the sites have ocean views, but you can hear the ocean roaring from every campsite.
2. **South Beach Campground** is just 3 miles away from Kalaloch and makes for a great backup plan if that campground is full.
3. **Log Cabin RV and Campground** has magnificent views of Lake Crescent. Full hookups are available, and the sites can accommodate larger RVs up to thirty-five feet.
4. **Fairholme Campground** is near Lake Crescent and is a perennially popular option for tent campers and those with small RVs.
5. **Sol Duc Hot Springs RV & Campground** is basically a parking lot with hookups in a terrific location right next to the trailhead that leads to Sol Duc Falls, which is one of the best waterfalls in the park.
6. **Hoh Rainforest Campground** is located in one of the most unique places in any national park. The Hoh Rainforest Visitor Center is nearby and so are some incredible and very easy hikes.

Cheap Eats and Affordable Fun in Port Angeles, Washington

Camping at the stunningly beautiful Salt Creek Recreation Area near Olympic National Park? Then make sure you head into the hip gateway town of Port Angeles for cheap eats, affordable shopping, and family fun.

▷ Start your day by getting coffee and a breakfast sandwich at the **Great Northern Coffee Bar**. Patrons love the unpretentious, outdoorsy vibe, and the coffee is served with love. The Bennigan breakfast sandwich is pretty epic—it comes with two scrambled eggs, Swiss cheese, sliced ham, and mustard sauce on a toasted pretzel bun.

▷ Head to the Port Angeles City Pier to visit the **Feiro Marine Life Center**. Admission is only a couple of bucks per person, and you get to meet the local marine life (think hermit crabs, sea stars, and much more) from the Strait of Juan de Fuca in a very up-close-and-personal setting. This is a terrific place for younger kids.

▷ If you need any supplies or just want to pick up a budget-friendly souvenir, head over to **Swain's General Store**—it has been a downtown institution since 1957. This is a terrific place to grab a raincoat or sweatshirt if someone forgot one, and it also has a pretty epic selection of outdoor goods for camping, hiking, and fishing. If you are heading into Olympic National Park but need some new gear first, this is the place to go.

▷ The burritos, tacos, and sandwiches at the **Little Devil's Lunchbox** are legendary among the locals, and the price is very good for such fresh and delicious food. The Beer Can Chicken Burrito and the Devil's Park Sandwich were our favorites.

▷ Catch a West Coast League ballgame right in downtown Port Angeles at Civic Field. This stadium has a beer garden and a kids play area, so everyone will leave happy after the last pitch is delivered. **Port Angeles Lefties tickets** are budget priced, and we love their team merchandise. Grab a T-shirt or a hat and wrap up your PNW souvenir shopping right there at the ballpark.

RECOMMENDED CAMPGROUNDS

⚲ BEST IN STATE   ○ ALSO GREAT

Madison Campground and Fishing Bridge RV Park
Yellowstone National Park, Wyoming

Colter Bay Campground, RV Park, Tent Village, and Cabins
Grand Teton National Park, Wyoming

Buffalo Bill State Park
Cody, Wyoming

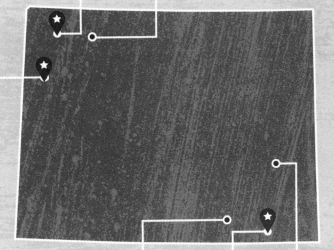

North Fork Campground/ Medicine Bow National Forest
Centennial, Wyoming

Curt Gowdy State Park
Cheyenne, Wyoming

Glendo State Park
Glendo, Wyoming

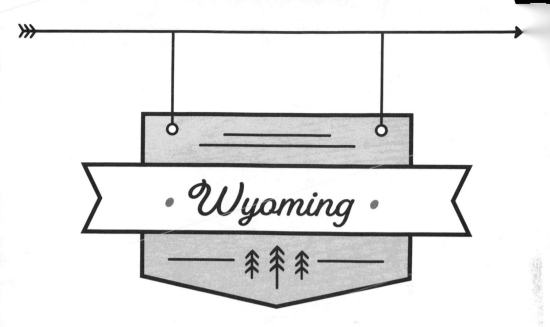

Wyoming

Picking the best budget-camping options in Wyoming is tricky work, to say the least. There are probably more excellent budget camping options in Wyoming than there are in the entire Northeast—and we say that as northeasterners who love camping in our neck of the woods. The sheer amount of public land in Wyoming is awe-inspiring—and so much of it is wild and beautiful. How is it even fair that Wyoming has two of the greatest national parks in the entire world situated right next to each other in the northwestern part of the state? To make things even more unfair, those astonishing national parks are surrounded by national forests with even more camping options. The rest of the state may get overlooked by Wyoming's hot corner, but there are terrific state park campgrounds everywhere you look. If you go to Wyoming once and you only get to Yellowstone and Teton National Parks, that is more than understandable. If you go to Wyoming twice and don't see some of the rest of the state, then shame on you. You are missing out on epic campgrounds surrounded by epic landscapes. Wyoming is a very long drive for most of us—so why not stay a while?

BEST IN STATE

Curt Gowdy State Park

▷ Cheyenne, Wyoming

▷ wyoparks.wyo.gov

▷ RV and Tent Sites, Lodge Rooms

▷ $

Curt Gowdy State Park belongs to an elite group of western state parks that offer camping and recreation on a grand scale. This campground is in Wyoming (conveniently located just 24 miles west of Cheyenne and 24 miles east of Laramie), but it is also just over two hours away from Denver, so the campground is often packed with Denverites and Colorado natives who (rumor has it) really love to head into Wyoming to go camping. All of that to say: Curt Gowdy gets crowded on the weekends. There are over a dozen campgrounds within Curt Gowdy, and they are spread around the park fairly evenly. Electric sites cost a few bucks more than primitive sites, and both are an absolute steal. The fishing and paddling opportunities on the park's three reservoirs (Granite, Crystal, and North Crow) are excellent, so make sure you get out on the water on a kayak or paddleboard while you are here. Also make sure to strap on your hiking boots and head to Hidden Falls—it's the most popular hike in the park by far.

Madison Campground and Fishing Bridge RV Park

▷ Yellowstone National Park, Wyoming

▷ nps.gov

▷ RV and Tent Sites

▷ $

Yellowstone National Park is a driving park. We drove more there than at any other national park we have visited—and that driving was immensely pleasurable and fun. If you think of it more as "touring" than "driving," then you will have the correct mindset for visiting Yellowstone. Picking a campground central to the things you want to do and see is very important here. There are twelve developed campgrounds in the park that can be reached by car, and here are a few of our favorite base-camp-type campgrounds for exploring the park. Madison Campground may be the best overall base-camp-type campground in the park. The campground is perfectly situated for exploring magical locations like Grand Prismatic Springs, Old Faithful, and dozens of the other miracles in Yellowstone's lower loop. Fishing Bridge RV Park was recently updated and overhauled, and it is the base camp in the park for RV owners who want hookups. Fishing Bridge is also centrally located and puts you into very good position to head right into the lower loop—but it also can easily serve as base camp for heading into the wild and wonderful upper loop.

------------------ **Budget-Camping Gear:** ------------------
Lodge Cast Iron's Camp Dutch Ovens

If camping in the Wild West doesn't make you want to bust out your Dutch oven and make a hearty stew for dinner or a sweet cobbler for dessert, then we don't know what will. Lodge Cast Iron makes camp Dutch ovens in a variety of sizes that are affordably priced and built to last for generations. If you are looking for tips and tricks to get started or great recipes for the campground, make sure you check out Cowboy Kent Rollins and his amazing YouTube channel. He has almost three million subscribers for a very good reason. When it comes to Dutch-oven cooking—and cast-iron cooking of all kinds—this man is the master.

Colter Bay Campground, RV Park, Tent Village, and Cabins

▷ Grand Teton National Park, Wyoming

▷ nps.gov

▷ RV and Tent Sites, Cabins

▷ $$

The various camping offerings at Colter Bay Village are not the most beautiful options in the entire park, but they are centrally located near many park highlights, and they are adjacent to park services and concessionaires that sell food, drink, coffee, souvenirs, camping supplies, and much more. Colter Bay Village is, in a sense, the capital city of Grand Teton National Park, and we heartily recommend it for your first trip to this magnificent national park located directly below Yellowstone. Colter Bay Campground is the most popular option in the village for tent campers with their own gear. There are no hookups at the sites. Colter Bay RV Park has full hook-up sites and is very popular with those who own motorhomes and travel trailers. The rental cabins in Colter Bay Village are excellent and offer a woodsy and glampy vibe for those who want total comfort right in the heart of the park. Colter Bay's Tent Village is not for tent campers with their own tents—instead it offers rustic "tent cabins" that have two log walls and two canvas walls and a canvas roof. They also have a potbelly wood-burning stove for those chilly Teton nights. We love all these options, and so do generations of visitors who come to Colter Bay Village every year. Book early no matter how you want to camp.

ALSO GREAT

Buffalo Bill State Park

▷ Cody, Wyoming
▷ wyoparks.wyo.gov
▷ RV and Tent Sites
▷ $

Driving through Buffalo Bill State Park will take your breath away. Camping there will steal your heart forever. There are two campgrounds here. Lake Shore is open year-round and North Fork is open during the summer season. The reservoir here gives life to the region and provides stunning views and water-based recreation such as boating and fishing. Both campgrounds and the reservoir are surrounded by rugged mountain views on all sides—and downtown Cody is nearby for food, coffee, camping supplies, and true out-west shopping that isn't too touristy. The Cody Night Rodeo is less than ten minutes away.

Coffee, Culture, Food, and Fun at Affordable Prices in Cheyenne, Wyoming

✧ Start your day in Cheyenne by grabbing coffee at **The Crooked Cup** on Carey Avenue. They roast their own beans and have a French press option. Their kolaches are also legendary—they are stuffed pastries with egg and cheese and other goodies hiding inside waiting for you!

✧ The **Cheyenne Botanic Gardens** wins huge points for the Paul Smith Children's Village. This permanent area features a secret garden, a tipi section, a wetlands area, and much more. Thanks to benevolent sponsors and the hard work of volunteers, admission here is always free.

✧ The cheekily named **Luxury Diner** in Cheyenne is a hole-in-the-wall inside of a dive that may be better known for breakfast, but we like it just as much for lunch. It serves up great burgers, burritos, hot roast beef sandwiches, and dozens of other midday meal options. The portions here are big, and the service is fast and friendly. It's downtown Cheyenne at its best.

✧ Stop by **Flippers Family Arcade** for an afternoon or evening of budget-friendly fun with an epic selection of pinball machines and classic arcade games. The burgers and bar food here are pretty darn good, and the beer selection is extensive.

Glendo State Park

▷ Glendo, Wyoming

▷ wyoparks.wyo.gov

▷ **RV and Tent Sites**

▷ **$**

Located far to the southeast of Yellowstone and Grand Teton is Glendo State Park, a beautiful state park beloved by those from the region but seldom visited by those from out of state. There are more than a dozen campgrounds here at Glendo—some are nestled in pine forests and others are right on the water. All of them are good, and all of them are cheap.

North Fork Campground/Medicine Bow National Forest

▷ **Centennial, Wyoming**

▷ **recreation.gov**

▷ **RV and Tent Sites**

▷ **$**

With sixty campsites, this is one of the larger National Forest Service campgrounds just about anywhere, and it is also one of the best, especially for RV owners who love its spacious sites. The ten waterfront sites nestled along the North Fork of the Little Laramie River are the best in show. Bark beetles killed many of the beautiful trees in this park a few years back, but the campground is coming back already with young trees taking root and wildflowers blooming everywhere in late spring and early summer.

Appendix A

BUDGET-CAMPING MEALS

H ere are some of our favorite time-tested meals for feeding a lot of people on a small budget at the campground. We also enjoy the timeless classics like hamburgers and hot dogs for dinner and pancakes and eggs for breakfast. Despite what you see on Pinterest, simple and unfussy campground meals are often the most enjoyable for everyone. We don't measure ingredients at the campground, and all these recipes can be adjusted for how many mouths you need to feed.

Meal plan in advance and shop in bulk at your favorite local grocery to avoid overspending. We also share meal responsibilities when camping with family and friends.

WALKING TACOS

Ingredients

- Ground beef or turkey
- Taco seasoning
- Black beans
- Individual-sized bags of Fritos or other corn chips

- ▷ Shredded cheese
- ▷ Chopped lettuce
- ▷ Diced tomatoes
- ▷ Diced onions
- ▷ Salsa, sour cream, or hot sauce for topping

Instructions

1. Heat a skillet over medium heat. Add the ground beef or turkey and cook until browned, breaking up any large chunks with a wooden spoon or spatula.
2. Add the taco seasoning and black beans to the skillet and stir to combine. Cook for an additional two to three minutes until the beans are heated through.
3. Crush the bag of Fritos or other corn chips and open the top of the bag.
4. Spoon the beef and bean mixture over the crushed chips.
5. Top with shredded cheese, chopped lettuce, diced tomatoes, and diced onions.
6. Add salsa, sour cream, or hot sauce.
7. Close the bag of chips and shake gently to mix all the ingredients together.

FOIL PACKETS _

Ingredients

- ▷ Heavy-duty aluminum foil
- ▷ 4 boneless, skinless chicken breasts
- ▷ Butter, cut into pats
- ▷ Minced garlic
- ▷ Dried thyme
- ▷ Dried rosemary
- ▷ Salt and pepper
- ▷ 4 cups of your favorite chopped vegetables (potatoes, carrots, onions, bell peppers, asparagus, or zucchini)

Instructions

1.   Light your campfire or preheat your grill to medium-high heat.
2.   Lay out four sheets of aluminum foil on a flat surface.
3.   Place a chicken breast in the center of each foil sheet.
4.   In a small saucepan, melt the butter.
5.   Add the garlic, thyme, and rosemary to the melted butter and stir to combine.
6.   Brush the butter mixture over each chicken breast.
7.   Season the chicken with salt and pepper.
8.   Divide the chopped vegetables evenly among the four foil packets, placing them around the chicken.
9.   Fold the sides of the foil up and over the chicken and vegetables, then fold the top and bottom edges of the foil over to seal the packet completely.
10. Place the foil packets directly on the campfire or grill grate and cook for twenty to twenty-five minutes, flipping once halfway through.
11. Use tongs to carefully remove the foil packets from the heat.

BREAKFAST BURRITOS —

Ingredients

▷   Bacon, diced
▷   Potatoes, peeled and diced
▷   Onion, diced
▷   Eggs
▷   Large flour tortillas
▷   Shredded cheese
▷   Salt and pepper
▷   Salsa, hot sauce, or sour cream (optional toppings)

Instructions

1.   Preheat your Blackstone griddle to medium-high heat.
2.   Add the diced bacon to the griddle and cook until crispy, stirring occasionally.

3. Remove the bacon from the griddle and set aside on a paper towel–lined plate to drain excess fat.

4. Add the diced potatoes and onions to the griddle and cook until tender and golden brown, stirring occasionally.

5. In a mixing bowl, whisk the eggs together with salt and pepper.

6. Push the potatoes and onions to one side of the griddle and pour the eggs onto the other side.

7. Scramble the eggs until fully cooked.

8. Once the eggs are cooked, mix them with the potatoes and onions on the griddle.

9. Divide the egg-and-potato mixture evenly among the tortillas.

10. Top each tortilla with a spoonful of cooked bacon and shredded cheese.

11. Fold in the sides of each tortilla and then roll it up into a burrito.

12. Place the burritos on the griddle and cook for a few minutes on each side until the tortilla is crispy and golden brown.

13. Serve with salsa, hot sauce, or sour cream if desired.

DUTCH-OVEN PIZZA _

Ingredients

▷ Pizza dough (store-bought or homemade)

▷ Pizza sauce

▷ Shredded mozzarella cheese

▷ Sliced pepperoni

▷ Any chopped veggies you prefer, such as bell peppers, onions, or mushrooms

Instructions

1. Build a campfire and allow the flames to die down to a bed of hot coals.

2. Using a pair of oven mits, preheat a 12-inch Dutch oven by placing it on the hot coals for about ten minutes.

3. Roll out the pizza dough to fit the bottom of the Dutch oven.

4. For a crispy crust, brush the bottom of the Dutch oven with olive oil before placing the dough in the pot.

5. Spread the pizza sauce evenly over the pizza dough, leaving about a half-inch around the edges.

6. Sprinkle the shredded mozzarella cheese over the sauce.

7. Add the pepperoni and chopped vegetables over the cheese.

8. Cover the Dutch oven with its lid, and place it on top of the hot coals.

9. Arrange a few hot coals on top of the lid to create an oven-like effect.

10. Cook the pizza for about ten to fifteen minutes, checking it periodically to ensure it's not burning.

11. Once the cheese is melted and bubbly and the crust is golden brown, use a spatula to carefully remove the pizza from the Dutch oven.

12. Let the pizza cool for a few minutes before slicing and serving.

STEAK AND GREEN BEAN STIR FRY

Ingredients

- 2 tablespoons vegetable oil
- ½ cup soy sauce
- 2 tablespoons honey
- 2 tablespoons cornstarch
- 1 tablespoon minced garlic
- 1 tablespoon grated ginger
- Salt and pepper
- Flank steak, seasoned with salt and pepper and thinly sliced
- Green beans, trimmed (or any other vegetables you prefer)
- 1 package of udon stir-fry noodles

Instructions

1. Preheat your Blackstone griddle over medium-high heat and add oil.

2. In a small bowl, mix the soy sauce, honey, cornstarch, minced garlic, grated

ginger, salt, and pepper. Or bring along a bottle of your favorite pre-prepared stir fry sauce.

3. Place the thinly sliced flank steak on the hot griddle and cook for about three to four minutes on each side, or until browned.

4. Remove the steak from the griddle and set it aside.

5. Add the trimmed green beans to the griddle and cook for about five to six minutes, or until slightly tender.

6. Add the noodles and the soy sauce mixture to the griddle and stir until everything is coated with the sauce.

7. Add the cooked steak to the griddle and stir until everything is well combined and heated through.

8. Remove from the heat and serve hot.

Appendix B

CAMPGROUNDS BY STATE

Appendix C

CAMPGROUNDS BY THE AFFORDABILITY SCALE

Appendix D

CAMPGROUNDS BY BADGE

Worth the Splurge

About the Authors

Jeremy Puglisi is the co-host of *The RV Atlas* podcast and managing editor of *The RV Atlas*. He is the coauthor of *Where Should Camp Next, Where Should We Camp Next?: Camping 101*, and *Where Should We Camp Next?: National Parks*. His work has been published in *RV Magazine, AARP The Magazine, ROVA*, and dozens of online publications. You can also check out his RVing shows on GoRVing's YouTube channel. He loves nothing more than camping with his wife and three sons, and he is always ready to hitch up and head out for the next RV adventure.

Stephanie Puglisi is the co-host of *The RV Atlas* podcast. She is also the coauthor of *Where Should We Camp Next?, Where Should We Camp Next?: Camping 101*, and *Where Should We Camp Next?: National Parks*. She most appreciates that RV camping has allowed her to embrace her semi-outdoorsy personality—sleeping in the great outdoors while simultaneously enjoying a hot shower and soft bed.

Notes on Your
Camping Adventures